# Out of Left Field

**DATE DUE**

| | | | |
|---|---|---|---|
| | | | |
| | | | |
| | | | |
| | | | |
| | | | |
| | | | |
| | | | |
| | | | |
| | | | |
| | | | |
| | | | |
| | | | |
| | | | |
| | | | |
| | | | |
| | | | |
| | | | |
| | | | |
| | | | |

# Out of Left Field

## *Jews and Black Baseball*

REBECCA T. ALPERT

OXFORD
UNIVERSITY PRESS

# OXFORD
## UNIVERSITY PRESS

Oxford University Press is a department of the University of Oxford.
It furthers the University's objective of excellence in research, scholarship,
and education by publishing worldwide.

Oxford   New York
Auckland   Cape Town   Dar es Salaam   Hong Kong   Karachi
Kuala Lumpur   Madrid   Melbourne   Mexico City   Nairobi
New Delhi   Shanghai   Taipei   Toronto

With offices in
Argentina   Austria   Brazil   Chile   Czech Republic   France   Greece
Guatemala   Hungary   Italy   Japan   Poland   Portugal   Singapore
South Korea   Switzerland   Thailand   Turkey   Ukraine   Vietnam

Oxford is a registered trade mark of Oxford University Press
in the UK and certain other countries.

Published in the United States of America by
Oxford University Press
198 Madison Avenue, New York, NY 10016

© Oxford University Press 2011

First issued as an Oxford University Press paperback, 2016.

Library of Congress Cataloging-in-Publication Data
Alpert, Rebecca T. (Rebecca Trachtenberg), 1950–
Out of left field : Jews and black baseball / Rebecca T. Alpert.
p.   cm.
Includes bibliographical references and index.
ISBN 978-0-19-539900-4 (hardcover); 978-0-19-061913-8 (paperback)
1. Baseball—Social aspects—History—20th century.   2. Racism in sports—
United States—History—20 century.   3. African Americans—
Relations with Jews—History—20th century.   I. Title.
GV867.64.A43 2011
796.3570973—dc22      2010042051

*In Memory of Rabbi Curtis G. Caldwell (1950–2013)*

# CONTENTS

# ACKNOWLEDGMENTS

Gratitude is a religious emotion for me. The opportunity to thank the many people who helped bring this work into the world reminds me of how much writing books depends on the kindness of friends and strangers, and fills me with a sense of awe and wonder about how interconnected and mutually dependent we all are.

Baseball researchers are a particularly generous and friendly group of people. I cannot believe how much time, energy, good ideas, and kindness Tim Wiles, Michael Lomax, Larry Lester, Larry Tye, Martin Abramowitz, Ben Green, J Michael Kenyon, Michael Haupert, Neil Lanctot, Jim Riley, Ray Mohl, Warren Weiner, Ron Taylor, David Brewer, Dennis Bidwell, Bob Bailey, Rich Westcott, Jonathan Eig, Kyle McNary, Joe Dorinson, Doug Stark, Leaden Bernstein, Dave Spenard, Paul Dickson, James Sturm, Leslie Heaphy, Gary Mitchem, Bob Luke, Thomas Garrett, and Brent Kelley extended to me, and I promise to pay it forward.

Walter Isaac introduced me to Rabbi Curtis Caldwell, who was my guide and partner as we navigated the community of Hebrew Israelites in Belleville, Virginia, that produced the great Jewish baseball team the Belleville Grays. Along with Matthew Caldwell, Jessica Reed, Khadijah Miller, Elder Ezra Locke, and Sheba Denby, he made my visit to Belleville both possible and pleasurable. I am also grateful to community members who consented to participate in oral histories: James Flippens, John Palmer, Hannah Penner, Joel Wagner, Leah Ringwood, Edmund James Brown, Jethro Martin, Howard Benjamin Prichet, and Carlton Moore. While in Belleville I was able to meet and contact others who knew the Grays and provided invaluable clues to their history: Thomas Burt, George Haskins, and Carl Haywood.

Writing history requires the assistance of far-flung archivists, researchers, and librarians. Terry Thompson, Jim Baggett, Jim Snider, Pam Sawallis, Marc Smilen, Robert Hitchens, Troy Valos, Bruce Bardarik, Michelle Chesner, Auburn Nelson, Jim O'Leary, Kathy Lafferty, Lisa DeBoer, and Joellen Elbashir, who work in cities from Birmingham to Brooklyn, were invariably helpful and wildly responsive to my odd long-distance requests. David Kelly, Pat Kelly, Freddy Berowski, Sarah Sherman, Carol Nishijimi, Ray Rodney, Barbara Dane, Terrie

Albano, Erika Gottfried, David Whitehead, Scott Johnson, Aslaku Berhanu, Leslie Willis-Lowry, Larry Lester, Bennett Rosner, Joel Wagner, Brenda Andrews, and Jerry Pollock graciously supported me during the challenging process of collecting photographs for this volume.

At home, the access and media librarians at Temple University provided consistent support and the highest quality assistance imaginable. Many thanks to Justin Hill, Nick Reynolds, Pam Austin, Eric Jeitner, and Sebastian Derry for their help retrieving and navigating the labyrinth of microfilm and old newspapers. Temple has a fine staff of research librarians as well, but none compares to Fred Rowland. Fred thought through research problems with me, stopping me on the stairs or e-mailing me with solutions sometimes sent in the middle of the night when we didn't find an answer right away. His engagement in my project often matched (and occasionally exceeded) my own. He taught research skills to my student assistants, found references for me I never would have accessed without his help, and was even willing to read a draft of my manuscript. (It turns out he's a rather good editor, too.) Without Fred's encouragement and skill, this project might never have been completed.

Others at Temple also supported this work. University Study Leaves allowed me the time to do the kind of sustained writing that's impossible in the midst of teaching and administrative responsibilities. The College of Liberal Arts provided funding for research assistants, and I am indebted to Kevin Delaney, Shawn Shurr, and Kim Riley in the Dean's Office, and even more to those students for their careful and often tedious labor: Kipp Gilmore Clough, David Krueger, Chris Dawson, Rachael Kamel, and Avi Alpert. Editors at Temple University Press, Alex Holzman, Micah Kleit, and Janet Francendese have taught me much about the ins and outs of academic publishing and have helped to guide this project in small and large ways. The Department of Religion took my project seriously. Linda Jenkins took care of the details that made doing this work possible. Terry Rey, Jeremy Schipper, and David Watt were actually interested in talking sports with me. Laura Levitt, my colleague not only in Religion but in Gender and Jewish Studies as well, does not talk sports, but does just about everything else, from coming up with ideas for readers and venues for presentations to adorning my office with baseball tchotchkes. Her friendship is a great gift.

I am also deeply grateful to my academic colleagues and friends in the field (broadly conceived) of North American religion who have been brilliant conversation partners: Deborah Waxman, Jacob Dorman, Walter Isaac, Jonathan Karp, Deborah Dash Moore, Jonathan Jackson, Lila Corwin Berman, Judith Weisenfeld, and Michael Alexander. Their work and ideas have inspired me and challenged my thinking. Friends Jacob Staub, Traci West, Lorene Cary, Adina Newberg, and Ruth Ost also provided intellectual support for the project along with many cups of tea and much sympathy.

Alex Holzman and Judith Weisenfeld read the proposal and portions of drafts. Both of them encouraged me to take the project to places I hadn't considered and broadened my perspective on the work. Christie Balka, Maynard Seider, Lori Ginzberg, Fred Rowland, and Lila Corwin Berman graciously read entire drafts and provided comments on contents and commas that were most wise and occasionally rather funny, too.

Theo Calderara is an extraordinary editor and a pleasure to work with. He saw the value in this project and gave me both the support and space I needed to get it done. Copy editor Steve Dodson, a wizard at baseball trivia in addition to the proper placement of commas, made many key suggestions and corrections. The staff at Oxford Press also deserve thanks for their careful and thoughtful attention to how to get this work out into the world.

Acknowledgment conventions suggest that it's important to say that no one mentioned above is responsible for errors, only the author. This is particularly true in terms of writing sports history. Mythic stories and accepted truths die hard, and good writers and researchers have perpetuated them. What I also learned from this process is that careful writers and researchers do in fact publish works that contain errors. Mistakes, especially within citations, abound as you follow footnotes, and while I'd like to think myself exempt from such problems, that is surely not the case.

This book is dedicated to my parents, Irving and Sylvia Trachtenberg, who took me out to my first ballgame, and to everyone else who has shared that pleasure with me since: Ken and Debby Rich, Roberta Yusba, Jed Somit, Joel Alpert, Robin and Adam Goldberg, Bruce Giuliano, Marcia Spiegel, Joy Levitt, Lee Friedlander, Linda Holtzman, Jacob Staub, Tamar Kamionkowski, Lance Laver, Lizzie Schmidt, Susan Schewel, Jon Pahl, Curtis Caldwell, Alex Holzman, the Bacharachs of Seattle, Corey Endo, Mick Woynarowski, Avi Rose, Joan Martin, David Watt, Laura Levitt, Arlene Stein, Nancy Solomon, Zach Luck, Rob LeFevre, Carol Tracy, Marsha Ray, Jeremy Schipper, Natalie and Steve Sondheimer, Eliza Ruder, Caroline Rober, Sasha Endo, and Danielle Ruttenberg. I hope they enjoyed the games and conversations as much as I have.

I am also deeply grateful to my son, Avi Alpert, whose interest in baseball was the driving force behind wonderful experiences of travel and research that I hope have given him as many fine memories as they have provided for me. My daughter, Lynn Alpert, who was never engaged in sports at all, has become, to my surprise and possibly her own, a true Philadelphia Phillies fan and wonderful companion when it comes to all things baseball.

My ultimate gratitude is to Christie Balka, my intrepid life partner, who has seen more baseball games with me than she ever could have dreamed possible. It was Christie who convinced me that writing about baseball was my destiny; she knows me better than I know myself.

Rebecca Alpert
Philadelphia
September 2010

# Out of Left Field

# 1

# Baseball Was America

It was my mother who taught me about Jackie Robinson, the first black man to play in the major leagues,[1] and what she taught me shaped my values as an American Jew. My mother interpreted Robinson's story as a morality tale about how the Brooklyn Dodgers changed America forever by ending segregation in the national pastime—her favorite sport. Under the courageous leadership of Dodger executive Branch Rickey and with the support of loyal (including many Jewish) fans in Brooklyn, the Dodgers were a paradigm for an America free from bigotry and prejudice. The message I got both from my family and from the Reform synagogue I attended as a child in the 1950s was that social justice is a primary Jewish value. Jews have an obligation not only to secure our own rights, but to overcome our own prejudices, root out the causes of injustice, and pass this ideal down through the generations. The story of Jackie Robinson has served as a powerful moral influence throughout my life.

I am not alone. The story of Jackie Robinson's integration of baseball has provided many Jewish writers and artists, rabbis and baseball fans, with a symbolic representation of their experience of assimilation into American society in the era immediately following World War II. The vast outpouring of popular accounts of the Jewish connection to the Robinson story, in film and television, graphic novels, children's literature and adult fiction, sermons, essays, and memoirs, reveals three themes: an identification with Robinson as a victim of oppression, an idealization of Robinson as a heroic figure whose success announced the possibility of an end to all bigotry, and a glorification of the role Jews played in bringing about Robinson's triumph.[2]

The Jewish connection to Jackie Robinson is part of the larger Jewish ideal of a special relationship between blacks and Jews, based primarily in the Jewish imagination and grounded in experiences of integration and assimilation. In the 1950s and beyond, Jews (and some African Americans) believed that African Americans could emulate Jewish successes. They saw Robinson's story and his own sympathy with Jewish causes as proof of this, and of a deep bond between blacks and Jews. Their perspective was unique. As historian Cheryl Greenberg suggests, despite Branch Rickey's claim to religious inspiration for his move to bring Robinson to Brooklyn, no one argues that they had a special black-Methodist relationship.[3]

But connecting Robinson's pioneering effort to the success of Jewish assimilation obscured the real differences between the fates of blacks and Jews in mid-twentieth-century America. Jews saw the American capacity for tolerance in their own experiences of assimilation to the white middle class, but they did not discern the enormous difference between America's brand of anti-Semitism and its pervasive antiblack racism. They did not comprehend the damage caused by the long history of slavery and the subsequent failures of reconstruction in the South. Nor did they see the impact of the dangerous jobs and segregated institutions that greeted blacks as they moved north in large numbers at the turn of the twentieth century, and that persisted throughout the half century preceding Robinson's triumph. They could not have known that, despite legal changes, structural racism would continue to impede the progress of black America even today. Baseball's unwritten ban against black players is a perfect example of the different way Jews and blacks experienced America. This did not make for any particular connection between blacks and Jews before the end of World War II.[4]

The Jewish nostalgia for the Jackie Robinson saga and the hope his story engendered in American Jews contrasts sharply with its meaning for black America. For African Americans, nostalgia is not the point. While they understand the importance of Robinson's achievement, blacks are conscious of its limitations as a narrative of liberation. Most black Americans today are also far less interested in recalling the bygone era of racial segregation in which the Robinson story is embedded. Baseball appeals to memory and tradition, and African Americans, for good reason, don't see the past as "the good old days."[5]

The promise of equality held out by Jackie Robinson's entry into baseball was never fulfilled. Before his death in 1972 Robinson spoke out angrily about the absence of blacks in baseball's leadership on and off the field, a problem that still exists. To this day no major league baseball teams are owned by blacks, and there are few black baseball executives or managers. Despite the ongoing efforts of Jackie Robinson's family and foundation to promote baseball to African American youth, only a handful of major league teams had more than three African American players on their opening day rosters in 2010. The relative paucity of blacks in baseball is referenced by commentators every year on April 15, the day major league baseball celebrates Jackie Robinson Day. Not surprisingly, the annual celebration was invented by the Jewish commissioner of baseball, Bud Selig who, like me, grew up inspired by the story of Jackie Robinson.[6]

This stark contrast is what led me to explore baseball's past in greater depth. What did Jews want to remember that blacks wanted to forget? Jackie Robinson was himself one of the greatest critics of segregated black baseball (usually referred to as the "Negro Leagues"[7]). But the world that he and other blacks were forced to inhabit during the era of Jim Crow is an important, and troubling, part of American history, and one that deserves serious attention.

Interest in preserving and celebrating the statistics of the Negro Leagues and recognizing their great players has been an obsession of dedicated baseball researchers, mostly white men, since the 1970s. Robert Peterson's *Only the Ball Was White* opened a public discussion that has produced many excellent studies over the past forty years. Players who spent their careers in this segregated institution, the men and women who ran the teams, and the sportswriters from the black press who covered and commented on their experiences have received some of the public recognition they deserve, and the difficult conditions under which they labored have been exposed.

As I began to examine this literature, I discovered that Jews came unexpectedly from "out of left field" to play a significant—although decidedly less heroic and more complex—role in the history of black baseball than I could ever have imagined. As Jews involved in an economically marginal but culturally significant black business, they had a great opportunity to wield power beyond what they could have achieved in the wider society in an era when they were subject to discrimination themselves. Examining their experiences in this segregated institution sheds light on the development of American Jewish racial, ethnic, and religious identity; the competitive and cooperative dimensions of the economic and social relationship between blacks and Jews during the Great Depression and World War II; and the Jewish commitment to social justice in mid-twentieth-century America.

## The Jews of Black Baseball: Entrepreneurs, Communists, and the Belleville Grays

Baseball, the national pastime, was an important entry point for white ethnics seeking to assimilate into American culture. Beginning in the Depression era, a few Jewish men, immigrants and children of immigrants, who had begun to make a career in the business of sport would wield economic and social power in black baseball—power that was still denied to them in other venues. They would negotiate that power and influence alongside the African American entrepreneurs who dominated that business. Black baseball provided the opportunity for a different model of black-Jewish economic and social relationships. Unlike other economic and social encounters between blacks and Jews in this era, where Jews assumed the economic upper hand as landlords, shopkeepers, and bosses, these Jews worked as equals and competitors with the predominantly black owners of Negro League teams.

Baseball historian Jules Tygiel referred to these men as the "Shylockian villains" of black baseball, who backed the game financially but were never committed to its growth as a rival to white baseball.[8] The black owners with whom they worked expected that their Jewish business partners would be "good with money," and they were. The Jewish entrepreneurs helped to stabilize the business of black baseball during difficult financial times and provided a decent living for the players in the face of the horrific conditions of Jim Crow America. Because these businessmen were identified as Jews and understood to have experienced oppression themselves, expectations that they would sympathize with black oppression meant that they were sometimes held to a higher standard of decency than other whites by the black press, a goal they did not always live up to. Commercial relationships did not necessarily conform to moral ideals.

Unencumbered by concerns about race pride that motivated black owners and journalists, the Jewish entrepreneurs produced a brand of comedic baseball based on vaudeville and minstrelsy that reaped financial benefits both for them and for those players willing to perform. But it also played a role in making these "showman" black players poor candidates for the serious game of major league baseball. The Jewish businessmen who owned and promoted teams did make efforts to cooperate with the black businessmen who ran the industry and made contributions to black baseball as a business, but their tactics and values also brought conflict and tension. More often than not, black and Jewish understanding of each other was mediated through stereotypes held by the larger society.

These entrepreneurs were not the only Jews whose roles in black baseball created opportunities for a different kind of relationship between blacks and Jews. These other Jews did not become interested in black baseball as a business enterprise, but were pioneers in the effort to end baseball's segregation. Although this group included politicians, writers, and even one major league owner, it was the Jewish sportswriters for the communist newspaper in New York, *The Daily Worker,* who literally came from out of left field to champion integration. These second-generation Eastern European Jews argued passionately and consistently in print for an end to baseball's segregation a decade before Jackie Robinson signed his first contract with the Brooklyn Dodgers. These men were also activists who used their access to the white baseball power structure, their political skills, and their connections to radical organizations to create a public grassroots campaign to end Jim Crow in baseball. These political radicals saw black baseball as an emblem of the failure of democracy in America. They worked cooperatively with sportswriters of the black press on this campaign, yet at times found themselves in a power struggle with them over control of these efforts, and conflicted between their allegiance to the Communist Party and their passionate desire to end Jim Crow practices in baseball.

Rabbi Curtis Caldwell of Temple Beth El, an international organization of Hebrew Israelites (often referred to as Black Jews) with headquarters in Belleville, Virginia, told me about a third group of Jews involved in black baseball. The

Belleville Grays were an independent black Jewish baseball team that was part of his community in the 1920s and 1930s. Like Eastern European immigrant Jews who learned about baseball in order to become American, black Jews also saw baseball as way of belonging to America. But for them, belonging meant being welcome only in the segregated world that black baseball embodied. The Grays achieved short-lived success, but the team was unsustainable in an industry built on cutthroat business dealings that were anathema to their religious values. As Jews were in the process of becoming "white" during this era, a black Jewish baseball team posed a threat to Jews who sought assimilation through white- ness. White Jews were also prone to reject the Jewishness of black Jews because their religious practices were different and therefore suspect. Black Jews them- selves, particularly those from a Hebrew Israelite background, were only mini- mally connected to the white Jewish world. The pride white Jews felt at the success of major league star Hank Greenberg did not extend to the Belleville Grays, whose successes they did not claim for their own but who add an impor- tant dimension to the story of Jews in black baseball.

These Jews (the players, the communists, and the businessmen) not only came to black baseball from left field but remained outsiders, intimately involved but never belonging. In the context of a black business, they both acted out and fell victim to pervasive stereotypes of Jews as greedy middlemen and hucksters, un-American communists, and privileged white men who themselves accepted society's stereotypes of blacks as lazy and ignorant, while the participation of black Jews remained unnoticed. Jews both wielded power in black baseball and at the same time were limited by their own lack of power in the dominant culture and their need to survive in American society where "Jewish" was still a suspect category.

The story of Jews in black baseball is more complicated than either the mythic story of Jackie Robinson or the tale of the avaricious Jewish middlemen might lead one to assume. This book shows how a small group of Jews of different class and national backgrounds negotiated the process of becoming American in the first half of the twentieth century through their involvement in the segregated world of black baseball. These various Jews had a profound influence on black baseball, both negative and positive. Their influence ended with the demise of black baseball in the 1950s, brought about by the social changes that permitted Jackie Robinson to integrate the major leagues and that made Jewish and black organizations interested in forming an alliance to fight discrimination on the basis of "race, creed, and color." But that change came at a cost. These ways of being Jewish—supporting radical causes, participating in complex cooperative and competitive partnerships in a black business, trading on stereotypes, devel- oping connections between white and black Jews—were all antithetical to the values of cold war liberalism that American Jews embraced in the 1950s. And while the changes in postwar America succeeded in making Jews comfortable and radically diminishing anti-Semitism, it was soon obvious that these changes would mitigate, but not end, the black-white racial divide. The alliance between black and Jewish organizations that flourished at this time, and the myth of the special relationship between blacks and Jews, fell apart in the 1960s under the pressure of a reconfigured black politics that recognized that securing legal rights alone would not end discrimination.

## Baseball: The Segregated National Pastime

Baseball is an understudied institution, but one that was central to American life in the first half of the twentieth century. It carried symbolic weight and advanced American civic values. Through a powerful public relations effort, the leaders of organized baseball created rituals that became part of the American calendar and stars who were venerated and celebrated as American heroes. Promoted as "America's game," baseball grew in popularity from its beginnings as a professional game after the Civil War through the first half of the twentieth century. Early in the 1920s, baseball was a big business that was exempt from antitrust legislation and legally defined as entertainment. Babe Ruth, considered baseball's greatest player, was a national icon and America's most popular celebrity. In 1939 the creation of the Baseball Hall of Fame provided the game with a shrine and an invented myth of its origins in Cooperstown, New York. Each baseball season began in the spring with the President of the United States "throwing out the first ball" at a game in the nation's capital, and ended in a "World Series" with the ballpark of the home team draped in red, white, and blue bunting. At the time, no other sport rivaled baseball's claim to be America's "national pastime."

Because of its role as part of America's civil religion, baseball provided an entryway for new immigrants to become absorbed in the American way of life. Jewish men became boxers and basketball players to protect themselves on the streets and to prove their masculinity, but playing or even following baseball made them American. Eastern European Jews who came to America in large numbers between 1880 and 1920 became passionate baseball fans, an expression of their desire to become integrated into the American melting pot by adopting its patriotic customs and values. The Yiddish press in New York, for example, reported on local games and provided explanations of the nuances of the game. Hank Greenberg, the first Jewish baseball "star" in the 1930s is the central mythic figure, the Babe Ruth of Jewish baseball lore. His stature was seen as proof that Jews were becoming part of the fabric of American life, even in the face of growing anti-Semitism. The Jewish baseball story is often told as the journey from Hank Greenberg to Sandy Koufax, the only other Jewish player in the Hall of Fame. Greenberg opened the door for Jews to be welcome in America, while Koufax, playing thirty years later, exemplified the success of

Jewish normalization. In those thirty years the status of Jews in America had changed dramatically. Greenberg, after consulting with his rabbi, played an important game on Rosh Hashanah and so introduced Detroit in the 1930s to the customs of the Jewish New Year. Koufax refused to pitch on Yom Kippur in the 1965 World Series, and his decision was also celebrated, but did not need to be interpreted to baseball fans because Jewish New Year observance had become part of the American calendar. Both men stood for the particular and universal aspects of Jewish life, recognized as Jewish heroes and American icons simultaneously.[9]

But the history of Jewish involvement in baseball is a complex tale. Jews were actively involved in organized baseball from not long after its beginnings in the 1840s. Teams of "Hebrews," as they were most often known, played in semiprofessional and sandlot leagues, representing clubs and community centers, and were an important dimension of Jewish communal life in the early 1900s. Dozens of Jews (primarily of German and Central European descent) played at the professional level—a Jew, Lipman Pike, was believed to be one of the first professional players—and several German American Jews owned nationally recognized teams as early as the 1870s. These owners were mostly urban businessmen who sought to gain status and respectability by running sport enterprises. Not unlike the Jews who built up the motion picture industry, they were able to gain entrance into a new business that at the time was not yet prestigious but still required capital to build ballparks and meet payroll. Andrew Freedman of the New York Giants (with important connections to Tammany and a very bad reputation in the baseball business for his unscrupulous dealings), Barney Dreyfuss of the Pittsburgh Pirates, Sidney Frank of the Baltimore Orioles, and Nathan Menderson, Julius Fleischmann, and Aaron Stern of the Cincinnati Reds all owned teams in the late nineteenth and early twentieth century. In the 1920s and early 1930s Sidney Weil owned the Cincinnati Reds, Judge Emil Fuchs owned the Boston Braves, and Albert Lasker owned the Chicago Cubs. Their participation tapered off, however, and Dreyfuss's son-in-law, William Benswanger, who inherited the Pirates, was the only Jewish owner for many years after the Depression, as baseball became a more conservative business.[10]

As much as baseball functioned as a tool of immigrant assimilation to white America, it also served as a primary symbol of the black-white racial divide from the end of the nineteenth century to the middle of the twentieth. In Jim Crow America, defined by a doctrine of "separate but equal" accommodation, an unwritten rule kept blacks out of organized baseball at every level, beginning in 1889. White team owners and baseball officials decided individual "borderline" cases based on a color line that they arbitrarily created in full consciousness of society's racial categories. European Jews, Italians, and Irish would be welcome. So would Native people and Latin Americans, provided that they did not appear

to have African ancestry. Men of African descent had to create their own separate teams and leagues if they wished to play America's game. "Equal" was out of
the question, as access to resources and monopolistic business practices
privileged the game played by whites.[11]

From its inception, the segregated world of black baseball was financed
and organized by both black and white men. European immigrants found
opportunities in marginal or newly developing businesses, especially entertainment and sports. The broad interest in baseball and the existence of a vast
number of local industrial and semiprofessional teams in both white and
black communities during the late nineteenth and early twentieth centuries
provided a variety of business opportunities that required only small capital
investments. Entrepreneurs, white and black, sponsored teams, sold uniforms and equipment, and leased or owned the parks and fields in which they
played. Sportswriters in the black press provided newspaper coverage and
attracted attention for local games. Sports promoters scheduled contests and
drew fans to the games. Former players and sportswriters and other small
businessmen who lacked the financial resources to own teams in organized
white baseball were in a position to make substantial sums in the undercapitalized world of black baseball.

Jews were not the first white ethnics to be involved in the business of black
baseball. During the late nineteenth and early twentieth century, most of the
whites who owned black baseball teams were of Irish and German descent. But
starting in the late 1920s, Jews replaced them, and with only one exception the
white men who ran, promoted, and served as booking agents for black baseball
teams after 1930 were Jewish. This transition followed a familiar economic
pattern of the successive waves of immigrants who came from Europe to America.
German Jews came to this country in the nineteenth century along with other
German immigrants, but not in large numbers. They quickly established themselves in business, and some became successful owners of white professional
and semiprofessional teams and were involved in other aspects of the baseball
industry. But without access to the kind of capital their German counterparts
were able to invest in white professional baseball, the children of the Eastern
European immigrants found a place in the business of sport as local promoters
and sporting goods salesmen and began to interact with the world of black baseball by scheduling interracial games and selling equipment in the early 1920s.

This access across the racial divide gave them the opportunity for a more
central role in black baseball during the Depression, when many of the earlier
white owners moved on. Other immigrant Jews did business in the black
community as merchants who ran pawnshops; liquor, grocery, and candy stores;
and butcher and tailor shops in the heart of the black neighborhoods. The competition between black entrepreneurs and Jewish store owners was an enormous
source of tension. Jews involved in the music and entertainment industry held

economic power over black artists. Jewish families hired black domestics to work in their homes, and were among the primary participants in white flight (even as they themselves were subject to restrictive covenants in the neighborhoods to which they wished to move). And in the privacy of their homes, they expressed disdain for "shvartzes."[12] Jews may have wanted to stand outside the racial system of the United States and deny the privileges that accrued as they assimilated to whiteness, but evidence suggests that they did not.[13]

While the involvement of the Jewish entrepreneurs in black baseball was necessary from a financial perspective, it was not always welcome. Some black baseball owners understood the necessity of working cooperatively with whites in order to make a profit, which of course mattered to the black entrepreneurs.[14] But black baseball, like its white counterpart, also carried cultural meaning in the black community. Black teams and leagues were viewed as sources of pride and communal endeavors that "lifted the race." It was a predominantly black-owned business that thrived in both the North and South, provided an important leisure activity, and proved that black men could live up to America's expectations of masculinity as equally gifted and skilled at the national pastime.

White promoters in black baseball were, as a rule, not interested in the deeper significance of baseball for the black community. They saw black baseball as a business through which to make a profit. One of those early promoters, and for a time the most powerful one, was known as "the Hebrew Menace," despite the fact that he was not Jewish. The assumption that he was reveals much about negative attitudes about Jews and business that would linger in the popular imagination, creating a difficult situation for the Jewish businessmen who were involved in black baseball. These men, Jewish but also white, were a bridge between two worlds, committed to the advancement of this African American business venture and also to maintaining their own advantage in an enterprise built on segregation.

## American Jewish Identity

For Jews of European ancestry, Jewishness in the modern era is characterized by a complex mix of common history and cultural practices as they evolved through a connection to a real or imagined past and a strong sense of genealogical "familialism," or belonging together. This identity incorporates, but isn't limited to, Judaism as religious practice. But Jewishness is also defined by how outsiders use the term, often as an effort to reinforce difference. Jewishness was often categorized by outsiders as an identity based on national origins, and Jews were compared to Irish and Italians more often than to Christians. In the early twentieth century, racial categories as defined by biology and anthropology entered others' definitions of Jewishness and contributed to perceptions of the Jew as inferior, weak, and morally degenerate. To sidestep those characterizations, modern Jews often avoided identifying as Jewish in the racial sense, preferring to emphasize the religious dimension by referring to themselves as Israelite, Hebrew, or of the Mosaic persuasion. It often did not matter. These characterizations were exacerbated by the influx of Eastern European Jewish immigrants at the turn of the twentieth century, as the growing numbers of Jews with different customs and languages threatened the assimilationist strategies of the earlier generations of American Jews.[15]

The Eastern European immigrant generation remained objects of stereotypes and discrimination. That generation maintained communal norms out of necessity, living together in neighborhoods and sharing occupational choices and networks that were cohesive and supportive. They spoke Yiddish and maintained many of their Eastern European (Ashkenazi) cultural and religious norms. The children of immigrants went to school, were influenced by the outside culture, and created new business opportunities for themselves. While the immigrant generation mostly pursued skilled labor or self-employment, the next generation moved into professional and managerial work. They survived the Depression and World War II. Although the children of immigrants grew up associating primarily with other Jews, their trajectories at work and school broadened their worlds and moved them away from exclusively Jewish neighborhoods and business associations. They rejected Yiddish, but understood it. Intermarriage was a rare choice, and one that would most often cast them out completely. By the second generation, Jews were no longer an isolated group, but they retained and shaped a new American Jewishness. Non-Jews still maintained boundaries and made Jews aware of their Jewishness, but it was no longer seen as negatively. Jewishness was an identity that they valued deeply and passed on to the next generation.[16]

The Eastern European Ashkenazi Jews who were involved in black baseball, all children of immigrants, were part of a cohort of Jews who are defined variously by scholars as "provisionally" or "conditionally" or "ambiguously" or "not quite" white. Jews did not shift fully into the racial category of whiteness until after World War II, when Hitler's racialization of European Jews rendered it necessary to begin the process of reconceptualizing Jewishness as a religious and ethnic and not a racial category. These arguments make good sense in reference to the vast numbers of Jewish immigrants from Eastern Europe from the 1880s to the 1920s, but do not really apply to the German Jews, who established themselves in this country in the mid-nineteenth century, and not at all to black Jews. In the white world, Eastern European Jews were a "middle category" in America's racial hierarchy. And, as cultural critic Michael Rogin and others have argued persuasively, shifting into the category of white meant disassociating themselves from being black, as enacted through performances in blackface in minstrel and vaudeville theaters. While this new identity was formed in the worlds of politics, music, and film, it also pervaded the worlds of sport and black business.[17]

This complex process of racialization played out in interesting ways for Jewish men in the context of black baseball, working closely but also competing with black owners, employing black players and managers, and negotiating power relationships on terms very different from those of the white world. In the world of black baseball, their whiteness was less provisional and more of an established fact. They were able to navigate comfortably in the white sports business world while they remained outsiders to black society. They worked among blacks, but they did not suffer the indignities of Jim Crow, nor did they refrain from their own racial prejudice and stereotypes. They took note of how blacks were treated, but placed themselves on the other side of the racial divide. But they were also Jewish, which meant that their business practices were often viewed through the lens of stereotypes about Jews and money. And they identified as Jews, both in private and public, maintaining at least minimal attachments to Jewish cultural and religious institutions. In this world these men were seen, and saw themselves, as both white and Jewish. And the two functioned as separate but connected identities that would shape the relationship these Jewish entrepreneurs had to the business of black baseball.

## Presumed Jewish

Nat Strong, the *Hebrew Menace* to colored base ball, will soon find out that Palestine will be a far better place for his activities than the western and some of the eastern sand lots. This octopus has tried to encircle every ball park in the country in his effort to control and keep down the race managers and owners.

"Pandora's Box," Norfolk *Journal and Guide*, February 6, 1921

Despite this black journalist's assumption,[18] Nathaniel Caldwin Strong, the "Hebrew Menace," was not Jewish. His parents, John and Sarah, were born in Ireland and Wales, respectively. He married a woman whose family came to the United States from Sweden, and they lived in the exclusive suburb of New Rochelle in Westchester County, New York. Strong belonged to the New York Athletic Club, which barred Jews and blacks from membership through the 1940s.[19]

The powerful language the author of the article chose to describe Strong tells us much about how Jews were viewed in the black community in the early part of the twentieth century. Referring to Jews as "Hebrews" and connecting them to Palestine indicates a familiarity with Jewish life and values. The assumption that Strong was Jewish is probably based on the growing prominence of Jews in small business, particularly in black neighborhoods. It reveals a discomfort with Jewish economic power that existed in the black community and beyond. Strong has often been held responsible for the early failures of the Negro Leagues by the black press, and scholars of black baseball have confirmed his role as villain.[20]

Beginning in the 1890s, Strong was the dominant figure in black and white sandlot and semiprofessional baseball in New York and most small towns in the Northeast. As head of the Nat C. Strong Amusement Company, he owned a number of the best parks and fields where games were played. To schedule a contest, particularly at a lucrative venue against a popular team, an owner had to deal with Strong's booking agency, in which he partnered with Walter Schlichter, a white newspaperman from Philadelphia. Both Strong and Schlichter also owned teams. Controlling teams, venues, and schedules gave Strong a virtual monopoly on semiprofessional (white and black) baseball in the Northeast.[21]

It was in Strong's financial interest to make sure that black teams were available to play against independent white teams in parks that he owned and operated. Cross-racial contests were often perceived as a "novelty," or a symbolic battle between the races, and drew large crowds. This presented a competitive challenge to black team owners, as Strong showed little interest in supporting their efforts to develop a distinct black baseball industry with its own teams and home fields. Strong worked behind the scenes to thwart efforts to develop the black-owned Lincoln Giants and Bacharach Giants in Harlem and the Bronx, where the teams would have a strong fan base and achieve independent financial strength. He came under considerable criticism for purchasing a black-owned team, the Brooklyn Royal Giants, and then booking them to play their games as the visiting, not the home team, thus denying them revenue (home teams generally received a larger percentage of the gate receipts) and the opportunity to develop a loyal fan base.[22]

In 1920, former black baseball star Andrew (Rube) Foster organized the Negro National League to challenge Strong's domination. Strong's response was to work with another black team owner from Philadelphia, Ed Bolden, to organize a competitive Eastern Colored League (ECL). Foster called the ECL "Nat Strong's Booking Agency," as three of the six teams in the league were either booked or owned by Strong. Foster employed business practices similar to Strong's, and he had disproportionate control of his own league, acting as both owner and booking agent. Neither man understood that for baseball to be a successful business, owners had to work cooperatively as well as compete. Although greater profit was achieved through fierce competition in the short run, lack of cooperation among owners ultimately prohibited the successful development of the industry. And although black owners were competitive amongst themselves, they did not appreciate competition from white owners.[23]

The leagues ultimately did not survive Foster's mental illness, Strong and Bolden's own power struggle, and the onset of the Great Depression.[24] Strong's agency still had power over teams and parks in New York, supported by the alliances Strong built with Bolden and Alejandro "Alex" Pompez, who owned the New York Cubans. But Bolden's own illness and financial troubles and Strong's death in 1935 left room for others, including the young Jewish entrepreneurs Syd Pollock, Abe Saperstein, and Ed Gottlieb, to gain a foothold in black baseball.

## Stereotypes of Jews

The assumption that Strong was "the Hebrew Menace" tells us much about the stereotypes of avaricious Jewish businessmen that were dominant in American society in the twentieth century, as well as the undercurrent of discomfort with Jews that existed in black baseball. Although Strong was not Jewish, the fact that he was perceived as Jewish, and as inimical to the advancement of black baseball, would influence how the Jews who did get involved in Negro League baseball were themselves perceived. Anti-Jewish stereotypes have had both religious and racial dimensions, but concerns about Jews and money were some of the most pervasive and powerful. As sojourners who were often unwelcome in ancient and medieval Christian societies, Jews had few occupational choices outside their own segregated communities. Jews turned to international trade and commerce and were given the task of serving as moneylenders, since charging interest was forbidden to Christians (and to Jews within their own community), and later as intermediaries between peasants and nobles. While Jews were not primarily in financial occupations, the archetypical image of the greedy and wealthy moneylender and financier, symbolically rendered in the popular imagination through the figure of Shylock in Shakespeare's *Merchant of Venice*, became ingrained in Western consciousness. The idea that Jews were skilled (and manipulative) in financial dealings was central to the anti-Semitism of men like Henry Ford and Father Charles Coughlin, who stirred fears of an international Jewish financial conspiracy in the United States during the Depression. Members of the black community saw Jewish merchants in their neighborhoods who charged high prices and didn't hire local blacks to work in their stores as manifestations of this stereotype. Men like Strong, and the Jews who followed him into the Negro Leagues, were suspect not only because they were white outsiders but also because they represented the avaricious Jewish businessman intruding into the black community.

Ironically, Jewish stereotypes about money led not only to the conclusion that Jews controlled capitalist financial systems but also to the identification of Jews as the driving force behind communist ideology. In fact, Jews were disproportionately represented in the Communist Party at different periods in Europe and America, perhaps because of their liberal commitments to economic equality, but also in reaction to the widely held assumptions about Jews and capitalism. Much anticommunist rhetoric in the 1930s and 1940s was fueled by anti-Semitism. Because of the strong association between Jews and communism fostered by anti-Semites, many Jews (and most Jewish organizations) became staunchly anticommunist in reaction. Nonetheless, association of Jews with "the red menace" would affect the ability of Jewish communist sportswriters to effectively pursue their fight to end segregation in baseball. Blacks, also accused of communist sympathizing, were fearful of associating themselves with anything related to radical politics.[25]

Another stereotype that would challenge Jews in the business of black baseball was the association of Jews with the entertainment industry, of which sports were part. Fear of the Jew in the world of entertainment stemmed from early anti-Judaic myths of Jewish pollution, in this case of culture. An issue of *Life* magazine in 1901 called the Jew a "contaminating influence," mentioning Jewish control over theatrical syndicates and influence on yellow journalism, and even the harm caused by Andrew Freedman, owner of the New York Giants baseball team, as a polluter of the "national game." Concerns over Jewish pollution of baseball were only heightened by the Black Sox scandal in 1919, when Jewish boxer Abe Attell, known as "The Little Hebrew," was named as the gambler behind the scheme for several of the Chicago White Sox to fix the World Series. Though never proven, it was widely assumed that Attell was working for notorious Jewish gangster Arnold Rothstein. Rather than blame the poor labor conditions that drove the players to seek additional income, the Jewish gamblers made convenient scapegoats.

In the 1920s, anti-Semitic rhetoric focused on the "Hebrews" who were involved in motion pictures. The "foreign-born Jews" were greedy, amoral businessmen who disdained true art. The perception of Jews corrupting American values was part of the basis for Henry Ford's anti-Semitic rants in the *Dearborn Independent*, where Jewish gamblers, the Jewish press, and Jewish entertainment industry executives were all understood to be involved in a massive conspiracy against Christian (and hence American) values. This discomfort with Jewish connections to the entertainment industry extended to black baseball. The Jewish entrepreneurs brought their business practices, including reliance on comedic traditions derived from minstrelsy, into black baseball, to the deep consternation of many journalists and team owners.[26]

These negative assumptions about Jewish practices and values were all associated with Jews of European ancestry. Black Jews would not enact these stereotypes or suffer from being associated with them. For black Jews, Judaism was a religious practice divorced from cultural or racial designation, and these stereotypes did not apply to them. But they would experience denial of their Jewish identity, both from the white Jewish community and from other African Americans who did not understand why they would want to associate themselves with the traditions of Judaism.

## The Jews of the Negro Leagues

In the 1930s, some black team owners revived efforts to create organized black baseball leagues. By this time, most of the early white promoters had left the business. They were replaced by a small group of second-generation Eastern

European Jews who came to occupy a central role in black baseball until its demise. These Jewish businessmen were not integral to this world; they were outsiders who lived on the other side of the racial divide. Their Jewishness sometimes made them the objects of skepticism and antipathy. But at other times, being Jewish, and their presumed business acumen, added to their power. Jewishness also occasionally inspired feelings of kinship based on the connection between oppressed minorities. While they unequivocally identified as Jews, and were occasionally targets of anti-Semitic comments from fellow owners and from the black press, they were also sometimes perceived simply as white men in a black business. Their Jewish backgrounds and identities complicated their positions. Their Jewish identities, however, were not so complicated. They were children of immigrants and Jews more by culture than religious practice.

## Ed Gottlieb

Isadore Gottlieb was born in Kiev in 1898. His family migrated to New York in 1902 and moved to Philadelphia when Gottlieb was ten years old. They spoke Yiddish at home, and "Izzy" Gottlieb listed Yiddish as his native tongue on census records into early adulthood. As a teenager, Gottlieb, like many children of immigrants, changed his name to the more American sounding Edward. Gottlieb was the one Jewish owner who was involved in the Jewish communal world. He belonged to a synagogue throughout his life, made philanthropic contributions to Jewish causes, was a public supporter of sports in Israel, and was recognized by the Jewish community of Philadelphia as a leading citizen.

Gottlieb was primarily known in the Jewish world as the organizer of the SPHAS basketball team, an acronym of the South Philadelphia Hebrew Association where the team got its start. As founder, player, and coach of the SPHAS, owner of the Philadelphia Warriors of the National Basketball Association, and NBA schedule maker, he earned a place in the Basketball Hall of Fame. But Gottlieb also played an important role in black baseball, both locally and nationally. As East Coast booking agent and officer of the National Negro League and co-owner of the Philadelphia Stars, his work behind the scenes in black baseball from the 1920s to 1950s earned him the honor of serving on the committee that chose the first Negro League athletes for Baseball's Hall of Fame.[27]

## Syd Pollock

Sydney Samuel Pollock was born in New York in 1901 to Jewish parents, Theresa Sussman and Edward Pollock, who had emigrated from Hungary in 1892. They raised Sydney, their eldest, along with five other children, in North Tarrytown, New York, where the family owned and managed a theater that showed silent films and staged vaudeville performances. They also owned a dry goods store

*Figure 1.1* Ed Gottlieb (1898–1979) (Temple University Libraries, Urban Archives, Philadelphia, Pa.).

along with other successful commercial properties. By age fourteen, Syd had quit school and was managing the theater along with his father. In 1923 he married a Catholic woman, Villa Carroll. According to the family history, Syd's mother, who kept a kosher, Yiddish-speaking home and considered herself Orthodox, threw Syd out of the house and sat shiva, mourning as if he had died, as was the custom in those days. Pollock's son Alan recounts the story of Syd's father throwing him down the stairs and telling him he was dead. But he was forgiven quickly, and seems to have continued his position in the family business. With the birth of their first child two years later, Syd was welcomed back into his parents' home. The children were raised Catholic, but Syd remained a Jew. Syd stayed connected to his family and made sure that, although he was buried next to his wife, there would be a Jewish star on his gravestone.[28]

*Figure 1.2* Syd Pollock (1901–1968) (courtesy of Jerry Pollock).

## Abe Saperstein

The most well-known Jewish entrepreneur in black baseball was Abraham M. Saperstein, owner of the Harlem Globetrotters basketball team. Saperstein was born in London and came to the United States in 1907 with his family, settling in Chicago. His parents, Anna and Louis, had moved to England from Poland. Saperstein, the eldest of nine children, grew up in a Yiddish-speaking household, listing "Jewish" as his first language/mother tongue on census records. The family did not participate in Jewish communal activities. At age twenty-eight he was still living at home and working for the Forestry Division. He was not interested in working in his father's tailoring business and began to develop an interest in sports, especially baseball and basketball.[29]

Saperstein was open about his Jewish ancestry, and was frequently identified as a Jew by others. In the film about Saperstein's life, over which he had significant editorial control, *Go Man Go*, Saperstein was played by Dane Clark, a Jewish actor who had himself changed his name from Bernard Zanville and shed his ethnicity. But Saperstein's Jewish background is highly visible in the film. His parents speak with Yiddish accents. His mother, when giving him advice, tells him that if he wants

*Figure 1.3* Abe Saperstein (1902–1966) (Harlem Globetrotters International, Inc.).

to make something good, he needs the right ingredients, "like gefilte fish without the freshest carp and eggs, where are you?" The scene of Abe's wedding takes place under a chuppah (Jewish wedding canopy) and is performed by a rabbi.

Saperstein gained fame as the owner of the Harlem Globetrotters. Often, the press referred to Saperstein and the Globetrotters as "a group of Negroes coached by a Jew." Saperstein made occasional connections between his Jewish identity and the life he lived among blacks, contending that he understood the black predicament as he, too, was part of a "persecuted minority." When Saperstein was one of only four white men inducted posthumously into the Black Athletes Hall of Fame in 1974, *New York Times* sports columnist Red Smith reported a story that Saperstein had told to him about traveling with the Globetrotters and being thrown out of a blacks-only hotel in Atlanta. Saperstein had argued with the owner to no avail; he was forced to dress and leave. "Those guys just wouldn't listen . . . Anti-Semitic, I guess." Saperstein took for granted that being Jewish gave him an insider's knowledge of antiblack racism.[30]

## Other Jewish Entrepreneurs

Two other Jewish entrepreneurs, Max Rosner and Harry Passon, played minor but important roles in black baseball. Rosner was a business associate of Nat

*Figure 1.4* 1917 Brooklyn Royal Giants. Back row, left to right: Nat Strong, Frank "Doc" Sykes, Max Rosner. Middle row, left to right: Andrew "Stringbean" Williams, Frank Charles Earle, unknown, Pearl Webster, Johnny Pugh. Front row, left to right: Louis Santop, unknown, Ernest Gatewood, Joe Hewitt, Frank Harvey. (Courtesy of Bennett Rosner, MD.)

Strong. He emigrated from Hungary to the United States in 1892 at age twelve. Like many Jewish immigrants, he began to work in cigar manufacturing and later owned his own factory. As owner of the white semiprofessional Brooklyn Bushwicks and their field, Dexter Park, Rosner provided a location and top-level opponent for Negro League teams for many years. Passon was a childhood friend and early business associate of Eddie Gottlieb. He came to the United States from Russia with his family at the age of nine. Passon owned a popular sporting goods store in Philadelphia, which he and Gottlieb had started together. Passon promoted Negro League games that were played at a park he leased, commonly referred to as Passon Field. He also owned the Bacharachs for a short time in the 1930s. Passon had never been publicly connected to the Jewish world, although his wife and children all identified as Jewish and his children married within the faith. Passon took his own life when his sporting goods business fell on hard times financially. He had not been involved in black baseball for many years.[31]

*Figure 1.5* Bill Benswanger (1892–1972), Pittsburgh Pirate owner (National Baseball Hall of Fame Library, Cooperstown, N.Y.).

The Jewish family that owned the major league Pittsburgh Pirates also played a role in the Negro Leagues. Barney Dreyfuss was a wealthy Jewish entrepreneur of German descent who made his fortune in the family distillery business. Dreyfuss was a powerful and visionary owner who organized the Pirates team in 1900. He had a close relationship with Cum Posey, owner of the Pittsburgh-based Homestead Grays and a major power in the revitalized Negro Leagues. The Grays played at Forbes Field beginning in the early 1920s. Posey once remarked that it was Dreyfuss who got him interested in baseball. He considered Dreyfuss a friend of the Homestead Grays, and noted that Dreyfuss not only attended most Grays games but paid to get in. Dreyfuss supported Posey by maintaining the Grays' exclusive rights to use Forbes Field, although he vigilantly maintained the color line and was criticized for never allowing the Pirates to play against the Grays. Despite this, Posey had a close relationship with Dreyfuss, and commented on the occasion of Dreyfuss's death that he would miss his support and companionship. The arrangements for the Grays to play at Forbes Field, however, would continue when the team was taken over by Dreyfuss's son-in-law, William Benswanger, who would figure prominently in the story of baseball's integration.[32]

## Jews and Blackness

The one other Jewish entrepreneur in black baseball was not subject to the problems that white Jews experienced in the world of black baseball because he was also African American. Of all the Jewish owners of black baseball teams, the one whose story challenges assumptions of white Jewish racial identity is Howard Zebulon Plummer. Plummer was the owner of the Belleville Grays and also the leader of a group of Hebrew Israelites, the Church of God and Saints of Christ (COGASOC), also known as Temple Beth El. The team, originally called the Saints, was started by Plummer's father William in the early 1920s for the purpose of communal recreation. H. Z. Plummer, generally referred to as Bishop Plummer in the black press and as Grandfather Abraham in his own community, was the religious leader of Temple Beth El from 1931 to 1975, and he professionalized the team. Although not an official part of the Negro "major" leagues, under Plummer's leadership the Belleville Grays were part of two lesser-known leagues (the Negro International/Colored Eastern League in 1939 and the Interstate League in 1940). They also played independently against local and Negro National and American League teams from the 1920s through the 1950s.[33]

Like other black Jewish (Hebrew Israelite) groups, Temple Beth El's self-identification as Jewish was questioned by Jews of European descent. The question itself implies an assumption that the rabbinic Judaism practiced by

*The Plummer Boys — "A Great Team"*
Judah, HZP, and John — 1924

*Wm. H. Plummer's Ball Team
— 1924*

L-R: T. Foreman, John Plummer, M. McClean, R. Madison, Judah Plummer, H. Young.
Matthew Hill, HZP, B. Garris.
L. Wails, N. Townsend, Mark Hill, F. Williams, P. Jackson, Wm. H. Plummer, L.
Thomas, J. Wagner, S. Gaines, Wm. Palmer, J. Murray.
8

*Figure 1.6* Top: H. Z. Plummer (center) and his brothers Judah and John in uniform.
Bottom: 1924 team photograph from Temple Beth El archives (Courtesy of Temple
Beth El, Suffolk, Va.)

Ashkenazi Jews is normative and all other versions of Judaism must be scruti-
nized for their similarities and differences to that standard before they can be
accepted as Jewish. Black Jews have often been invisible to the outside world, as
Jewish and white identities have been understood as intertwined. White Jews,
anxious to assimilate, shunned contact with black Jews, often claiming that
Hebrew Israelite religion was a version of Christianity and not Judaism. The

*Figure 1.7* The Belleville Grays, ca. 1920 (courtesy of Joel Wagner).

question that Walter Isaac pointedly asks, "why a group of Christians would refuse to accept any religious affiliation with Christianity," is both pertinent and unanswered by those who choose to exclude this group from the mythical world-wide Jewish community.[34] Including H. Z. Plummer and the Belleville Grays in the story of Jews in black baseball restores them to their rightful place in the history of American Jews in the twentieth century.

It is not surprising that little is known about African American Jews, whose traditions arose out of the period of enslavement. As a survival technique, blacks concealed much from white society during slavery, and emancipation did little to alter that. The archetype of the trickster, derived from African myth, would reinforce the awareness that guile and deception, mixed with humor, would be useful survival tools in a racist society. What leading black thinker W. E. B. DuBois termed "double consciousness" would help blacks manage the intrusive gaze of the white world. So would secret societies like the Masons, and non-Christian religious traditions like Judaism and Islam.

What we do know of slave religion in the American South was that it successfully incorporated elements of African traditions (including Jewish, Christian, Muslim, and indigenous customs) and mixed them with the version of Protestant Christianity that was taught by slave masters. This new religious system was based mostly on Hebrew Bible references to liberation from slavery and the images of the chosen people. Preferred Bible passages were those that highlighted the liberatory story of Moses, the hopes of the Psalms, and the redemption of the Christian scriptural book of Revelation. Slaves prayed to a God who delivered Moses, David, and Daniel, and were decidedly disinterested in the life and story of Jesus. Psalm 68:31, "Nobles shall come out of Egypt; Ethiopia shall hasten to stretch out her hands unto God," encapsulated hope and emphasized the legitimacy of their African heritage.[35]

## Masonic Roots

Prince Hall founded black Freemasonry in America in the eighteenth century. Like many of his contemporaries, he identified the black experience in America with the suffering, chosenness, and ultimate redemption of the Israelite slaves of the Exodus. Black Freemasonry began in the American colonies when Prince Hall's petition for a Masonic order was rejected by white colonists in Massachusetts. Hall went to an Irish Freemason group in the British Camp and was granted a provisional charter to start African Lodge No. 1, later renamed the Prince Hall Lodge in his honor. Their official charter came from the Grand Lodge of England in 1787. Prince Hall Masons, along with other African American groups, found themselves identifying strongly with Egypt and Ethiopia. Black Freemasons linked their genealogy back to the traditions of Moses in Egypt, claiming that tradition as a source of ancient Jewish traditions in black Masonic rites. Prince Hall himself claimed an Ethiopian ancestry for Freemasonry. Like white Masons, they identified as craftsmen and builders of Solomon's Temple. Hall's cofounder John Marrant believed in a theology based on the return of displaced blacks back to "African Ethiopia." Masonic ritual practices of secrecy gave them an important hiding space and enabled them to preserve traditions outside of the watchful eye of the white public.[36]

These early Masons were precursors to black Jews and Muslims, black nationalists and Garveyites, in creating a vision of a black community with roots in an African past and a promise of the future. Their influence was broad. Virtually every free black male leader in the nineteenth century was a Mason, and Prince Hall Masonry was at the time the province of elite blacks only. A rapid expansion after 1900 made the Masons less exclusive but more socially active. They were looking to establish a caste of communal leaders and fight stereotypes of black inferiority.[37] For many black men, North and South, Masonry gave them an education and broadened their horizons. It also gave them prestige denied to them in white society, and opportunities to lead, dress elegantly, and develop business skills, while providing communal supports such as credit unions, insurance systems, charity, and scholarship funds.

## Temple Beth El's Jewish Identity

The Masons and slave religion influenced the thought of William Saunders Crowdy, the founder of the Church of God and Saints of Christ (COGASOC). Crowdy was the first to take the metaphoric association with Israel literally. African American religious historian Albert Raboteau calls COGASOC a "heterodox" version of Judaism that was one of many efforts to solve the dilemma of racist Christianity. Crowdy founded the movement in 1896. A former sharecropper and the son of former slaves from Maryland, Crowdy became a soldier in the Union Army during the Civil War, and subsequently purchased land in Guthrie, Oklahoma. In 1893 he experienced a vision from God that the Negro race was descended from the ten lost tribes of Israel. His theology emphasized that blacks needed to recapture the concept of corporate salvation and peoplehood of the Old Testament and move away from Christian individualist doctrine. He quit his job and moved to Lawrence, Kansas, where he founded his church in 1896. By 1901 he had moved his headquarters to Philadelphia. In the 1906 census of religious organizations, COGASOC reported forty-eight organized groups in fourteen states with 1,823 members and seventy-five ministers. Their basic doctrine combined Jewish and Christian teachings and practices. The group followed the Jewish calendar, using Hebrew names for the months and observed Jewish holy days, particularly Passover, the New Year (Rosh Hashanah), and a Sabbath that lasted from Friday to Saturday, sundown to sundown. They also followed standard Baptist practices, confessing faith in Christ, practicing foot washing, and tithing. They engaged in Christian holiness practices such as abstinence from wine and profanity, endogamous marriage, and censorship of printed matter. The group also followed Masonic custom in their military style of dress, use of special colors, decorative adornments, and secret ritual practices. Crowdy and all subsequent leaders of the group were active Masons. The roots in Masonry were important for black religious movements that connected Africa to biblical history.[38]

William Crowdy's following grew. The 1916 census of religious bodies reported ninety-four organized groups with thirty-seven buildings (there was only one building in 1906). By 1936, the community consisted of two hundred and thirteen groups, seventy-nine buildings, and 37,084 members. They also reported groups in the West Indies and an evangelical presence in Africa. In addition to Philadelphia, the group had a major center in Plainfield, New Jersey, and in 1903 purchased a plot of land near Portsmouth, Virginia, that they called Belleville, and that became their international headquarters in 1920. The leader whom Crowdy appointed as one of his successors, William H. Plummer, developed Belleville, which was the community's "Canaan land" and a remarkable accomplishment. In rural Virginia in the 1920s, Plummer's several-hundred-acre development ran on its own electricity. It housed a sawmill, a building for religious services, communal dining hall, music hall, barbershop, laundry, printing plant, auto repair, blacksmith and carpentry shops, and dormitories for the Belleville Industrial School that ran from kindergarten through high school and conducted industrial, farming, and religious training. While the rest of the facilities were for community members only, the school (and later a home for widows and orphans) was open to the public. To sustain itself, the community produced lumber for sale and did poultry and dairy farming, along with producing crops of wheat, corn, and peaches.[39]

## Religious Observance

After Crowdy's death there was a split in the group as some adherents moved closer to Christian practices while others focused primarily on the Jewish dimensions of Crowdy's teachings. William Plummer led the group that gravitated towards Jewish observances and called themselves Temple Beth El. They proclaimed that they adhered to the religion *of* Jesus, not *about* Jesus, although not all the Christian elements were eliminated. Their English prayers are adapted from the old Reform *Union Prayer Book*, although they also incorporated readings from Christian scripture, especially Revelation. They also maintain their own versions of Jewish practices. Men and women sit separately. They perform a Torah service, although they do not read from the Torah or remove it from the Ark; the scroll is treated like a venerated object. Until the 1950s, their Passover celebration incorporated the sacrifice and communal eating of a lamb as described in the book of Exodus. The Passover meal, eaten at midnight in a public ritual, was often compared in newspaper accounts to the Last Supper. Quite a few of the Temple Beth El congregations have adopted more traditional Jewish practice, including holiday and life cycle celebrations. Some members of Temple Beth El communities today refer to themselves as Jewish, but others still call themselves Hebrews or Israelites. Although that terminology was originally adopted from American Jews who referred to themselves in similar terms in the nineteenth century, today it serves to differentiate them from the Ashkenazi Jewish world.[40]

Since the 1940s, their leaders have been called either rabbis or elders. Similar shifts toward Ashkenazi Jewish practices took place in other black Hebrew groups beginning in this era, and were primarily influenced by contacts with other Israelite communities, with American Ashkenazi Jews, and with Ethiopia and its Jewish community, Beta Israel.

For Temple Beth El, the main Judaizing influence was Ethiopian rabbi David DeKollscritta. DeKollscritta was born in Eritrea in 1892, arrived in the United States in 1913, and made his residence in Brooklyn. He claimed to have been raised as a member of the Beta Israel community in a monastery in Eritrea because his parents did not have the money to redeem him as the firstborn, an ancient biblical custom practiced by Ethiopian Jewry. The Jews of Ethiopia have been in contact with European Jewry since the early twentieth century. Their origins are debated, but their traditions indicate ancient roots either as descendents of the biblical Israelites or tribal people who refused to adopt Christianity in the fourth century, or religious dissidents from the Judeo-Christian Ethiopian society some centuries later. They follow biblical kosher laws, male circumcision, and the Sabbath, along with ancient practices of monasticism and female circumcision common to other Ethiopian religious traditions.

DeKollscritta was recognized as a rabbi and written about in the black press, where black claims to Jewish identity were for the most part treated as a simple matter of fact. In 1943, at the invitation of Howard Zebulon Plummer, DeKollscritta spent several weeks in Belleville and at other Temple Beth El communities in the South, teaching classes in Yiddish and Hebrew to the children and also to their teachers at the "Belleville Ethiopian American Hebrew School." Teaching Yiddish indicated DeKollscritta's interest in connecting Temple Beth El to the recognized symbols of the Ashkenazi Jewish world. Community members remarked that he visited Belleville frequently and was considered an important teacher for the community. According to newspaper reports, of the many black and Ashkenazi Jewish groups he came into contact with, DeKollscritta chose Temple Beth El as the version of American Judaism that most closely resembled his own in Ethiopia. He singled out their use of the Hebrew calendar and observance of Jewish holidays, their denial of the divinity of Christ, and their claim of descent from the lost tribes of Israel.[41]

Although Saperstein, Gottlieb, Pollock, and Plummer were all Jews, the racial dimension of their identities defined their experiences in the world of black baseball. As white Jews, Saperstein, Gottlieb, and Pollock were racial outsiders. Being of African descent, Plummer was not identified as a Jew by those outside his community. But it was his religious commitments that defined his worldview and limited his participation as a baseball entrepreneur, as he found himself discouraged by the business practices of league play and unwilling to compromise on his religious beliefs to stay involved in the game that he loved.

## Jews and the Commitment to End Segregated Baseball

Jews and blacks shared some common experiences in early twentieth-century America that explain why Jews imagined a special kinship between themselves and Americans of African descent. The simultaneous Jewish migration from Eastern Europe and black migration from the South (known as the Great Migration) found Jews and blacks newly arrived in the same Northern cities. Both groups suffered from race hatred. Both experienced a surge of separatism in the forms of Zionism and Garveyism. Religious blacks identified with the liberation struggle of the Jews of the biblical Exodus. Both groups created defense agencies to fight against discrimination.

American Jewish historian Hasia Diner has emphasized how, in the first part of the twentieth century, Jews of all types, at least in the North, championed the African American cause. Distinguished Jewish leaders like Stephen Wise, Lillian

Wald, Emil Hirsch, Louis Marshall, and Felix Frankfurter all signed the call that would result in the founding of the NAACP, professing their belief in extending full equality to African Americans. Philanthropists like Jacob Schiff, Lessing Rosenwald, and Felix Warburg (the same German Jews who funded the acculturation of the Eastern European immigrants) gave unstintingly to historically black colleges and were the financiers of the major African American civil rights institutions, the NAACP, the Urban League, and the Congress of Racial Equality. In the short term, Jewish embrace of the antilynching movement and other causes was appreciated by African Americans. But this alliance also revealed differences. Although by the 1920s Jews had achieved sufficient economic and political power to support black causes, they did not feel secure in American society. Their efforts extended into the 1930s as Jewish lawyers Joel and Arthur Spingarn became significant figures in the NAACP leadership and in their legislative battles. Jewish labor organizers formed alliances with black union

*Figure 1.8* Lester Rodney (1911–2009) (Communist Party of the United States Photographs Collection, Tamiment Library, New York University and Ray Rodney).

leaders like A. Philip Randolph, founder of the Brotherhood of Sleeping Car Porters. Jews in the Communist Party championed Paul Robeson and fought for the integration of baseball as part of this effort.[42]

Many theories have been advanced to suggest why so many Jews were so deeply committed to fostering the legal rights and integration of African Americans in the first half of the twentieth century. The religious foundation of a commitment to justice that is deeply ingrained in Jewish textual tradition and the theology of a just God who will deliver the oppressed from bondage played important roles. The liberation narrative of the Exodus story is certainly what attracted enslaved Africans to the Hebrew Bible and black Jews to choose to embody that metaphorical connection, identifying the lost tribes of Israel as their ancestors and Moses as their liberator.

Jewish values of social justice and ties to political radicalism motivated some Jews to get involved in the fight to put an end to segregation in baseball. Saperstein, Pollock, and Gottlieb both impeded and contributed to the effort, as did Pirate

*Figure 1.9* Nat Low (Communist Party of the United States Photographs Collection, Tamiment Library, New York University).

owner William Benswanger. Journalists Walter Winchell, Shirley Povich, and Roger Kahn and politicians Isadore Muchnick, a Jewish city councilman in Boston, and New York mayor Fiorello LaGuardia, whose mother was Jewish, played small roles which scholars have attributed to their Jewish consciousness.[43] Some, but not all, of the Jewish fans in Brooklyn supported Jackie Robinson and the other black Dodgers, and those who did remembered and interpreted the event years later through the lens of Jewish values. But the only consistent and fundamentally moral stance against segregation and on behalf of justice was taken by three Jewish sports reporters for the communist newspaper *The Daily Worker*.

Beginning in 1936, Lester Rodney, Nat Low, and Bill Mardo combined their principled stand with an activist campaign that foreshadowed Jewish efforts on behalf of civil rights twenty years later. Rodney, Low, and Mardo came from

*Figure 1.10* Bill Mardo (1923–) (Communist Party of the United States Photographs Collection, Tamiment Library, New York University).

Jewish families in the New York metropolitan area. They found themselves attracted to the values of communism that bore a deep affinity with the Jewish commitment to social justice. As the sports department of *The Daily Worker*, they fought for better conditions for working people (and athletes in particular) and set down a critique of the racial divide in America under Jim Crow as exemplified by the ban against blacks in organized baseball. But they inevitably found themselves frustrated by the lack of credit they received for their passionate and relentless campaign spanning two decades.

Still, these writers benefited from the same white privilege that gave the Jewish entrepreneurs in black baseball the opportunity to navigate in both the white and black worlds. Rodney, Low, and Mardo had access to major league owners and public attention for their efforts to end segregated baseball. Their experience working with the black press on this issue was mixed. Some journalists appreciated their efforts, while others didn't want the campaign for integration associated with communism. As with the other Jews involved in black baseball, larger social forces would determine how much power they exercised and how their efforts would be interpreted by the black community and the dominant culture.

## The "Special Relationship" between Blacks and Jews after Jackie Robinson

The integration of baseball came at the beginning of a brief era when there actually was a special relationship between black and Jewish communal organizations. World War II brought about major changes in the way the United States would deal with the problem of minority groups. Fighting Hitler and fascism abroad shed a new and negative light on segregation and hatred at home. How could America object to Hitler's racist policies against the Jews and other groups in Europe if we practiced racial politics against Jews, blacks, and others right here in America? The war made it obvious to many, especially the young men and women who had served in the military, that change was necessary. Before the war, racial and ethnic segregation was the norm, and bigotry was not only tolerated but presumed. World War II marked an end to virulent and public anti-Semitism. Jewish agencies still maintained a defensive posture, worrying about Jews as a target for anti-Semitism especially because of their associations with communism under the threat of McCarthyism. But the organized Jewish community also learned from the destruction of European Jewry to mobilize public opinion and counter stereotypes, working for legislation against bigotry and fighting discrimination in the courts and the press.

Jews were also committed to ending discrimination against blacks. The Jewish commitment was based on the "unitary theory of bigotry," which suggests that in order to end one form of oppression, all oppression must be eradicated. Therefore, a fight against anti-Semitism would by definition include working against all forms of racial and ethnic injustice. In the Jewish mind, blacks became surrogates for Jews in the fight for integration. Jewish and black organizations found common ground, and fought together to end legal discrimination in housing, voting, employment, and education for African Americans as well as an end to social discrimination in housing, education, and employment for Jews on the basis of "race, creed, or color."

Jews understood the oppression of African Americans because they had experienced anti-Semitism, and they often drew parallels between these experiences. But their motives were not based only on altruism or identification, but on communal self-preservation. Fighting against racism also helped the Jews maintain their identity in the face of assimilation. The dream of equality that the enlightenment had promised was in its final stages. But the bargain of the enlightenment came at a price: for individual freedom, Jews had to struggle to maintain their cultural identity. In exchange for equality, Jews were expected to assimilate. One way Jews could justify their existence as a distinct cultural group was by fighting for the rights of others. As Murray Friedman suggests, "work[ing] for a society in which economic disadvantage and intolerance would have no place became a religio-cultural obsession."[44]

Yet, however comfortable Jews were, anti-Semitism was still a factor in American life. In 1947 a major Hollywood motion picture, *Gentleman's Agreement*, depicted the range of anti-Semitic attitudes and behaviors that Jews experienced in America at the time. Gregory Peck played a journalist (Phil Green) posing as a Jew to write an article about anti-Semitism. Green and his Jewish friend (a soldier returned from the war) faced barriers in housing, employment, and social connections. Green's son Tommy was beaten up and taunted with racial slurs. His secretary, a Jew who changed her name to get a job, illustrated the problems faced by Jews who tried to hide their identities. The film was poignant and well-received, and contributed to the process that marked the beginning of the end of publicly acceptable anti-Semitism of the type the film illustrated. The message was clear: if no one could really tell that Gregory Peck was not, in fact, a Jew, then there was no reason to hate. Seth Forman characterized the point succinctly: "Tolerance is necessary because we're all the same."[45]

*Gentleman's Agreement*, which depicted the problem of anti-Semitism as a current issue, appeared at a time when anti-Semitism was starting to decline in America. But at mid-century the fight against antiblack racism would have a slower and more volatile trajectory. The idea that we're all the same was not at all the message of another Hollywood film, *The Jackie Robinson Story*. Starring Jackie Robinson himself, this film was made in 1950, three years after *Gentleman's Agreement* won the Oscar and Robinson played his first game in major league baseball. The film told the story of Robinson's life and of the racism he encountered in the process of becoming the first African American since 1889 to play in the major leagues. The film portrayed Robinson's experiences as a ballplayer dealing with Jim Crow laws in the South, and illustrated some of the racial incidents he faced in his first few years in the major leagues, including death threats and intimidation by fans. But the Hollywood version of Robinson's story omitted many of the injustices he experienced, including a court-martial when he was in the U.S. Army during World War II for refusing to move to the back of the bus, even though the Army had by then made segregated seating illegal on its vehicles. And the movie ended with Robinson's testimony before the House Un-American Activities Committee, in an effort to underscore his allegiance to this country where he was now allowed to play ball with whites and where the loyalty of black citizens was being questioned by anticommunists. While *The Jackie Robinson Story* tried to present a message of tolerance similar to *Gentleman's Agreement*, it was clear that tolerance for Jews and blacks meant two different things. Jews were understood as the same as other whites; blacks were seen as different. Jews could assimilate, but there were conditions placed on Robinson's acceptance as a black man in a white world.

These films illustrate the different fates of blacks and Jews in twentieth-century America. Comparing them gives us a sense of why Jackie Robinson's story was read by Jews as symbolic of the potential promise of equality in America, but also of where the similarities end. The experiences of Jews in black baseball explain the historical roots of those differences, and the complicated relationships between Jews and blacks in America in the first half of the twentieth century. Jews and blacks in this world got along, but they also saw each other through the lens of stereotypes. The Jews of black baseball competed, cooperated, and were compassionate supporters of African Americans; some were African American themselves. As would happen again with the rise of the black power movement years later, the blacks with whom they worked in black baseball did not necessarily want the unintentionally patronizing help white Jews offered. The story of Jews in black baseball reminds us that the relationship between blacks and Jews was complicated and highly nuanced, defined by their similar status as "oppressed people" and by the stereotypes each had of the other, and filled with good will that was not always well expressed or received.

All of these changes made the various manifestations of the Jews of black baseball an embarrassment to the postwar Jewish community. Abe Saperstein, Ed Gottlieb, and Syd Pollock, the businessmen who made their living from a segregated institution and traded in old-style Jewish vaudevillian humor with traces of minstrelsy, fit most uncomfortably into a postwar Jewish community that emphasized liberal religious values and the importance of working against discrimination. The communist Jews were likewise unwelcome. While Lester Rodney, Nat Low, and Bill Mardo campaigned for the same values that undergirded postwar American Jewish life—the end of segregated baseball as an affront to American democracy—their affiliation with the Communist Party put them outside the range of what the Jewish community wanted to claim as their own.

Ironically, one additional consequence of blacks and Jews working together politically was that the Jews working in relation to blacks could only be white; what else could "black-Jewish relations" mean? In that framing, black Jews could not be Jewish, and their particular blend of Jewish religion and African ethnicity would force them to remain outside the category. Jews were fully white—successful immigrants in a pluralistic society.

The story of the Jews who came out of left field and into the world of black baseball provides a unique vantage point through which to interpret the complex economic and social negotiation between blacks and Jews in the first half of the twentieth century, tell the story of black Jews, and understand Jewish efforts at social justice in a business that was defined and constricted by the black-white racial divide.

# 2

# The Business of Black Baseball

Professional sport is a business, and black baseball experienced the same challenges that other black businesses faced in segregated America. Entrepreneurs had neither a history of business expertise nor financial resources to draw on. Banks often refused loans, and there was little access to credit or start-up capital. Because Jim Crow reigned in both North and South, blacks needed their own hotels, transportation, and leisure activities to cope with the reality of segregated spaces. But even to support segregated institutions blacks were compelled to forge financial connections with whites. And when black businesses did achieve success, whites were always ready to enter and take over.[1]

Although other white ethnics were instrumental in creating and promoting black baseball teams around the turn of the century, Jewish entrepreneurs began to fill these roles beginning in the 1920s. Anti-Semitism made Jews, and Eastern European immigrant Jews in particular, unwelcome in many traditional white businesses. As a result they often found themselves involved in innovative or otherwise undercapitalized enterprises, including black baseball. As a small business, black baseball required a modest capital investment, and it provided a good return on that investment, so Jewish sports entrepreneurs were eager to invest in teams or provide financial backing for black owners. The Negro Leagues used booking agents to schedule games and rent or lease ballparks, and Jewish entrepreneurs who had experience as middlemen gravitated to this work, following the path of other immigrant groups before them. It was an ideal location for Jewish entrepreneurs to succeed. Black team owners mostly welcomed Jewish business expertise, though they were also concerned by the competition these men offered.[2]

Compared to major league baseball, black baseball was not a stable enterprise. From World War I until the 1960s, major league baseball generally consisted of two leagues of eight teams each. More than eighty teams were involved in eleven different Negro leagues over the history of black baseball (roughly 1887–1953), plus an additional twenty-seven clubs that played independently. Purchasing a major league franchise cost more than four hundred thousand dollars in the 1920s, while in the same era a successful and well-financed team like the Hilldale

Daisies in the Eastern Colored League was organized with a capital investment of less than ten thousand dollars.[3]

While major league schedules were coordinated by the leagues, Negro league teams were independent contractors. Most teams played the majority of their games against nonleague opponents, frequently white teams, because these exhibition games were more lucrative. Nonleague games were negotiated on a cash basis, and profits were highly variable. Rain or a bad turnout at the gate could make the difference between a profitable and nonprofitable season. Teams could make a good return on investment if they made wise business decisions about traveling schedules, purchasing equipment (and rain insurance), scheduling games against strong opponents at popular times, leasing accessible and inexpensive venues, and promoting games effectively. They could also make some money on side ventures like selling peanuts and programs.

Player salaries were also an important variable. The Negro League owners had neither the financial resources to pay the players well nor the legal status of the major league "reserve system," which allowed teams to own a player's contract for life. And players, former slaves and their descendents, were not prepared to surrender their freedom to choose their employer so easily. The monopoly over players on major league teams was further strengthened in the 1930s when Branch Rickey invented the "farm system," making exclusive arrangements that turned minor league teams into a feeder system for his major league club, a system other teams quickly adopted. Black baseball existed outside that protected environment, although segregation provided its own "reserve clause," as Negro league players could not sell their talents to white teams, although they could (and did) leave to play in the Caribbean and in South America, where the color line did not exist.[4]

Major league salaries ranged from four to twenty-eight times higher on average than in the Negro Leagues, with the more equitable ratios occurring during World War II. Yet given the limited options for employment for black men in the United States, players also made more money than they would have doing the kind of unskilled labor that was available to them. Negro League players earned about one and a half times as much as other black wage laborers, and even occasionally surpassed the pay of unskilled white wage laborers. Typical salaries for the six-month season ranged from several hundred dollars in the late 1920s to as much as eight thousand dollars during the mid-1940s, although these salaries dropped precipitously after integration.[5]

Although the large number of teams provided a lot of job opportunities, most teams could not afford to carry more than twenty players, and players themselves served as coaches, managers, and often bus drivers. Not all teams offered salaries and contracts, and some played under the "co-op" system, in which players received a percentage of the team's earnings. This could be advantageous when the teams did well, but did not provide a reliable income. Undercapitalization also meant teams suffered from a shortage of personnel to help train players and advance their skills. Despite these difficult conditions, black baseball survived, and was at times and for some owners and players a lucrative business, especially in the years after the Depression.

The Negro Leagues also remained loose affiliations, with little power over owners or players. Owners lacked the capital to build stadiums and establish local loyalties for their teams. Although teams were nominally associated with cities and towns, without their own parks they could not control their schedules and could only play "at home" when the white teams from whom they rented were out of town. They were often at the mercy of local booking agents to make those arrangements. Most teams "barnstormed," setting up games against whatever competition they could find rather than adhering to a league schedule. That included white teams, who were eager to take on black competition because of the high quality of play and because a racially charged environment attracted fans. To ensure a profitable season, teams had to travel on the cheap, often in a bus that also carried their equipment and occasionally served as a "hotel" when Jim Crow made meals and sleeping accommodations unavailable. Without formal contracts, owners could not depend on player loyalty and often lost players in midseason to independent teams. Despite these difficult conditions, black baseball provided a livelihood for players and owners, and exciting entertainment for black communities.

## The Beginnings of Jewish Involvement: The 1920s

Jews became involved in black baseball in the 1920s. Ed Gottlieb and Syd Pollock were introduced to black baseball through their associations with Nat Strong, the so-called "Hebrew Menace." Teams of Jewish players, black and white, played against black teams, which also created opportunities for Jews to enter the business of black baseball as owners and promoters.

Beginning in the late nineteenth century, black baseball was a popular leisure activity for African Americans and a thriving business in many cities with large black populations, North and South. In the early 1920s, two black entrepreneurs, Andrew "Rube" Foster, a former Negro League player based in Chicago, and Ed Bolden, a post office employee and the executive of the successful Hilldale Daisies from the Philadelphia area, created rival Negro National and Eastern Colored leagues. Foster's league was an effort to challenge the power of Eastern promoters, especially Nat Strong. Unlike Foster, Bolden was willing to work cooperatively with Strong, who played a central role in half of the teams in the Eastern Colored League. Although the leagues succeeded financially during the 1920s, neither survived the Depression.

Ed Gottlieb got involved in sports at a young age. He started out as an athlete in high school, playing varsity basketball and semiprofessional baseball on the weekends. After high school, Gottlieb, along with teammates Harry Passon and

Hugh Black, organized a semipro basketball team under the auspices of a social club, the South Philadelphia Hebrew Association. The SPHAS became one of the premier semiprofessional basketball teams in the country and Gottlieb's central preoccupation.

In 1920, in search of better uniforms and equipment for their basketball team, Gottlieb, Passon, and Black opened their own sporting goods store, PGB Sports, in downtown Philadelphia. It was through the store that Gottlieb made connections to Negro League baseball. As early as 1921, one of his best customers was Ed Bolden, proprietor of the Hilldale team. Gottlieb and Black sold the business to Passon a few years later, and Gottlieb focused on sports promotion and started a booking agency in an office above the store.[6]

Both Passon and Gottlieb scheduled games for black and white teams, taking a percentage (usually 10 percent) of the gate. Gottlieb explained that he really became a promoter by accident. Aware of Nat Strong's reputation, Gottlieb asked Strong to send the House of David, a popular traveling team of white players from Michigan that wore long beards, as was the custom of the Messianic Christian community that sponsored them, to play an amateur (white) team Gottlieb managed, the Philadelphia Elks. Strong told Gottlieb he'd send the House of David if Gottlieb arranged four games for them in Philadelphia. According to Gottlieb, "I lined up four games and became a promoter." Among the teams that played against the House of David was Ed Bolden's Hilldale club of the Eastern Colored League. With this success, Gottlieb had gained entry into the world of black baseball.[7]

Syd Pollock began his career booking baseball in North Tarrytown, New York, in the early 1920s, working for "Bloomer Girls" novelty teams, which were extremely popular in independent baseball from the 1890s through the early 1930s. These teams were composed predominantly of women players, with a few men in drag who usually performed the pitching and catching duties. Pollock also organized and played for the local white (male) Westchester Blue Sox until he was injured in 1923, and promoted many other local teams.

As his promotional work expanded, Pollock set up a booking agency in emulation of, and as a rival to, Nat Strong's. Breaking into the highly competitive baseball scene in New York wasn't easy. By 1924, he was receiving public notice:

> The Middletown State Hospital baseball team…has discontinued booking through Sid Pollock, of Tarrytown NY, and will now book exclusively through Nat C. Strong of New York City NY, who handles only heavy semi-professional teams.[8]

Strong probably put the notice in the newspaper, although Pollock would likely have welcomed the attention, on the theory, key to Pollock's business philosophy, that there's no such thing as bad publicity.

The rivalry between Pollock and Strong escalated when Pollock began to book a Cuban team, the Havana Red Sox, in 1928. Nat Strong and his Afro-Latin business associate, Alex Pompez, did not welcome another entry into what was already a fiercely competitive field. Teams from Cuba had been touring the United States since the early 1880s, and they had reputations for playing high-quality baseball. Black teams from the United States often used Cuba or Havana as part of their names and sometimes pretended to speak to each other in Spanish. These teams may have been paying homage to the great Cuban teams, or they may have thought that if they passed as Cuban they'd find more opportunities to play. They may also have been honoring the Cuban system that permitted mixed-color teams. Lighter-skinned Cubans who chose to stay in the United States were able to play ball in the white leagues, but darker-skinned Cubans had no choice but to play in the Negro Leagues. Strong and Pompez had been bringing Cuban touring teams to the United States since 1906, when the U. S. occupation of Cuba made the island more accessible to booking agents based in the United States. Sponsoring the Havana Red Sox was Pollock's first venture into the world of black baseball.[9]

Booking and later owning the Havana Red Sox was Pollock's main business interest for several years. Bringing a team from Cuba required a substantial financial investment, including obtaining visas and posting bond with immigration to insure that the players would have enough money to return. Pollock put together a strong team that relied exclusively on Cuban players (including Cuban pitching great Luis Tiant, Sr.), many of whom had played with teams that Pompez and Strong had organized. Newspapers hinted that Pollock was hoping to gain entry into Bolden and Strong's Eastern Colored League, though that league was in the process of dissolving. After the 1929 season, Pollock became discouraged by immigration problems and competition from Pompez and decided to focus his efforts on finding African American talent.[10]

Although the team compiled many wins while touring the South and Midwest, Pollock had a difficult time getting owners in the East, most of whom were working with Nat Strong, to take his team seriously. Pollock used black newspapers to publicly challenge his critics. "Our record is clean . . . our business methods held in high esteem," he told the *New York Amsterdam News*. Among his many detractors was Cumberland "Cum" Posey, a newspaper columnist for the *Pittsburgh Courier* who was also a player, manager, and owner of the Homestead Grays, one of the most popular black baseball teams. Posey would often contend that Pollock and other Jewish owners were only in the game for the money. To this accusation Pollock replied, "The writer [meaning Pollock himself] does not have to depend upon baseball for a living." Like Posey, but unlike most of their Jewish and black counterparts in black baseball, Pollock could rely on family money. His father had done well financially as the owner and operator of vaudeville theaters. It was this freedom from financial constraints that allowed Pollock to carve out a career of his choosing while he continued to live in North Tarrytown and work in the family business. But the family fortune would not have sufficed to purchase a major league team, and Pollock enjoyed the niche he found combining his interests in sports and entertainment.[11]

In addition to Jewish promoters and owners, Jewish teams also played a role in black baseball in the twenties and early 1930s. Ed Gottlieb was the catcher and manager of the Philadelphia SPHAS—or Hebrews, as they were often called—composed of players who were also on his basketball team of the same name. They frequently played against black teams at home in Philadelphia but also traveled to New York to play against Negro League teams like the Lincoln Giants and New York Black Yankees. And when Gus Greenlee, owner of the famous Pittsburgh Crawfords, wanted to convince Ed Gottlieb to bring his black Philadelphia Stars into the Negro National League in 1933, he requested a match between the SPHAS and the Crawfords, whose roster included future Hall of Famers Oscar Charleston, Judy Johnson, Josh Gibson, and Satchel Paige. The SPHAS lineup included several Jewish players from the basketball team, such as Cy Kaselman, Max Posnack, and Hymie Bernstein. The pitcher, Rube Chambers, was Catholic. Gottlieb had no problem mixing religions on his team, as long as the players were white. The Crawfords won, 5–2, and the *Pittsburgh Courier* called it an "upset," so the SPHAS must have been considered a powerful team. Another team known as the Bronx Hebrews played frequently against the Lincoln Giants in 1925 and 1926. There is also a newspaper report of a "Hebrew All-Star Nine" playing against a Ku Klux Klan team in Washington, D.C., in 1926.[12]

By the early 1920s, William Plummer's team of black Jews from Temple Beth El was playing organized baseball against local teams in Virginia. Plummer's vision of a healthy community included athletics, and Sunday, Tuesday, and Thursday were set aside for sports. The community built tennis courts and a wooden baseball stadium on their vast lands. Plummer himself had played baseball at school while he was growing up. According to communal lore, the team he started was originally called the Belleville Clod Hoppers and then the Belleville Industrial School team, but it was referred to in the press as the "Saints." The team was finally known as the Belleville Grays, named after the attractive, professionally made gray uniforms that Plummer purchased, but possibly also in tribute to Cum Posey's Homestead Grays, who were gaining a national reputation for their fine play. The Belleville team prided itself on using only the best equipment. They played every Sunday afternoon throughout the 1920s, and community members who attended as children remember these games being festive occasions that drew two or three thousand people from the Tidewater region. The games were an important source of entertainment for the local black community, which, in the Jim Crow South, had few opportunities for public social gatherings. Owning their own stadium and fielding a high quality team was an important part of the public contributions the team made to the black community of Portsmouth.[13]

The team is first mentioned in the sports pages of the Norfolk *Journal and Guide* (the local African American newspaper) in 1924 as the Belleville Industrial School "Saints." All the players were community members, including Plummer's

*Figure 2.1* Wooden stadium built by William Plummer, Belleville, Va. (courtesy of Joel Wagner).

three sons. William Plummer was not interested in baseball as a business. Under his leadership the team played for recreation and competition, as did the other teams of white Hebrews in that era. But in December 1931, Plummer died, and new leadership in Belleville would change the Belleville Grays into a team that would play a surprising role in the history of black baseball during the Depression Era.

## The Depression Era: 1931–1936

The Great Depression brought many changes to black baseball. As the economic opportunities of the '20s began to disappear, black baseball entrepreneurs had a harder time finding fans, as few people had discretionary income to spend at the ballpark. Many of the successful teams of the 1920s went out of existence, and many of the owners of that era, particularly the white ethnics, moved on to other interests. But a new group of African American owners would find opportunities in this era of hardship that would reinvigorate the black baseball business.

Many of these owners made their money from gambling and nightclubs. While the numbers game was illegal, it was a well-run part of the underground economy and the forerunner of the state lottery. Individuals bet on daily numbers, and the winning digits were based on some published figure, often related to the stock market. Numbers "kings" were well respected in black communities, admired for their wealth and appreciated because of the jobs that they created. Owning baseball teams provided them with legitimate businesses.

Most of the new owners were gamblers, but others relied on family wealth or the capital investment of Jewish promoters. Two of the most successful gamblers were Abe Manley, who, with his wife Effa, owned the Newark Eagles, and Gus Greenlee, owner of the Pittsburgh Crawfords, named after Greenlee's nightclub. Greenlee was also the founder of a new Negro National League and inventor of the most important and lucrative event of the black baseball calendar, the East-West All-Star game. Of those who remained involved from the earlier era, Cum Posey, owner of Greenlee's rival team in Pittsburgh, the Homestead Grays, relied on family wealth and then, after his family business was ruined in the Depression, co-ownership with numbers man Rufus Jackson. Alex Pompez, the Afro-Latin associate of Nat Strong and owner of the New York Cubans, also had funds derived from family wealth and gambling enterprises. Ed Bolden worked in the post office. Bolden and others would rely on financial support from Ed Gottlieb and Abe Saperstein.

Apart from the Jewish entrepreneurs, all of the Depression-era owners were African American, with the exception of J. L. Wilkinson and T. Y. Baird, the proprietors of the Kansas City Monarchs. Wilkinson and Baird were respected for their well-run organization, which had sunk deep roots in Kansas City's black community. But Wilkinson was also a complicated figure with connections to novelty baseball. Wilkinson owned an "All-Nations" team that toured with an orchestra and wrestlers as well as Bloomer Girls teams. He financed the House of David and other traveling novelty teams. Recent scholarship has suggested that the Monarchs co-owner T. Y. Baird was a member of the local Kansas City Ku Klux Klan chapter.[14]

Nonetheless, Wilkinson was singled out as a "good white," while Syd Pollock, Ed Gottlieb, and Abe Saperstein were more controversial. As Jews they replaced Nat Strong as the "Hebrew Menace." But they played strategic roles in the business of black baseball. They owned teams both publicly and as silent partners with black owners. They were deeply involved in shaping the future of the Negro Leagues through their outspoken ideas and bias towards seeing sport as entertainment. The one owner who was both black and Jewish, Howard Z. Plummer, was also interested in contributing to the development of the leagues, but found the business did not fit well with his religious principles.

## H. Z. Plummer and the Belleville Grays

William Plummer died in December 1931. In January, his eldest son Howard Z. Plummer, then thirty-two years old, was named to lead Temple Beth El. H. Z. Plummer faced a difficult challenge early in his leadership when an article in *The Crisis* (the official magazine of the NAACP) described the Belleville community as "communistic" and a "cult." H. Z. responded in an article he wrote for the *Pittsburgh Courier* that corrected the "inaccurate and unfair statements about the Church of God and Saints of Christ." He described the Industrial School, chartered by the State of Virginia, which welcomed nonmember students who studied "entirely free from any religious constraint." The experience of being criticized in such a high-profile venue, combined with a general lack of understanding of Hebrew Israelite traditions, made Plummer's community wary of discussing their beliefs in public and very protective of their privacy. But it also made him seek out ways to bring positive attention to other aspects of communal life. The Belleville Grays would serve this purpose. The team continued to bring crowds to "the Saints place," but most local people were unaware that the community identified as Israelites.[15]

In 1932 the *Journal and Guide* began to refer to the team as the "Grays of the Belleville Industrial School." One of their star pitchers, Josiah Wagner, was raised at the school. Josiah's son Joel remembered his father's stories of traveling with the team and their refusal to play on the Jewish Sabbath. Plummer began to professionalize the team. They trained in Florida, and became members of the Tidewater Associated League. The Grays toured that summer, winning many games, including one against another Jewish team from the Paterson, New Jersey, Young Men's Hebrew Association. A newspaper recounted: "On Sunday the Grays batt[l]ed the Y.M.H.A of Paterson [NJ] and defeated the Yiddish boys by batting the pill to all corners of the lot." Of course, only the Paterson team was seen as Jewish by the press.[16]

H. Z. Plummer brought other changes to the Belleville Grays. In 1932, for the first time, local baseball players who were not raised in the community joined

*Figure 2.2* Josiah Wagner, pitcher for the Belleville Grays (courtesy of Joel Wagner).

the team. Pitcher Roy Watford and second baseman Albert "Buster" Haywood came from a renowned local team, the Portsmouth Firefighters. Borrowing players for important games was common in independent baseball, although it was a controversial practice in the Negro Leagues. The top players, who were paid per game and not under contract, moved around to make additional money. Plummer's brother Judah, an excellent catcher, also played for the Firefighters, as did the best-known Negro League player from the Portsmouth area, Buck Leonard. In his autobiography, Leonard credits Buster Haywood with cautioning him not to leave the relatively well-paid and steady opportunities available locally to try out for Ben Taylor's Baltimore Stars, where the players were paid a percentage of the gate rather than a salary. But Leonard did leave, and Haywood was himself enticed a few years later to seek more competitive and lucrative opportunities. In 1935, Haywood went to Jacksonville to try out for a new professional team that would become part of the Negro National League, the Brooklyn (later Newark) Eagles, owned by Abraham Manley and managed by the same Ben Taylor. Taylor was a stellar first baseman and also manager for many years for a number of Negro League teams. He was elected to the Baseball Hall of Fame in 2006. These contacts would encourage Plummer's interest in league play and would bring his team attention outside the Portsmouth area.[17]

## Syd Pollock's Independent Team

Despite the economic challenges of the times, Cum Posey, owner of the Homestead Grays, decided to start a new league in 1932. Although his East-West League was a short-lived financial failure, it paved the way for a new Negro National League the following year, started by his Pittsburgh rival Gus Greenlee. Despite past disagreements, Posey invited Syd Pollock and his team, now called "Syd Pollock's Cubans," to join the league. The move to include Pollock's team was controversial, since it was a traveling team without a home base. Sportswriter Rollo Wilson was critical of including such a team in league play, calling it "the first weak spot in the armor." In reply, Pollock made a point of distinguishing his club from earlier traveling teams run by Nat Strong, Alex Pompez's Cuban Stars and Brooklyn Royal Giants. "I wish to assure the many followers of my activities in the baseball world that Syd Pollock is NOT a Nat Strong. I believe in building and not in destroying." Pollock's business strategy was not like Strong's. Strong operated a network of black and white teams, and many in black baseball believed that he provided more advantageous conditions for the white teams. But Pollock was not focused on building a sports promotion empire. He was primarily interested in operating traveling teams and believed that the world of black baseball was well suited to his business plan.[18]

Pollock was interested in finding out whether a traveling team could function within a league structure, and appreciated Posey's invitation. He argued that including a traveling team would benefit the other league entrants, since they would have to travel less. And he expressed an earnest desire to be part of black baseball's building efforts. Going against the common wisdom that a team needed a home city in order to develop loyal fans and a steady income, Pollock believed that his traveling teams, like circuses and other forms of traveling entertainment, would attract attention with a novelty angle. He planned elaborate travel arrangements that included regular annual visits to towns across the country supported by strong advance publicity. Over the years Pollock's plan succeeded. But he would continue to draw criticism from the black press and from other owners for his iconoclastic practices.[19]

Despite adverse financial conditions and the doubts of the black press, Posey's league got off to a strong start, and Gus Greenlee's Pittsburgh Crawfords and the New York Black Yankees considered affiliating. Pollock's regular press releases enthusiastically reported that his team had beaten every league team at least once, and was doing well considering that the players had to deal with the adversities of travel. By the end of June, Pollock's team was third in the standings in the eight-team league after the Baltimore Black Sox and Posey's Homestead Grays, compiling a twelve and fifteen record. The Cubans played as many games as the other teams, despite their onerous travel schedule.

But the league was not able to sustain itself and folded midseason. Pollock wrote a postmortem in praise of the league that was published in several of the black newspapers. He described the financial problems besetting baseball and put the league's demise in context, suggesting the league would have done well had it started in better financial times. All of baseball was suffering from the effects of the Great Depression. Pollock vowed to finish out the season on the road and pay his players even if he had to take a loss. He closed with his usual optimism: "let's hope for future seasons which will bring a better fare to baseball and all other business enterprises in general, all of which are now undergoing a severe strain." Pollock's efforts and his role as an outsider who seemed to care deeply about black baseball were gaining positive attention. Columnist Romeo Dougherty gave over his "Sportopics" column in the *Amsterdam News* to Pollock's essay, calling him:

> . . . one of the few men in baseball that can take his pen in hand and give a comprehensive account of the game as it concerns the Negro. And this despite the fact that Mr. Pollock is a member of the opposite race.[20]

Pollock's commitment to working within the league structure soon wavered. In July 1933 his Cuban team was invited to join the National Association of Professional Baseball Clubs (later, the Negro National League) that Gus Greenlee had organized in the wake of the demise of Posey's East-West experiment. Pollock's team would "serve as a traveling attraction" to replace the Homestead Grays, who were suspended from the league because of the ongoing rivalry between Cum Posey and Gus Greenlee. But he resigned from the league soon after his team was admitted. Pollock realized that being part of the league was curtailing his profits by limiting his team's traveling schedule and paying lower guaranteed rates for games. To the disappointment and anger of the other owners, Pollock got involved in a legal battle with the owner of the Columbus team, Arthur Peebles, over how much Pollock's team was to receive for games they played. Peebles argued that he paid the league standard fee, since the Cubans were a league team when he made the arrangement. Pollock was demanding higher fees, as would be appropriate for an independent team, and filed suit for breach of contract and damages for disrupting their schedule. This episode would mark the beginning of a rupture between Pollock and African American owners that would continue throughout Pollock's long career in black baseball. Owners of league teams resented his maverick style and his lack of commitment to league play. He would remain outside the black baseball power structure.[21]

Pollock did play an important role in advancing interracial baseball, however. Hoping to promote his team, Pollock attempted to enter the Cubans in the prestigious white-only *Denver Post* Tournament of independent baseball in 1932, but the offer was rejected when he informed the organizers that the club was composed of "dark-skinned Islanders." Tournament organizer C. L. Parsons of the *Denver Post* told Pollock that he rejected the Cubans because some of the Southern teams in the tournament might object to their presence. Pollock sent the information to the black press. It was presented not as an outrage, but a simple matter of fact. Although he didn't succeed in gaining entrance to the tournament, Pollock's effort opened the door. Two years later Satchel Paige pitched for the white House of David and defeated a black all-star team composed of Negro League standouts, breaking the race barrier in the Denver tournament.[22]

Although teams in organized baseball would not hire black players again until 1947, the world of independent baseball was financed by interracial play, and even included a few integrated teams in the 1930s. Paige and others played on integrated teams in the Northwest in the 1930s, and the novelty "All-Nations" teams also featured black players, as did the House of David on occasion. Although integrated teams remained rare and predominantly located in the western part of the country, black and white independent teams frequently played against each other. These interracial games drew large crowds of blacks and whites, and occasional attention from the white press. The popularity of these contests encouraged the Commissioner of Baseball, Judge Kenesaw Mountain Landis, to curtail the practice. Many believed he did so to avoid having white teams of major leaguers defeated by supposedly inferior black teams. But even after the ban, black teams continued to play against all-star teams from the major and minor leagues after the baseball season and in winter leagues in California and Latin America.[23]

## *Abe Saperstein and Interracial Baseball*

Pollock was not the only Jew who was involved in promoting interracial baseball in the 1930s. Like Pollock, Abe Saperstein focused his attention on independent teams and was a master at publicity. Saperstein began promoting sports in Chicago in the 1920s, and became associated with black baseball as a result of his friendships with former Chicago Giants players Walter Ball and Robert Gilkerson, who had organized touring teams when their playing careers ended. Saperstein was well connected to black players and began his career in black baseball creating opportunities for them to make money outside the structures of league play.

The first baseball team Saperstein owned was a novelty team known as the Cleveland All-Nations, which toured in 1933. It was modeled on Monarchs owner J. L. Wilkinson's 1912 All-Nations team. Saperstein considered Wilkinson his mentor in devising attractions that would bring crowds. All-Nations teams featured players based on their race and nationality. Saperstein's team consisted of "Irish, German, Austrian, Indian, Italian, French, Mexican, Polish, English, Slovak and two Race stars." He advertised it as a "true product of the American melting pot." Saperstein's team toured the Northwest and Canada, and played against several black teams as well as white teams.[24]

As a result of his baseball and basketball connections in the Northwest, Saperstein was responsible for getting Satchel Paige and other black players to North Dakota in 1933 to play on the first professional interracial teams since the 1880s. Neil Churchill, the owner of a white team in Bismarck, North Dakota, was looking for a player to help his team beat a rival club in Jamestown that had hired a few black players. Churchill placed a call to Saperstein, who sent Quincy Trouppe from the Chicago American Giants, Red Haley from the Memphis Red Sox, and Roosevelt Davis, who was pitching for the Pittsburgh Crawfords. Churchill's team still could not beat Jamestown pitcher Barney Brown, so Churchill contacted Saperstein again, and asked him for the "best negro pitcher in baseball" according to Satchel Paige's own recollections.[25]

Saperstein was also responsible for getting the attention of the white press for an event that would keep the Negro Leagues financially solvent for many years: the East-West All-Star game. This annual event would become the Negro Leagues' greatest attention-getter and moneymaker. Patterned on the major league All-Star Game, which also began in 1933, the East-West All-Star game was played at Comiskey Park in Chicago for thirty years. Sometimes a second game was played on the East Coast. The game was the invention of Pittsburgh

*Figure 2.3* Satchel Paige (National Baseball Hall of Fame Library, Cooperstown, N.Y.).

Crawford staff member Roy Sparrow and owner Gus Greenlee, who believed that the top players from the black teams should be showcased like their major league counterparts. Greenlee also provided the initial financial backing. From its inception, it attracted crowds of over twenty thousand. Attendance would swell to fifty thousand at the height of the game's popularity in the 1940s, providing the main source of revenue to run the leagues. The game was the most popular event of the year in the world of black sports, and it attracted the elite of the black community, not only from Chicago but around the country. It also drew the attention of the white community to the high caliber of play in the Negro Leagues. The game made Chicago a key center of black baseball and increased the circulation and prestige of the two most important black newspapers, the *Chicago Defender* and the *Pittsburgh Courier*, through which fans voted for players to be in the game. It also built Abe Saperstein's reputation as an important—and problematic—figure in black baseball.[26]

Saperstein was also known to be one of the "men 'behind the guns'" for the East-West game because he secured the Chicago White Sox's field, Comiskey Park, over Charles Comiskey's objections. Saperstein was credited with (and paid well for) making sure the daily (white) newspapers in Chicago publicized the event. As a result, Saperstein developed a reputation in the black press as someone who had "done more toward building Race baseball in Chicago than many a fellow you and I could name." But Saperstein would give most of his attention to creating opportunities for individual players and owners that he drew into his circle. Although he would become closely involved with individual teams in the Negro American League when it was founded in 1937, Saperstein was not interested in supporting the leagues, and was frequently in conflict with them.[27]

## Black Baseball in Philadelphia

Although Pollock and Saperstein disdained league play, Philadelphia Jewish entrepreneurs Ed Gottlieb and Harry Passon took a strong interest in Greenlee's new league. While this marked the beginning of Gottlieb's long association with the Negro National League, Passon's participation lasted only a few years. Passon's short-lived experience in black baseball illustrates the difficulties fair-minded businessmen had in this contentious world. He could not compete with the new alliance Ed Gottlieb forged with the most powerful black man in Philadelphia baseball, Ed Bolden, leaving his old partner Passon behind.

In 1931, Harry Passon started his own black baseball team. He called them the Bacharach Giants to capitalize on the name recognition of the successful and popular team that had played in Ed Bolden's Eastern Colored League the 1920s. That team had originated in Jacksonville, Florida, and then moved to Atlantic City, where they took the name of the Jewish mayor of the town, Harry Bacharach. Passon's Bacharachs were based in Philadelphia and played at the field he leased, which came to be known as Passon Field. In 1933, as interest in the team grew, Passon made improvements to the field, adding a grandstand, clubhouse, and lights. The team was made up of veterans who had played for teams like Hilldale and the St. Louis Stars. "Sleepy" Joe Lewis, who would become the manager of the Belleville Grays in later years, was the catcher.[28]

By this time Ed Gottlieb had become the premier booking agent in Philadelphia. Ed Bolden had relinquished ownership of Philadelphia's main professional black baseball attraction, the Hilldale Daisies, but wanted to return. Hilldale, now owned by John Drew, joined Cum Posey's East-West League in 1932. Drew didn't want to use Gottlieb's booking services, so Gottlieb made sure that the team would not have opportunities to play in Philadelphia. Bolden and Gottlieb made a powerful alliance. To further secure their power, they started a new team, the Philadelphia Stars, in 1933. Their partnership lasted until Bolden's death in 1950. Webster McDonald, who pitched for and managed the Stars in their early years, remembered Bolden and Gottlieb as "two partners, one colored, one white," and that is often how they are described in the black baseball literature. Bolden, who had worked in prior years with Nat Strong, knew very well that Gottlieb's affiliation with Strong would make it possible to get good dates for games in New York and New England as well as in Philadelphia. With Gottlieb's financial backing and connections to the Nat Strong Booking Agency and Bolden's baseball expertise, the Stars easily became the top black baseball team in Philadelphia.[29]

The Stars played independently for a year, and then joined Gus Greenlee's Negro National League in 1934. Gottlieb had already been booking games for the Stars as well as for the other Negro National League teams when they traveled east of Pittsburgh. The League, like its 1920s predecessor, Rube Foster's Negro National League, did not want to deal with Strong as a booking agent, but had no choice if they wanted to play white semipro teams on the east coast. Greenlee, like Bolden, was willing to work with Strong through Gottlieb, however. Greenlee's Pittsburgh rival Cum Posey worried that Gottlieb would soon encroach on his territory in western Pennsylvania and suggested that the league's problems were directly related to the power that Strong and Gottlieb exercised. Posey would be a frequent critic of Gottlieb's power and scheduling activities throughout their years of association in the Negro National League, often accusing Gottlieb of lacking concern for the welfare of the league and being interested only in having teams he booked make money. But Posey was also interested in turning a profit, and he and Gottlieb would become allies in later years.[30]

Posey recruited Harry Passon's Bacharachs to join the Negro National League in an effort to counter Gottlieb's power. Passon was enthusiastic about bringing his team into organized play. He applied for league membership and attended several organizational meetings. But the other owners rejected Passon's application, bowing to the desires of Bolden and Gottlieb, who did not want two league teams in Philadelphia. Passon, who still worked closely with Gottlieb at the sporting goods store and other promotional activities, was surprised by their opposition. Cum Posey saw this as a personal defeat. He expressed his disappointment with the decision, pointing out that as long as the clubs did not play in Philadelphia on the same date, the Bacharachs, who could draw on the road, would be an important attraction for the league. Posey got his way eventually, and the Bacharachs were accepted. But Passon could not compete with Bolden and Gottlieb. By the time the League owners met in the winter of 1935, Passon had decided to quit. He offered to sell the franchise for $400, which was the amount that he had advanced in player contracts. One of the owners suggested that it really wasn't necessary to make good on those contracts, leaving Passon uncomfortable with the way the league was doing business and ready to leave.[31]

But Passon kept his contractual obligations to the players and won the admiration of the black press for how he conducted business. Rollo Wilson, who was both a sportswriter and a commissioner of the league, devoted an entire column to praising Passon's "sportsmanship" and "intestinal fortitude." Wilson appreciated how Passon supported his players, even those who made purchases from his store they didn't pay for and didn't play the caliber of baseball he was expecting them to. Passon paid salaries, met obligations, and wanted his team to succeed. Passon's association with Negro league baseball continued in a limited way. His sporting goods store supplied league equipment, and the Worth ball he sold became the official ball of the National Association in 1935 and 1936. But Passon discovered, as Howard Z. Plummer would learn a few years later, that black baseball was a rough business, and other Jewish and black owners and promoters provided tough competition.[32]

The unexpected death of Nat Strong in 1935 created an opportunity to improve the conditions for black baseball in New York, and an opportunity for Ed Gottlieb to extend his reach. Although the owners discussed hiring a new booking agent after Strong's death, Gottlieb retained the position. He would continue to work in affiliation with Nat Strong's agency and with Strong's successor William Leuschner, who played a background role. Together with Max Rosner, the Jewish owner of the popular white semipro Brooklyn Bushwicks, they would exercise a great deal of power over bookings in New York and access to ballparks there that would cause conflicts in the years to come.

Gottlieb's multiple roles—as owner of the Stars, booking agent for the league, and head of his own booking agency—gave him a lot of power in the Negro National League. While at times the other owners valued his contributions and believed that he was an asset to the league, they would also continue to perceive him as an avaricious Jew and an outsider who, like his predecessor Nat Strong, sought his own financial gain at the expense of the other owners.

## Coming Out of the Depression: 1936–1940

In the years leading up to World War II, black baseball gained momentum. New leagues (including the Negro American League, the midwestern rival to the

NNL) and new independent teams expanded the reach of the game. The Jews involved in black baseball started new teams and became more deeply involved in the business of the leagues as booking agents, owners, even officers. But as they gained power their status remained complicated. Their own business agendas came into conflict with the goals of other owners. Sometimes those conflicts were simply over money and turf. But other situations arose when issues of racial pride and self-respect became paramount and stereotypes took the place of real understanding. This era also marked the further professionalization of the Belleville Grays. Black Jews, unlike their white counterparts, were also motivated by racial pride. A well-respected baseball team would gain recognition for the Temple Beth El community and enhance the status of black Jews in the black community as well as making them a credit to the race.

## *The Belleville Grays*

The boundary between league and independent play was porous. Teams and individual players shifted from one to the other, sometimes in the same season. New leagues formed and dissolved frequently. The Belleville Grays are a case in point. H. Z. Plummer gained respect for his own business dealings from the black press, but his aspirations to gain national recognition for the Grays would be tempered by the realities of the business of black baseball.

Plummer saw building the Belleville Grays as a positive investment that would bring respect to his community, make an economic contribution to the region, and bring honor to the race. E. B. Rea, sports editor of the leading black newspaper in Virginia, the Norfolk *Journal and Guide*, admired Plummer's goals. He praised Plummer and the team, and urged fans to support them. He pointed out the financial benefits organized black baseball brought to the community, noting that each team carried twenty-two players as well as a business and managerial staff that kept black men employed in hard times. He also reminded his readers that this work "is not of the lowest calling, but a part of the national entertainment offered throughout the country." Baseball carried prestige and status. Plummer believed this effort to build his team would bring recognition and acceptance to his community and refute the idea that his group was "communistic" or a cult, as had been suggested in the national press.[33]

The team began to travel extensively and to receive overtures from leagues. Maintaining a hectic schedule while respecting their religious commitments would be difficult to do, but Plummer made every effort. Benjamin H. Young, community member and now manager of the team, announced in the black press that they were looking for opponents, and they would play "any day excepting Friday and Saturday." He also noted that they had hired local star Eugene "Sook" Lawrence and brought the former Negro League catcher Buster Haywood, who had played for them in the early 1930s, back to their squad to underline their commitment to high-quality baseball. When they returned from a trip to play teams in North Carolina, H. Z. Plummer commented: "The club is getting along fine, but it is not quite up to standard. But before I have finished I am going to place a team in the field second to none." The newspaper pointed out that Plummer "travels with the team and appears in uniform at every game. He is a former star of Belleville teams of the good old days." To prepare for league play, Plummer scheduled contests against top-notch teams such as Ben Taylor's Washington Royal Giants, the New York Black Yankees, the Baltimore Black Sox, and Alex Pompez's New York Cubans.[34]

Plummer also hired a local booking agent with national connections, John B. (Brady) Johnson, to arrange games. Johnson attempted to schedule games with the Pittsburgh Crawfords and the Newark Eagles. In a letter to Abe Manley of the Eagles, Johnson claimed the Grays were the "best club" in the area, perhaps not as strong as the Negro National League clubs, but "a big favorite" in Norfolk and Portsmouth. As part of the offer, Plummer would provide guest accommodations at the Belleville Industrial School, and was suggesting a $100 guarantee with options of a 40 percent net for the visiting team. Although there are no records of the Grays playing either the Eagles or the Crawfords that season, former Crawford catcher Leon Ruffin was added to the lineup late in the season, as Plummer began to look for players who could fulfill his promise of making the Grays "second to none."[35]

Leon Ruffin came from Portsmouth, and grew up deep-sea fishing around the ports. He came home after the 1938 season, leaving the Pittsburgh Crawfords when the team moved to Toledo. Ruffin was a catcher with a strong arm. He played intermittently for the Newark Eagles and, after serving in the Navy, was the starting catcher on their 1946 Negro League championship team. Adding Ruffin to the team at the end of the season foreshadowed the efforts Plummer would make in the 1939 season to build the Belleville Grays into a contending team.[36]

In 1939, Plummer continued his efforts to make the Belleville Grays a top ball club. In January, the black press reported that one of the local teams that the Grays played against, the Washington Royal Giants, was planning to seek admission to the Negro National League. The application was brought to the January meeting of NNL owners, but was tabled until the spring. Instead of waiting for a decision from the NNL, Royal Giants owner W. M. Josephs decided to join a new league consisting of teams from Virginia, North Carolina, and the Washington, D. C., area, to be known as the Negro International League. John Brady Johnson, the man who promoted games for the Belleville Grays in 1938, was named president. H. Z. Plummer agreed to serve as treasurer and enter the Belleville Grays into this league. They announced their intention to play a split season, from May 1 to July 4 and then July 4 to Labor Day, with a championship series between the winners of the two halves, as was customary in the Negro

National and American Leagues. Seven teams joined, including the Washington Royal Giants, managed by the former Negro League star and future Hall of Fame member Ben Taylor. His involvement was an indication of the seriousness and high level of expectations for the new league. Plummer and his associates were hoping to create the "third colored diamond body," to rival the Negro National and American Leagues.[37]

The Belleville Grays would also be managed by a former Negro League player, "Sleepy" Joe Lewis. Lewis, who came from Maryland, was a catcher for the Lincoln Giants, Baltimore Black Sox, Bacharachs, and Hilldales in the 1920s. He caught the attention of sportswriter Rollo Wilson, who called him a "hard-working and conscientious athlete" who was often the backup catcher for stars like Biz Mackey. Lewis ended his playing career with Harry Passon's reorganized Bacharach Giants in 1933. He settled in Portsmouth and became manager of the Belleville Grays, serving in that position in 1939 and 1940. By 1942, Lewis had become the promoter of all Negro League games played in the Tidewater area, a job he would retain through the 1950s.

Plans to organize the league continued. Brady Johnson again sought games for the Grays with the Negro National League teams the Homestead Grays, Newark Eagles, New York Cubans, and New York Black Yankees. In March the Grays went to Jacksonville, Florida, for spring training. Final plans for the league were made at a meeting at the end of April. At the meeting Plummer, along with the owner of the Baltimore Black Sox, Joseph Thomas, suggested the league's name be changed to the Eastern Colored League. Plummer's and Thomas' argument was that calling the league "international" created a false impression for "an organization operated among players of one race and in one section of the country." Plummer and Thomas prevailed, and the name was changed. To those aware of Negro League history, the new name would echo the Eastern Colored League that had been organized in the 1920s by Ed Bolden to compete with Rube Foster's Negro National League, and perhaps that was what they had in mind. The organization also developed plans to play Tidewater area games at stadiums in Portsmouth used primarily by local white minor league teams, Bain Field and Sewanee Field, not at the old Belleville grandstands. They also agreed that each team would carry sixteen players. Umpires would be paid and selected by the home team, and the gate would be divided sixty-forty between the home and away teams.[38]

The Grays played exceptionally well in the month of May in league games, posting a record of nine wins and two defeats. A team photo in the *Journal and Guide* ran under the caption "Leaders in the Eastern Colored League." In a short time, Plummer had achieved the prominence and national attention for the team he had hoped for. D. E. Ellis, columnist for *The New York Age*, reported small crowds for these games, despite the high caliber of play, and exhorted his readers to support "Negro teams of the Eastern Colored League, and their associates, insted of crowding into the ofay parks." Competition from white baseball would continue to plague all of the black leagues.[39]

To build a strong team, Plummer invited players who were not part of the Belleville community. In addition to Roy Watford and Buster Haywood, who had played for the team in prior years, Plummer added pitchers Vernon "Big Six" Riddick, Tony Spruill, Lefty Stewart, and Gentry Jessup. Position players James

## The Cream Of Tidewater Baseball Clubs

he best equipped team in Tidewater, Virginia, is the Belle- rays, pictured above, owned and operated by Bishop H. Z. ier of Nansemond County, near Portsmouth. Owner Plum- is recruited some of the best players in this section to make ganization one of the strongest in Virginia. The club is ing for an extended tour into the North and East during ionth. Shown above, are, left to right, front row: A. "Buster"

Haywood, Luke Fears, Calvin Wooten, Matt Hill, J and Thomas Stephenson (center) mascot. Second row feries, James "Rip" Wilson, Billy Jackson, W. Plum- ris, Sam Dotson and Roy "Big Boy" Watford. _Thi Hill, Benjamin H. Young, manager and coach; Bis Joe Oakley, Will Bradley and Eugene "Sook" Law stone Photo).

### uis-Schmeling Fight Broadcast ɔnsored By Buick Over NBC

V YORK—The world's
v e ight championship
between Champion Joe
and Max Schmeling, for-
ampion, at the Yankee
m. Wednesday night,

Corporation. Clem McCarthy,
veteran NBC sports announcer,
will describe the blow-by-blow
progress of the fight over one
of the most extensive radio net
works ever arranged for a

in 1935, the Louis-Schmeling
fight in 1936, the battle in
June 1937, when the brown
bomber won the title at
Chicago from James J. Brad-
dock, and the Tommy Farr-
Louis fight in August 1937.

### Armsti
### Expect:
### Troubl

NEW YORK—Fe
Welterweight Ch
Armstrong is not

Figure 2.4 The Belleville Grays team photo, 1938. Manager H. Z. Plummer is wearing a suit in the last row. (Photo used courtesy of *New Journal & Guide*, Norfolk, Va.)

"Rip" Wilson, James Mickey, and Tommy Sampson were also recruited. But community members were actively involved. William Plummer and Jesse Jose would serve as umpires for the league. Luke Fears, Jasper Elam, and Calvin Wooten (a relative of COGASOC founder William Saunders Crowdy) played regularly. The star pitcher was Belleville community member Nathaniel "Sonny" Jeffries, who went on to play in the Negro Leagues before and after a stint in the Army in World War II, and was given a tryout for the white International League St. Louis Cardinals' farm team after baseball's integration. Most other community members were reluctant to try out at higher levels, however, as leaving would undermine their connections to their Belleville home.[40]

This team stayed together for the rest of the season, but not as part of the Eastern Colored League. Although high-level Negro League play was most desirable, its business made Plummer uneasy. The controversy that caused Plummer to withdraw his team from the league began in late May, when Ben Taylor's Royal Giants beat the Grays 6–3, with Sonny Jeffries taking the loss at Griffith Stadium, Washington's major league ballpark. The Royal Giants also played and won a second game against the High Point Red Sox from a rival league that day.

Finding it peculiar that the Royal Giants would play the High Point Sox and the Grays the same day, sports columnist Sam Lacy investigated the matter. He learned that the Belleville management (and particularly Plummer as a league officer) was disturbed at a report from the team in Charlotte that the management of the Royal Giants had padded expenses for advertising and the cost of balls when they played in North Carolina. The Grays had announced that they would not play the Royal Giants unless the dispute about expenditures could be resolved, so the Giant owners secured a second game against the Red Sox in case the Grays did not come to Washington.[41]

The Royal Giants' backup plan to substitute the High Point team disturbed Plummer even more, because it undermined the integrity of league play. On Friday morning, before the game, Bishop Plummer and Benjamin Young traveled to Griffith Stadium for a discussion with representatives of the Royal Giants—Josephs and Taylor—hoping to resolve the dispute. Washington Senators' owner Clark Griffith negotiated a settlement between the clubs, and Plummer agreed to have his team return to Washington on Sunday to play. Plummer closed the session, according to Lacy. "'I do not want to let it be said that my club disappointed the Washington fans or failed to live up to its pledge to the league,' the Bishop said." But having to negotiate petty controversy deeply disturbed Plummer's sense of propriety and his religious principles. That would be the last league game the Belleville Grays played.[42]

Although Plummer's experience with league play was difficult, it enhanced his national reputation as an honest businessman and gentleman. The same edition of the *Baltimore Afro-American* that carried Lacy's report made the official announcement that three teams had pulled out of the Eastern Colored

League: the Belleville Grays, the Norfolk Black Tars, and the Baltimore Black Sox. The next week, the *Afro-American* reported other inappropriate financial dealings, this time involving league president John Brady Johnson and secretary W. M. Josephs. During the winter, as the league was getting organized, Josephs paid Johnson's hotel bill in exchange for using his influence to get the Giants into the league in place of their local rival, the D. C. Hilldales. Josephs also took seventy-five dollars from the owner of the Giants, James Page, for the franchise fee, but that fee was never paid to the league. *The New York Age* also covered the story and lauded Plummer's decision to leave. "Bishop Plummer, founder and generally acknowledged backbone of the league . . . [is] to be commended for not tolerating 'unclean' dealings."[43]

The Belleville Grays finished their schedule as an independent team. They ended the season with a 45–8 record, playing other local independent and some Negro League teams. They did finally meet the Newark Eagles, and lost to them by the score of 3–1 in early July. Darrell Howard, in his study of black baseball in Virginia, wrote: "It was a rarity for the professionals to play the locals during a promoted tour, but Belleville's reputation now preceded it." In his estimation, the loss "highlighted the prowess of Belleville as they were able to hold a professional team to a respectable margin." The Grays were scheduled to play the Eagles again in August, according to a telegram from Abe Manley to Brady Johnson, who, despite his continuing affiliation with the league, still handled booking arrangements for Plummer's team. The games were to take place in Norfolk on August eighth through the tenth. Belleville was to provide a hundred-dollar guarantee, with an option of 40 percent net for the visiting team, and free lodging at Belleville. There are no records to verify that the second series of games took place, however.[44]

Plummer's experience with Negro League play left him alienated from black baseball's power elite. While other owners either overlooked, or were themselves involved in, the petty financial disagreements that were common in a small business like the Negro Leagues, Plummer wanted no part of it. As a religious leader he was not comfortable with the kind of shady dealings that were required, and would not allow himself or his team to be part of that world.

But the Grays made an important contribution to black baseball by providing a training ground for several players who would become Negro League standouts. Their careers attest to the quality of the team that Plummer created. T. H. Hayes, an African American funeral director from Memphis, had, with the backing of Abe Saperstein, recently taken ownership of the Birmingham Black Barons of the Negro American League. They were looking for players for their new team, and convinced four Belleville stars to join them in 1940. Shortstop James Mickey played only one season for the Black Barons, but for second baseman Tommy Sampson, pitcher Gentry Jessup, and catcher Buster Haywood, their tenures in Birmingham marked the beginning of outstanding careers in the Negro Leagues as players and, for Sampson and Haywood, distinguished careers as managers. Jessup and Sampson made repeated appearances in the East-West All-Star game.

Sampson was born in Calhoun, Alabama in 1912 and grew up in West Virginia, where he attended Du Bois High School in Mt. Hope and worked in the coal mines. He played on independent black teams in the area and then:

> I went to spring training with the Bellville Grays in 1939 in Portsmouth. It was a Christian organization. After the season was over, we barnstormed down through Georgia and to Florida. We played a team out of Birmingham—the Birmingham Stars—and they told me they was gonna have a team in Birmingham in 1940 and they asked me would I come down and join 'em...So they sent a car up there to pick up a bunch of us: Buster Haywood, James Mickey, Gentry Jessup, myself...

Sampson knew he was playing for a religious community, but he had no idea the Grays were a Jewish team. Plummer and his community, concerned about having their religious beliefs misrepresented, hid their identity as Hebrew Israelites.[45]

Sampson became the regular second baseman for the Birmingham Black Barons and was selected as an All-Star several times. In September 1944 the course of his career was changed drastically by a serious car accident, in which he suffered a broken leg and head injuries. He was hospitalized much of the winter. Doctors assumed that his career was over, and although he continued to play and later manage, he was never the same player. He would remain close with Abe Saperstein, who would provide advice and financial support for Sampson's own baseball business efforts.[46]

The Birmingham team also took Joseph Gentry Jessup from the Grays. Jessup was born in Winston-Salem, North Carolina, and attended school in Scranton, West Virginia. He pitched in Birmingham in 1940 and was expected to return. But when the manager, Ben Taylor's brother Candy Jim, moved to the Chicago American Giants, Jessup followed. Jessup became a premier pitcher for the Giants and was frequently referred to as "one of the best pitchers in the league." Fay Young reported that Jessup was being scouted by the White Sox. But as was often the case with Negro League veterans, the White Sox didn't even give him a tryout. Jessup went on pitching for the Giants through the 1949 season, and played in the off-season in California and Mexico. During the following three seasons, Jessup pitched in Canada for the Carman Cardinals of the Mandak League, winning twenty-seven games for a thousand dollars a month pay, a salary that was much higher than he could have received in the Negro Leagues after integration.[47]

The other player to leave the Grays for Birmingham was local star Albert "Buster" Haywood. Haywood had by far the most interesting career of the three former Belleville stars. A modest and quiet man, Haywood has attracted little notice from Negro League researchers. But his long career tells us much about the business of Negro League baseball. Haywood was born in Whaleysville, Virginia (a small town near Portsmouth), the son of Robert E. Haywood and Mary Goodman. Haywood's mother was a hospital dietician and his father worked in the shipyards at Portsmouth. He was laid off when Albert was sixteen, so Albert worked odd jobs to help support the family. He attended I. C. Norcom High School, founded in 1913 as the first high school in the region for black students.[48]

*Figure 2.5* Buster Haywood, star of the Belleville Grays and Ethiopian Clowns (National Baseball Hall of Fame Library, Cooperstown, N.Y.).

Haywood played baseball for independent teams in the Portsmouth area in the early 1930s, with Belleville in 1932, and also with the Portsmouth Firefighters and the Berkeley Black Sox. He tried out for the Brooklyn Eagles (later the renowned Newark Eagles) when Abe Manley organized the team in 1935, and won a spot on the roster as backup catcher. Haywood played a few games with the team, but ultimately the manager Ben Taylor judged him to "need a little seasoning," so Haywood returned to Portsmouth and the Belleville Grays. He became the star of the team, and his individual accomplishments—both at bat and behind the plate—during this period were often chronicled in the sports pages of the black press. He frequently garnered headlines for scoring or driving in the winning run. He hit at the top of the order, an unusual spot for a catcher.[49]

Although the Black Barons were part of the Negro American League and therefore playing at a higher competitive level than the Belleville Grays, the salaries they offered did not compete. In search of better wages, he left the Barons by mid-May to join the Ethiopian Clowns. The Barons were paying Buster ninety dollars a month when the Clowns came to town in 1940. The Clowns were averaging two hundred dollars. Although they had no contracts and played on a percentage basis, Haywood judged it worth the gamble.[50]

Haywood continued to play baseball for the Clowns through the 1953 season. As the manager from 1948 to 1953, he was responsible for scheduling spring training. In his last year with the Clowns, he brought the team to the Portsmouth area, where they slept and trained in Belleville at Bishop Plummer's place:

> We stayed at Bishop Plummer's about ten miles outside Portsmouth.
> He was minister at my church. There was an old diamond near his place.
> I played there against Buck Leonard and Skinny Barnhill as semi-pro
> back before I joined the Birmingham Black Barons. We trained two
> days. We opened against the Norfolk Palms in Norfolk.[51]

This is the only indication Haywood ever gave that he considered himself a member of the Temple Beth El community. Like other players, and even some community members, he used common Christian language to describe the group to outsiders, to whom the connection of "black" and "Jewish" would probably make no sense. Although Haywood played for the Belleville Grays and was their star for many years, and following their communal practice never smoked, drank, or cursed, he is not listed among official community members, and no one from his family remembers him mentioning his affiliation with COGASOC or any other religious organization. But his positive connection to the Belleville community was obviously strong and continued over time.[52]

Although Jessup, Sampson, and Haywood, the team's stars, were now gone, Bishop Plummer made one more attempt at league play in 1940, in response to an invitation from *Afro-American* sports editor Art Carter, who was organizing a new Interstate League. Carter aimed to bring the best teams in Maryland and Virginia together to form a minor league for the Negro National and American Leagues. He also invited Dr. Joseph Thomas, now head of the Edgewater Black Sox in Baltimore, and Plummer's close associate, to join. Thomas agreed immediately, while Plummer failed to reply for some time. He was clearly ambivalent about making another effort at league play.[53]

Manager Joe Lewis finally communicated with Carter on behalf of Bishop Plummer, indicating that the Grays would join the league in time for the season's start on May 26. They played their first game, but Plummer, hesitating still, had not paid the franchise fee. Carter sent several letters to Lewis asking for the financial commitment, but it was not forthcoming until Carter wrote to Plummer directly. Carter's letter indicated that he had spoken both to Lewis and to Plummer's friend John Murphy, owner of the *Afro-American* and Carter's boss, about Plummer's doubts. Carter acknowledged that both he and Dr. Thomas knew that Plummer might be hesitant after his previous difficulties with league play. But he reassured him that no one who had been involved in that league, with the exception of Dr. Thomas, would be connected with the new league. The letter, dated Friday, June 8, received an immediate response. Plummer came up to Washington on Sunday, paid the franchise fee, and fixed a schedule of play.[54]

The Grays played well enough, but were not the team they had been the prior year. With the exception of community member and outfielder Mark Hill, the team was composed primarily of young college men from the Portsmouth region. At the end of July they had won four and lost four in league play, and were in third place. Earlier in July, Joe Lewis thought they would have to drop out of league play because they couldn't always find enough personnel for the Sunday games. Although as victors of a late season tournament they were named the official state champions of Virginia, the 1940 season was not a successful one for the Grays. The Interstate League folded at the end of August.[55]

Yet H. Z. Plummer's influence gained him a strong reputation as an honest man who would have been an asset to the Negro Leagues had he wished to become more involved. Plummer's commitment to the game was brought to national attention that summer by *Pittsburgh Courier* reporter Randy Dixon, who thought Plummer could resolve the fights among owners that plagued the Negro National League:

> There's an esteemed gentleman with dough and a patriot's love of the game, who is willing and eager to enter a league with them. He's Bishop Plummer of ecclesiastical fame. . .The entry of. . .Plummer into the pastime would prove bromatic.[56]

This high praise did not persuade Plummer. Although he achieved his goal of creating a team that was "second to none" in Virginia, he would take the effort no further. Plummer's business adventure with organized black baseball had come to an end. Centerfielder and serious baseball enthusiast Mark Hill kept baseball alive in Belleville with community teams that played on a field he designed. Teams like the Indianapolis Clowns and All-Star teams organized by Roy Campanella and Jackie Robinson after the regular baseball season continued to stay at Belleville in guest quarters and play in the area at least through the 1953 season. But H. Z. Plummer was not inclined to become the arbiter of the very difficult relationships among the owners of the Negro League teams.[57]

## Eddie Gottlieb, Officer of the Negro National League

Had Bishop Plummer agreed to become involved in the Negro National League, he would have also encountered Ed Gottlieb. By 1938 Gottlieb was gaining the trust of the other NNL owners. Cum Posey, describing Gottlieb as highly professional and experienced, called on the league to appoint him to chair a committee to clean up its finances and also to design uniform player contracts, the absence of which would plague the league for the next decade. Posey also encouraged league owners to send box scores to Gottlieb so he could keep proper records. Gottlieb was also given the task of assigning umpires, and served with two other owners on an arbitration committee. He even held league office as recording secretary. As the only white owner in the NNL, he was given a lot of responsibility, and it is clear that at this stage the owners were willing to rely on him. Gottlieb would often host league meetings at his Philadelphia offices. He worked to get the league on firmer financial footing, improve relationships with the press, and raise the standards of umpiring.[58]

Despite Gottlieb's growing responsibilities, his loyalty to the league was often questioned by owners who believed that his interests as an owner of the Philadelphia Stars and as a booking agent created conflicts of interest and gave him too much power. Such conflicts often put Gottlieb in a difficult position. The situation surrounding the sale of the Pittsburgh Crawfords is but one example. By 1938, Gus Greenlee was in financial straits. The previous year had been difficult. Many of Greenlee's star players were lured away by Rafael Trujillo to play in the Dominican Republic. Like many other Negro League owners of the 1930s, Greenlee used his income from the numbers game to support his various businesses—the Crawfords team, the Crawford Grill, Greenlee Stadium, and his boxing ventures. Toward the end of the 1930s, however, a confluence of factors left Greenlee without capital. The Depression was of course a major factor. But like other black numbers bankers, he lost much of his business as former Jewish and Italian bootleggers shifted into the numbers business after Prohibition

*Figure 2.6* Annual Meeting of Negro National League in Baltimore, January 1941. Back row, left to right (seated): Charles Brown and Edward Witherspoon of Washington, D. C.; Alex Pompez, Cuban Stars; Thomas Wilson, Baltimore Elite Giants; Effa and Abe Manley, Newark Eagles; Cum Posey, Homestead Grays; J. B. Martin, Negro American League official. Standing: Rufus Jackson, Homestead Grays; Art Carter, sports editor; Jim Semler and Jock Waters, New York Black Yankees. Front row: William Leuschner, Nat Strong Agency; Ed Gottlieb, Philadelphia Stars; See Posey, Homestead Grays; Frank Forbes, Eary Brown, and Douglas Smith, Baltimore Elite Giants (NoirTech Research, Inc.).

ended. Gottlieb thought Greenlee was a stabilizing force in the league, and sought to keep him involved.

Gottlieb single-handedly organized a campaign to keep Greenlee from having to sell the Crawfords by raising money from the other owners to pay Greenlee's league fees. But other owners weren't willing to lend Greenlee the money, and the Crawfords passed into the hands of Hank Rigney, a white businessman from Toledo. Unlike Greenlee, Rigney didn't understand how to operate a baseball team, and Gottlieb thought him a dishonest man who would not follow league procedures. Effa Manley expressed private fears that Gottlieb was being difficult about the team moving to Toledo because it would reduce his booking opportunities as more games would be scheduled in Ohio, out of Gottlieb's eastern territory. Rigney was dissatisfied with the arrangements, and in a few months the Toledo Crawfords moved to the Negro American League. Gottlieb was convinced that his own interests and the interests of the league were one and the same.[59]

Gottlieb became the center of another controversy over power that saw Negro National League owners ultimately divided into pro- and anti-Gottlieb factions. National League president and owner of the Baltimore Elite Giants Tom Wilson awarded Gottlieb the task of negotiating with the New York Yankees to use Yankee Stadium for Sunday doubleheaders, a job that had formerly belonged to Greenlee. Greenlee's original plan called for all the league's teams to be showcased in New York, and Gottlieb was eager to follow through. He believed that the success of these ventures (especially when Satchel Paige was pitching) encouraged other owners of major league ballparks to offer reasonable rents, to the benefit of all the NNL teams.

Gottlieb put together a deal with Yankees general manager Ed Barrow for five Negro League doubleheaders at Yankee Stadium for 1939. Gottlieb's arrangement saved the league $12,500 in rental fees. For his work, Gottlieb received a 10 percent booking fee. The owners had all agreed to Gottlieb taking the percentage when he took on the Yankee Stadium promotion, and Gus Greenlee had taken 10 percent booking fees when he had negotiated the contract originally. At the time, only the Manleys opposed giving Gottlieb the commission, and in the end the Eagles participated in the lucrative arrangement. Gottlieb, as promoter, put up all the advance money, and the clubs involved gained over $16,000 in profits. For his work, Gottlieb received a total of $1,100.[60]

But the New York owners—James Semler of the New York Black Yankees, Abe and Effa Manley of the Newark Eagles, and Alex Pompez of the New York Cubans—did not like the fact that Gottlieb was awarded the contract. At the winter meetings in 1940 they banded together to fight the reelection of Tom Wilson as president of the league. Abe Manley stated that their opposition to Wilson's return as president was the fact that he was too weak to oppose Gottlieb. Semler, Pompez, and the Manleys saw Gottlieb's booking of Yankee Stadium as an incursion into their territory, for which they should have been compensated or brought in as partners. They, not Gottlieb, should get the 10 percent booking fee. Supported by Wilson and Cum Posey, Gottlieb fought back, arguing that the New York owners "were in the same position as a patient who applies for medical aid and then curses out the doctor when he charges him a sum for curing him."[61]

Effa Manley escalated the debate when she told the press that this was "something bigger than a little money! We are fighting for a Race issue. In other words what we are doing here has become more important than we." The fact that Effa Manley herself was white complicated the matter. As a woman who was raised by a white mother and black stepfather and married to a black man, Manley was seen as an insider. Gottlieb was not. Manley's comments were dismissed by some because of her gender, and Cum Posey was reported to have left the room in anger, refusing to return until Abe Manley promised to leave his wife home "where she belonged." But for others, Manley provided an opportunity to raise concerns about Gottlieb's control of the Negro National League.[62]

Because this was a fight over who would control the lucrative New York market, Nat Strong, the "Hebrew Menace," cast a long shadow. Since Strong's death, Gottlieb and his associate from the Nat Strong Agency, Bill Leuschner, realized profits of less than $2,400 each year, and their contract required that they give a quarter of their earnings back to the league. Their agencies were useful for the league because they had full-time offices that could handle all the work involved in scheduling and booking for all six NNL teams, an expense that the other teams could not afford. According to Cum Posey, Gottlieb and Leuschner were "experienced and fair" and their work necessary to the functioning of the league.[63]

Yet it was not Strong's New York successor Leuschner but Gottlieb who was the focus of the anger. The association between Jews and money simmered under the surface of some of the accusations against Gottlieb. Gottlieb was a carpetbagger, "bringing his white staff over to Harlem every time a league promotion is held at Yankee Stadium, packing his black bags full of coin and scooting back to Philly." He was charged with paternalism; "pulling the strings" and turning Posey, Wilson, and Bolden into his puppets. It was common knowledge that Gottlieb exercised power in the league because of his position as team owner, league booking agent, and proprietor of one of the most powerful sports promotion agencies in the country. But there was one more factor that explained his dominance. Gottlieb gained leverage over the owners by lending money to them, and providing credit for equipment purchased from Passon's Sporting Goods store. Cum Posey assumed that was the basis of Gottlieb's support and advised him "Don't lend in 1941, then see the friends you will be able to keep." Jewish economic power, always suspect, interjected into a struggling black business would make a simple quarrel over money into an issue of race.[64]

For some sportswriters this was also an opportunity to air their problems with Gottlieb as the owner of the Stars. Sportswriter Ed Harris lamented in the *Philadelphia Tribune* that Gottlieb's ownership was hurting the local team, because the other owners didn't want to do business with him. Gottlieb was also held responsible for the poor conditions at the Stars home field, which he leased and ran. The former home field of the Pennsylvania Railroad team, Penmar Park was located in a Jewish neighborhood, but convenient to transportation. Unfortunately it was also close to the train tracks, and therefore noisy and often covered with soot from the trains. Press box accommodations were poor, and Gottlieb employed white staff there, including young Jewish boys from the neighborhood. Concerns were also raised about the power Gottlieb wielded over promotions in Philadelphia. Gottlieb, "genial and suave," had, over the years, put himself in the position of booking so many facilities in the area that a team couldn't play without going through his agency. His connections with Strong's agency in New York strengthened his hold on any team, black or white, that wanted to play in lucrative venues in the Northeast.[65]

Gottlieb also received support from the black press. Fay Young did not approve of Effa Manley bringing up race at a time when whites were beginning to pay attention to black baseball. Art Carter defended Gottlieb as a businessman who was entitled to do the best he could for himself and not be obligated to the

*Figure 2.7* Penmar Park, home of the Negro League Philadelphia Stars (Library of Congress, Prints & Photographs Division, FSA/OWI Collection, LC-USW3- 056196-E).

common good. But Gottlieb saw no distinction between his own financial advancement and what was good for the league. He would remain its most powerful and controversial figure.[66]

Ultimately, the problem was settled by compromise. At the next league meeting, Wilson was confirmed as president, as Pompez abstained from voting, giving Wilson's side a majority. Gottlieb was reprimanded and removed as recording secretary, but allowed to keep the Yankee Stadium promotions for one more year. For the sake of harmony, Gottlieb agreed to relinquish the Yankee Stadium promotions after 1940 to New York Black Yankee owner Jim Semler, who was also granted permission to book one game for the Black Yankees and New York Cubans in that venue in the coming season. With Gottlieb doing the booking, the Manleys chose not to play in Yankee Stadium in 1940 in protest. Peace was declared. Effa Manley retracted her statements about the racial nature of the disagreement. When asked whether she opposed white ownership, she replied, "Certainly not. Some white owners are the best of men. I even admire Gottlieb's business ability. He would be all right if the chairman [Wilson] could handle him. He needs to be whipped into line." Gottlieb, the talented businessman, was welcome to help, and the black owners were ready to take advantage of his skills. But Manley believed that Gottlieb had too much power and did not want him to control the league. What on the surface was a small matter over a small amount of money became a symbolic question of Gottlieb's place as a white Jew who was the most powerful man in the Negro National League.[67]

## Pollock and Saperstein and the Negro American League

Like Ed Gottlieb, Abe Saperstein was a key figure in black baseball who took on roles as promoter, booking agent, and silent partner for black baseball teams. While Gottlieb was the most powerful figure in the East, Saperstein would be the force to reckon with in the Midwest. Abe Saperstein's Sports Enterprises had grown from a one-man operation to a large company with a full staff of secretaries, team managers, and assistant promoters. While his agency also promoted white sport enterprises, his main business was promoting black sports. In 1937 a group of independent black baseball teams in Saperstein's territory got together to form the Negro American League (NAL), and he became their official booking agent. Like Gottlieb in the NNL, Saperstein's relationship to the NAL would be contentious.[68]

One of the attractions Saperstein promoted that would cause him trouble with other league owners was an independent team, Syd Pollock's Ethiopian Clowns. Pollock had given up on Cuban teams a few years earlier and begun working in novelty baseball, primarily with black teams. In 1936 Pollock announced that he was going to be promoting a tour of the Ethiopian Clowns. The team was owned by two black entrepreneurs, Hunter Campbell and Johnnie Pierce, although Pollock would take the major promotional and organizational role. Pollock's announcement was accompanied by a photo of baseball players in tribal headdress and long gowns, holding bats like spears, with the caption "It's the War Influence on Baseball" and the description "First American Tour Ethiopian Clowns Baseball Tribe." The short article went on to list their African "names," saying that they were heading north to tour and would play daily after finishing their training in Florida. Calling a team the "Ethiopian Clowns" was a disturbing attempt to capitalize on the presence of Ethiopia in the news as a result of the Italian invasion of that country.[69]

The modern and ancient kingdom of Ethiopia held a sacred place in the hearts of African Americans. Psalm 68:31 ("Nobles shall come out of Egypt; Ethiopia shall hasten to stretch out her hands unto God") was used as a proof text for Ethiopia's importance in biblical history, as was the story of Solomon and Sheba. "Ethiopia" was the term used in sacred and secular black writing to signify Africa's proud heritage. American blacks often referred to themselves proudly as Ethiopians. In 1896 when the Ethiopians held off the Italian Army, modern Ethiopia came to the attention of American blacks, and it was a strong influence on W. E. B. DuBois's philosophy of black empowerment and Marcus Garvey's Back to Africa movement. When Ethiopia became Africa's first independent nation after Haile Selassie's coronation in 1930, black America again took notice. Selassie, the self-proclaimed "Lion of Judah," traced his own ancestry back to Solomon and Sheba, reinforcing the mythic qualities of Ethiopian heritage. Black pride in Ethiopia was a powerful antidote to the evils of Jim Crow America. As newspaper columnist J. A. Rogers noted, Selassie was "a veritable earthquake for those whose mental picture of black peoples is as clowns." Ethiopia's freedom and power were endangered by the Italian occupation of the country from 1936 to 1941. To field a team of Ethiopians who were also called Clowns was a profound insult to the heritage of that country and also to the pride of black America.[70]

Pollock thought calling the team Ethiopian was a smart business decision that would bring attention to the team. To him the Clowns were simply a baseball team with great show business potential that would help him advance his strategy for independent baseball. In the winter of 1937, Pollock announced that Johnny Pierce and Hunter Campbell would be assembling not only the Ethiopian Clowns but the Borneo Cannibal Giants (also called the Borneo Zulu Cannibals), images of Africa that traded on even more degrading views of that continent. To Pollock, it was all the same, and he was proud to be their exclusive booking agent. To further his ambitions, however, he would need to become the owner of the team. By the time the season began Pierce was no longer involved. Campbell would also run into financial difficulties, and Pollock assumed the role of the Clowns' financial backer. His press releases began to refer to the team as

"Syd Pollock's famous Ethiopian Clowns baseball club," although he would not buy out Campbell's share for another year, and Campbell would remain affiliated with the team as business manager until 1942. But for all practical purposes, by 1938 this was Pollock's team. He booked games for the Clowns with other novelty teams, but they also played against Cum Posey's Homestead Grays, who beat them several times thanks to the hitting of Negro League greats Josh Gibson and Buck Leonard.[71]

While calling the team the Ethiopian Clowns would continue to be a matter of contention with Negro League owners and the black press in years to come, Pollock's business practices were a more immediate problem. Several players on the 1937 Clowns, including manager Thadeus Christopher, had been under contract to Gus Greenlee's Pittsburgh Crawfords. The league threatened not to play the Clowns unless Christopher was returned, and Pollock cooperated to avoid the boycott.[72]

Pollock continued to draw the ire of league officials with other affronts. Toward the end of the 1938 season Pollock began to refer to the Clowns as the "Independent Colored World Champions," a dubious claim, as the team lost the Florida Baseball championship series to the Jacksonville Red Caps. Despite the losses, "Syd Pollock's Ethiopian Clowns baseball club" was advertised the following spring as having "won every game played against leading league and independent teams . . . thus establishing their claim to the 1938 world championship, by virtue of their undefeated record." By this time Pollock was calling the team "the world champion Ethiopian Clowns." But the Memphis Red Sox had won the league "world championship" in 1938. Pollock used these advertising tactics to draw attention to his team, but his competitive style did not please the other owners or the sportswriters who valued cooperation with the league as a way to advance the race.[73]

In 1939 Pollock got into deeper conflicts with the league when he enlisted Abe Saperstein as the Clowns' booking agent. This role conflicted with Saperstein's position as official booking agent of the Negro American League, which he'd held since the league began operating in 1937. Saperstein, seeing the lucrative opportunities that booking the Clowns offered, began to give Pollock's team priority over league teams in the many parks throughout the Midwest over which Saperstein had control. In response, at the March 1940 Negro American League meeting the owners removed Saperstein as the official booking agent, replacing him with Kansas City Monarch co-owner Tom Baird, although Saperstein was invited to continue booking games as Baird's assistant if he chose. Cum Posey, representing the NNL at the meetings, approved of this plan. He saw Saperstein as an outsider who was using the Leagues to his own advantage. Posey thought the Leagues ought to "have any extra money which may be made given to those who have their money invested in Negro baseball." It is also likely that Posey was concerned that Saperstein, who controlled most of the scheduling and ballparks in the Midwest, would soon be making inroads into his territory in Pittsburgh.[74]

Saperstein's power in the NAL was not diminished, however. Despite losing his official status, Saperstein, described in the Atlanta sports columns as "the clever Jewish promoter and booking agent extraordinaire," would continue his booking activities on behalf of many of the Negro American League teams because many of the owners would not have access to the parks without his intervention.[75]

In addition to losing his status as official booking agent, Saperstein's financial cut from the East-West game came under scrutiny. During the 1930s, the value of paying Saperstein to promote the East-West game in the white dailies, and especially the *Chicago Tribune*, was taken for granted, as the revenues generated were modest. But when times began to improve in 1940, Saperstein's cut appeared inappropriately large. Fay Young, sports editor of the *Chicago Defender*, who would later become one of Saperstein's staunchest defenders, wrote several strong articles questioning the value of his contribution in publicizing the East-West game. Young asked why neither the players nor the umpires were being paid and yet Saperstein was receiving what Young assumed to be "five percent of the receipts" for his role, "a lot of money for one man, white or black." Young expressed anger that the contract with Saperstein, which "might have looked good when the game was first started eight years ago," had not been renegotiated. And he was most concerned that Saperstein's office was not even sending out correct information about the game.[76]

Cum Posey expressed his objections to Saperstein's cut for the East-West game, too. He pointed out that Saperstein's share was as large as those of the *Chicago Defender* and *Pittsburgh Courier* put together. These papers were important to the game not only because of the coverage they provided, but also because they were the vehicle for fans to vote for players. Of course, this added subscribers to the papers and functioned to their advantage no matter how much Saperstein made. Posey concluded that the real reason the Negro American League owners wanted Saperstein satisfied was to make sure that he continued to provide them with favorable bookings in the vast number of parks he controlled. Despite, or maybe because of, the fact that they had recently demoted Saperstein from the status of "official booking agent," all the NAL owners supported continuing his percentage for the East-West game.[77]

Saperstein continued to provoke discord. His power came from booking games and promoting individual players. Saperstein and Pollock thought that black baseball would be financially successful based on good publicity that highlighted the game's star players, such as Satchel Paige. They were not interested in developing the leagues. Saperstein convinced the Chicago American Giants to lend pitcher "Lefty" Bowe to the Clowns to help them gain an advantage in the *Denver Post* Tournament in 1939, a violation of league rules. As the 1940 East-West game approached, Saperstein was encouraging the league owners to permit Satchel Paige to pitch in the game because his presence would increase the ticket sales. Because Paige was not pitching in the league but for an all-star team that Saperstein set up for him and that was touring with the Clowns, he was technically not eligible to play. Paige was also demanding that the owners pay his train fare to get to the game. Since the players weren't compensated for their travel, Saperstein's proposal was bound to create ill will. Sportswriter Fay Young assumed that Saperstein's motive was to create disagreements between the players and owners to disrupt the functioning of the leagues. He suggested that ending league play would work to Saperstein's advantage because he would then be able to book independent games with whatever teams he chose to bring in and get his 5 percent booking fee, which he did not receive for league games. This judgment may have been excessive, but not inaccurate. Saperstein was cynical about the value of league play.[78]

Saperstein was involved in brokering the use of major league baseball parks for Negro League games as a way of increasing attention to black baseball and generating revenue. He encouraged the major league owners in Cincinnati to rent Crosley Field. But rather than reserve it for a team in the leagues, Saperstein wanted to use the venue as a possible home for the Clowns. It was publicized as an effort in "building up Negro baseball," given the Clowns' ability to draw crowds. But it would not please the other black baseball owners, who were already enraged that Saperstein was booking the Clowns in profitable venues instead of setting up games for league teams.[79]

The Cincinnati venue would be the sixth major league park to be used by the Negro League teams. (Yankee Stadium, Comiskey Park, Griffith Stadium, Forbes Field in Pittsburgh, and League Park in Cleveland were the others.) In 1941 the opportunity to rent major league ballparks created an advantage, because it brought increased opportunity for publicity and attendance. Although it brought in money in the short term, in retrospect it was harmful. Major league teams continued to raise rental fees, which became a drain on Negro League teams' finances. It also served as an impediment to integration, as the major league owners became dependent on the revenue the Negro League games generated.

The 1941 season was also a turning point for Syd Pollock. At the joint meeting of the Negro American and National leagues in Chicago in February, the Clowns were banned for signing a league player (Lefty Bowe) and for sending out publicity calling the Clowns the "independent champions of colored baseball." Describing the meeting in his column, Fay Young assumed Pollock was "well-meaning" and had a right to his interest in booking his club and making money. Young was open to Pollock's presence in black baseball if he would agree to work with the leagues, respect their contracts, and stop calling his club "colored world champions."[80]

To gain sympathy, Pollock wrote to Effa Manley, joking that he wasn't "as bad as those fellows out in Chicago, or even my friend, Fay Young, painted me." He said he understood that the Manleys couldn't do business with the Clowns because of the ban, but also questioned why he was being singled out. At the time of the league ruling against him, he claimed not to have had any league players. He also had no idea why it would offend Cum Posey and Fay Young for him to refer to the team as champions or Ethiopians. "It all sounds so silly, especially coming from people that are supposed to be highly intelligent," he wrote. Pollock had worked for years among blacks, and saw discrimination firsthand. He also saw himself as subject to discrimination based on race. But he had no understanding of how offensive his attitudes were.[81]

At the joint meeting of the NAL and NNL in June 1941, Cum Posey, aided by Alex Pompez, again proposed to remove Abe Saperstein as the publicity agent for the East-West game. Posey said Saperstein was "a bad influence" because he booked and promoted the Ethiopian Clowns, "a group of colored players who travel over the US with their faces painted to represent the mythical natives of the African jungle." In a curious political alignment, Effa Manley, along with Eddie Gottlieb, declined to vote. Manley and Gottlieb's abstentions were crucial for Saperstein, as the western teams all voted to keep him. The owners were not prepared to get rid of Pollock and Saperstein completely. Perhaps Pollock's communications with Effa Manley had some influence, but it is possible that Gottlieb and the Manleys, too, put their financial interests over their political concerns.[82]

Posey stepped up his attack. He again targeted Saperstein and Pollock for calling the Clowns "Ethiopians," an insensitive act of "ridiculing a defenseless nation and the Negro race in general." In an open letter, Posey laid out his other complaints against Saperstein, both that Saperstein was making money by promoting Satchel Paige as an individual performer rather than supporting teams and the league and that he was using his position as promoter of the East-West game to inflate his reputation and gain contracts with major league parks while charging exorbitant booking fees. Posey concluded by saying that he was "committed to the total obliteration of all opportunists out of organized Negro baseball."[83]

Posey's efforts to get rid of Saperstein were supported by E. B. Rea of the Norfolk *Journal and Guide*. Rea agreed that something should be done about Saperstein and other "slick promoters," and vowed to get involved in the fight "to break this monopoly that threatens to stifle pro baseball." Posey also accused Saperstein of heading a powerful organization that included Negro American League owners and sportswriters like Fay Young, who defended Saperstein because they were on his payroll. Posey was convinced that Saperstein posed a serious threat and was one of many who were "attempting to edge into professional Negro athletics and to eventually control them." He declared that he and others would fight to overcome the threat posed by Saperstein and his supporters.[84]

During the season, Pollock exacerbated Posey and Pompez's concerns. He did not abide by the ruling that banned the Clowns from playing against league teams, but instead negotiated with J. L. Wilkinson to play the Monarchs. Posey expressed his anger that the league presidents were going to allow the Monarchs and Clowns to play, but did not criticize Wilkinson for his role. Pollock, meanwhile, was sending out press releases to emphasize the importance of these games, calling them a "showdown" to settle which team is the "best Negro ball team in the country if not the universe this season." Kansas City beat the Clowns two games out of three. For the remainder of June the Clowns toured the Midwest with the Havana Cuban Giants, a team that Pollock pulled together, consisting mostly of African Americans, not Cubans. At times, the touring entourage also included Paige's All-Stars, further antagonizing the black baseball establishment. A rematch between the Clowns and Monarchs took place later in the season, again without league approval. On occasion, Paige pitched for the Havana Cuban Giants against the Clowns. Paige and the Clowns drew big crowds, so Pollock and Saperstein could not pass up any opportunity to showcase them. The Clowns won the *Denver Post* Tournament on their third try, in 1941, and Saperstein again booked them to play in Cincinnati at the end of the season. Pollock proclaimed his team the first organized black club to win the tournament, since the black team that had won in 1934 was an all-star team and therefore not "official." He now dubbed his team the "newly-crowned national semi-pro champions." At least this title was legitimate.[85]

By the end of the season Pollock and Saperstein had made a lot of money promoting Satchel Paige and the Clowns. They had also completely alienated the Negro American League owners. The league finally took action against them at their winter meeting. They had achieved a level of notice that moved the owners to ban them not because of minor infractions but because the face painting and clowning (a topic we will examine at length in chapter 4) was "a detriment to Negro league baseball." In a response to Pollock's "Cuban Giants" team, which was composed primarily of African Americans, the leagues also banned all teams claiming to be Cuban except Alex Pompez's league team, the New York Cubans.[86]

World War II would provide even greater opportunities and challenges for Negro League baseball and the Jewish businessmen who were gaining power and wealth through their involvement in it.

# 3

# World War II and the Advancement of Black Baseball

World War II created enormous opportunities for black baseball and the Jewish businessmen who were central to its operation. Black baseball was less debilitated by the war than the white leagues. Restrictions on travel and gas rationing were mitigated by efficient scheduling. Limits on the numbers of black men who were drafted into segregated army units meant there were more players available. Defense jobs also led to more discretionary income in the black community, and that boosted attendance. White patronage increased because of better publicity and because major league owners' need for the revenue meant more games were played in major league stadiums. In addition, because so many major league players enlisted or were drafted into the armed services, the quality of play declined significantly, giving an opening to the Negro Leagues. These factors also led major league baseball to create the All-American Girls Professional Baseball League to attract customers, although this league would also exclude women of African descent. For the first time, the Negro Leagues began to operate at a profit. As the business of black baseball became more lucrative, acrimony would only increase as black and Jewish owners vied for economic power.

## Showcasing Satchel Paige

Saperstein's work publicizing the Negro Leagues also increased interest in the game. Saperstein continued booking Satchel Paige as an individual performer with various league and all-star teams, much to the ongoing irritation of the other owners. The owners of major league ballparks, on the other hand, eagerly welcomed these showcase events. Although adding black players to their rosters would have been a logical solution to their wartime problems, the major league owners preferred the option of booking Negro League teams in their stadiums instead. For Saperstein, this was a great opportunity. He arranged for Paige to pitch against white all-star teams led by star major league pitchers Dizzy Dean and Bob Feller, games that drew crowds of over 20,000 in Chicago and Washington, D.C.

Saperstein arranged a second contest between Bob Feller's all-star team and Paige, to be held in Indianapolis and advertised as supporting the Navy Relief Fund. Baseball Commissioner Kenesaw Mountain Landis, realizing that the games major leaguers were playing against Paige were drawing a good deal of attention, canceled the game on the pretext that it was not a military fund-raiser but a commercial enterprise. The cancellation enraged black sportswriter Halley Harding. He noted that he was "very familiar with the workings of Abe Saperstein, one of the promoters of those two games and I know he will use any implied or real motive to get people into a park." But he went on to say that there was real interest in this game because many people, white especially, wanted to see blacks play.[1]

Ed Gottlieb also believed that showcasing Satchel Paige was the key to pro-moting black baseball to white audiences. He ran into opposition from fellow owners because of it. Gottlieb continued to serve as the booking agent for Yankee Stadium, despite the prior agreement to give the work to Jim Semler of the Black Yankees. Gottlieb asked for league approval to borrow Paige from the Monarchs to pitch for the Black Yankees in Yankee Stadium contests, but was turned down. Despite the fact that he wasn't authorized to do so, Gottlieb arranged with Semler to pay Paige three hundred dollars to pitch (with Monarch owner J. L. Wilkinson's tacit approval, of course), explaining afterwards to Effa Manley that this "was very cheap, as he was largely responsible for the crowd, and helped all of us to make money." But paying Paige against the express wishes of the league sent Effa Manley into a rage against "the powers that are," who "certainly don't mind showing how little respect they have for us." She suggested to Cum Posey's brother Seward, the Grays' business manager, that they make an alliance that could "stop Gottlieb, Wilkerson, Leuschner, Saperstein and all the other Jews who want to join them where Negro Baseball is concerned." If she or her hus-band were presiding over league business, "these Jews would be stopped in their tracks...the 10% Gottlieb puts in his pocket, and Saperstein puts in his, would set up a nice treasury." [2]

## Jewish Power in Black Baseball

Of the men Manley listed, all were white, but only Saperstein and Gottlieb, her main targets, were Jews.[3] Manley was uncomfortable with the economic power Gottlieb and Saperstein exercised in a business owned and operated by blacks. The improved finances of Negro League baseball exacerbated the conflicts among Negro National League owners. Their battles over economic control were often expressed through stereotypes. Manley's comments anticipated the struggles between blacks and Jews in the civil rights movement decades later and revealed the fault lines in the supposed "special relationship" between Jews and blacks. References to "the Hebrew menace" and the desire to "stop the Jews in their tracks" came from the widespread cultural perception, prevalent in the black world as well as the white, that Jews were good with money, which itself led to the illogical conclusion that anyone who was good with money had to be a Jew. Just as Jews began identifying as white to become more American, blacks would use anti-Semitic rhetoric to gain some advantage with the white power structure that also found itself uncomfortable with Jewish economic power.

Opinion was mixed on whether Gottlieb and Saperstein cared about black baseball and had a right to make their living from it. Norfolk *Journal and Guide* columnist Lem Graves thought that Gottlieb, like Saperstein, was making too much money. St. Claire Bourne defended Gottlieb as the man with the resources who was entitled to make decisions. Cum Posey also stood up for Gottlieb, arguing that he only brought Paige to pitch to benefit the league's revenues, since Gottlieb had agreed to return profits from Yankee Stadium promotions to the league. But, not surprisingly, he was critical of Paige, who got "$50,000 worth of publicity," and even more critical of Abe Saperstein for "making more money using Satchel than Satchel gets for Satchel." Posey distinguished between Gottlieb, a fellow owner who was making an effort to support the league, and Pollock and Saperstein, who were interested only in the money. Manley didn't care that Gottlieb was also an owner; she was unhappy with the strategy that privileged the individual player and owner over the collective enterprise.[4]

Posey's support of Gottlieb, given his antipathy for the other Jewish owners, was not surprising in the context of league politics. Posey disliked the New York owners, and thought he could control Gottlieb and his close associate Tom Wilson, league president and owner of the Baltimore Elite Giants. One sportswriter suggested that Posey was "just slick enough" to have instigated Manley's feud with Gottlieb to keep Gottlieb under his thumb. An exchange of letters between Manley and Posey supports that contention. Manley wrote to Posey suggesting that the league try to get the Yankee Stadium promotion away from Gottlieb again. In response, Posey acknowledged to Manley that Gottlieb was "getting too big" and blamed Gottlieb for instigating fights between Manley and himself so they wouldn't notice what he was planning. The politics of the Negro National League involved constantly shifting alliances based on power, economic self-interest, and racial stereotypes that were difficult to disentangle.[5]

Effa Manley's outburst about Jewish involvement in the league had no effect on her business dealings. In the winter of 1942, while contemplating leaving the league and having the Newark Eagles play independent baseball, she contacted Saperstein about becoming their agent. He responded enthusiastically, asking if she was able to fly out to see him since his office was "jumping...with basketball efforts." By the time Manley replied by mail two days later they had already talked by phone. In her letter she acknowledged that the move outside league play would give the other owners the ability to sign Eagle players with impunity, but she was willing to take that risk "to tie up with someone [like Saperstein] who knows the ropes."[6]

Sensing the urgency of the deal, Saperstein suggested that Syd Pollock come down from North Tarrytown to talk to her and her husband. Pollock followed up with a letter to confirm a visit he would be making to the Manleys' home the next day. He planned to supply them with facts and figures that would convince them to work through Saperstein's office and "eliminate many headaches, squabbles at league meetings, and make yourself just as much money...if not more than you ever did playing league ball." Pollock went on to say that "Saperstein and his staff in the Chicago office outshine all others" at booking and promoting. He emphasized that the Eagles "would fit perfectly into plans Saperstein has in mind and briefly outlined to me several weeks ago when he was in NYC." The plans, for a new league that Saperstein was creating, would serve the Manleys well.[7]

Nothing came of the visit, and the Newark Eagles stayed in the Negro National League. Two weeks later, Saperstein sent Mrs. Manley a note wishing her the best of luck. He left the door open for further conversation, saying he "would welcome word from time to time as to how you progress," and suggested that they get together when he was in New York touring with the Globetrotters. A few days later, he received a cordial reply from Mrs. Manley, blaming her husband for wanting to stay with the league, and suggesting a business proposition. Manley wanted Saperstein to book the Eagles into Briggs Stadium, the major league park in Detroit, against the New York Cubans. She also recommended a strategy to make it look like the Manleys did their own booking. She told him that working together would be "a swell opportunity to get some satisfaction for both of us." In his reply, he indicated his interest in pursuing conversations with her but said he did not expect he could do anything at Detroit, since "everyone in the business has contacted the Detroit management regarding the park." Manley, like the other owners, was looking for opportunities for her own team. She obviously believed that Saperstein controlled all of the parks in the Midwest, and sought to work with him to her own advantage. But contrary to popular belief, his powers with major league owners were not as robust as they appeared, and they did not extend to Detroit.[8]

The Manleys used this opportunity to announce to the press that they were considering withdrawing from the league. They did not reveal that they had consulted with Saperstein and Pollock, but suggested their dissatisfaction with Ed Gottlieb was the main reason they were considering independent play. New York sportswriters Joe Bostic and Dan Burley seized on the opportunity to discuss the problems Gottlieb caused. They repeated the accusations that Gottlieb controlled the league because he handled the money, took commissions on promotions at Yankee Stadium, and promoted exhibitions (like the ones with Satchel Paige) rather than league games.[9]

## Saperstein, the Clowns, and the Negro Major League

While Syd Pollock failed in his mission with the Manleys, he was making plans to improve the image of the Clowns in the black community. Unlike Gottlieb or Saperstein, he normally used public venues to communicate, placing open letters and press releases in black newspapers advertising himself as well as his team. But in 1942 Pollock was under attack in the press, and needed a new strategy in order to maintain his team's popularity. He began to reinvent the Clowns as a black-owned and -operated business, removing his name from publicity. He promoted Hunter Campbell as "veteran owner and traveling business manager," although Campbell was ill and no longer traveled with the team. He hired a new field manager, McKinley (Bunny) Downs, and all the advance publicity for 1942 described Campbell and Downs as the team's organizers. He spread word of offers the Clowns received to play in Canada, Mexico, Cuba, and South America, encouraging the belief that they didn't really need the business of the other Negro League teams. And he advertised that the team would be offering to do free exhibitions for military personnel, also to improve the Clowns' image. Although they were still the "Ethiopian" Clowns, Pollock often referred to them as the Miami Ethiopian Clowns, hoping in vain to diffuse some of the tension surrounding their name.[10]

But Abe Saperstein had other plans for the Clowns. They were to be the centerpiece for his new Negro Major League. Saperstein believed that the success drawing crowds at Crosley Field made it logical for the Clowns to use Cincinnati as their home base. Hoping to avoid some of the more unpleasant conflicts over the team's name, they would become the Cincinnati Clowns.

Saperstein had some support for his new league in the black community, including from Major (Robert) Jackson, who had served as Negro American League commissioner from 1939 to 1941. Neither Saperstein nor Jackson liked the way the NAL had treated them the previous year, and setting up a rival league would provide them some satisfaction. Although Jackson's involvement ended abruptly with his death in June, Saperstein had gathered other prominent blacks to serve as officers of the league. Sports editor Russell Cowans of the *Michigan Chronicle* became secretary, and independent team owner Dr. Joseph Thomas (Bishop Plummer's old friend) from Baltimore was treasurer. The league was to be composed of the Cincinnati Clowns; the Chicago Brown Bombers, a local independent team that Saperstein helped to finance; the Minneapolis-St. Paul Gophers, managed by Saperstein's old friend and former Negro League star Jim Brown; and teams in Detroit and Boston. Saperstein was listed as the league's promotional director, but it was generally assumed that he was the power behind the league. He was the manager, booking agent, or part owner of at least three of the teams.[11]

Cum Posey called the league "Abe Saperstein's Protective Association," echoing the words used by Rube Foster in the 1920s to describe the Eastern Colored League and Nat Strong. He assumed the league was organized as a way for Saperstein to keep control of black baseball in the Midwest and to prove to white park owners that he was the dominant power. But Posey was willing to accept the Clowns without the "Ethiopian" moniker. If Pollock's team would drop the term "Ethiopian," and if they had no players who were on league contracts, Posey was prepared to consider them a legitimate entity. He explained that he could never really forgive Pollock ("a swell person, personally") for "capitalizing on the rape of Ethiopia when that country was in distress," suggesting that "Syd not being of the same race to which we belong, can not understand this feeling." Posey, like other blacks, did not have high expectations for whites, nor did he imagine that Pollock's Jewish background could have made him more sensitive. He was not willing to forgive him. But he was ready to move on.[12]

*Courier* reporter Wendell Smith continued to criticize Pollock's business practices. He pointed out, accurately, that the Clowns would mostly be on the road, still performing as the Ethiopian Clowns. Smith encouraged fans in Cincinnati to support the local black-owned Buckeyes and not the Clowns, and area newspapers also voiced concern that the Clowns and Buckeyes would be competing for local fans. Smith was worried that the new Negro Major League would provide unwanted competition for the other league teams and their black owners. He reported an oft-repeated rumor that Saperstein was planning to "control all Negro baseball." Smith claimed to "have nothing against Mr. Saperstein in his baseball promotions. I know him and think he is sincere and honest." But he viewed this league as a serious threat.[13]

The new league did extend Saperstein's power. In St. Louis, Saperstein's team overwhelmed local competition. Allen Johnson, owner of the St. Louis Stars, left the club to join James Semler as co-owner of the New York Black Yankees, claiming that he had trouble getting bookings in St. Louis because Saperstein controlled the parks there. Sportswriter Joe Bostic viewed Johnson's move as part of the larger picture of Abe Saperstein's domination of Negro League ball. Like Cum Posey, he compared Saperstein to Nat Strong, two white men who controlled and profited from the work of blacks. He was further incensed that the black team owners were complicit in their own domination. He credited the Eastern owners with at least trying to stand up to Saperstein by demanding that the teams not play against Pollock's teams.[14]

Sportswriter Lem Graves was also worried about Saperstein's power grab, especially since Pollock did publicity that was much more useful and professional than what newspapers received from the NNL or NAL. For a Negro Major League game in Portsmouth between the Clowns and the Chicago Brown Bombers, Pollock sent his newspaper "mats, pictures, biographical data, line-ups, prepared releases and every other thing needed for coverage of the games. He's made it easy for the scribe to handle it." And Pollock sent short pieces with the game results, too. The newspapers may have wanted to ignore the NML and write only about the other leagues, but could not. Without the funds for travel, the papers relied on the kind of reporting that Pollock routinely did and the other teams failed to do. Pollock's articles and photos filled space and provided the kind of coverage the newspapers needed.[15]

Despite Saperstein's plans and journalists' fears, the Negro Major League was not a financial success. The Clowns did not prove to be as great a draw as anticipated, and the league disbanded in midseason. Although the NAL ban against playing the Clowns was still in effect, the Clowns played against the Birmingham Black Barons, Memphis Red Sox, and Kansas City Monarchs in August 1942.[16]

## Saperstein's Contributions

Moving on from his failed adventure with the NML, Saperstein returned to the Negro American League and began to receive positive press. Dan Burley, once a staunch critic, wrote a column extolling Saperstein's virtues. The column began depicting Saperstein with a "portrait of Abe Lincoln on his walls," a not very subtle allusion to Saperstein as a white hero who supported black causes. Burley credited Saperstein with helping black sports achieve status and recognition, supporting individual black athletes, especially Satchel Paige, both personally and financially, and praised Saperstein's contribution to opening major league ballparks to Negro League games. The column contrasted so dramatically with the criticism Saperstein usually received that the *People's Voice* printed the following response from their sportswriter Joe Bostic:

> Hey Dan Burley, you've got all the guys guessing as to what is the angle on the Abe Saperstein business. Maybe he's OK, but that hasn't been the general concept up to now. What goes? Is he an exploiter or isn't he?

Even Cum Posey acknowledged that ultimately Saperstein had done a good job booking teams, and pointed out that most of the league owners "were glad to be booked by Saperstein." It is possible that the failure of the NML combined with the unprecedented financial successes the NAL was experiencing during the war had made those involved with black baseball less threatened by Saperstein's power and more open to cooperation.[17]

Saperstein also got more involved with team ownership and was widely praised for working with T. H. (Tom) Hayes to turn the Birmingham Black Barons into a successful team that would win its first championship in 1942. Saperstein lent Hayes the financial support necessary to start the team in 1940. His relationship with the Black Barons was solidified in 1941 when Winfield Welch became the manager. Welch had been working for Saperstein as road manager of the Harlem

Globetrotters and remained a trusted colleague and partner of Saperstein's for many years. He was an excellent business manager, often representing Saperstein at meetings. Saperstein, Welch, and Hayes shared financial control, splitting profits for nonleague bookings 30 percent for Saperstein, 20 percent for Welch, and 50 percent for Hayes. That would have been a fair deal, as Saperstein did the booking and Welch actually ran the team in Birmingham and on the road while Hayes lived in Memphis, where he owned a funeral business.[18]

According to Negro League great Double Duty Radcliffe, Saperstein made money for himself and the Barons by booking them into venues that they'd never played before. Radcliffe recalled: "Every time the Yankees would leave, Birmingham would be in Yankee Stadium with twenty-five to thirty thousand people." Several of the Black Barons' players, including Radcliffe, Paul Hardy, and Piper Davis, began to play for Saperstein's Harlem Globetrotters basketball team in the off-season. Nonetheless, Hayes, Welch, and Saperstein quarreled about finances, and their relationship was never smooth.[19]

*Figure 3.1* Abe Saperstein with T. H. Hayes (Memphis and Shelby County Room, Memphis Public Library and Information Center).

*Figure 3.2* The Ethiopian Clowns (National Baseball Hall of Fame Library, Cooperstown, N.Y.).

With the failure of the Negro Major League, the growing financial successes of the Negro American League, and their relocation to Cincinnati, the Clowns applied for entrance into the NAL at the 1943 winter meetings. League owners gained concessions from Pollock. The Clowns were accepted into the league with the understanding that they would not paint their faces, would not use the name Ethiopian, would use only the players' real names, and would dispense with their comedy and play straight baseball. The Buckeyes would move to Cleveland so the Clowns would be the official Cincinnati team. Despite promises, the Clowns continued to clown. They were occasionally referred to as the Cincinnati (Ethiopian) Clowns, and old photos of them in war paint were still being published, at least in papers in the South.[20]

The Negro American League welcomed the Clowns in deference to Abe Saperstein and because they believed the Clowns would be an asset in attracting fans. The National League remained concerned about Pollock's business practices. In May 1943, at the joint league meeting, the NNL owners complained about the Clowns entering the league and criticized the NAL teams that had played against the Clowns the prior year in violation of their agreement. Pollock managed to smooth things over by ironing out disagreements with other owners over players and their unfulfilled contracts.[21]

Despite his disdain for league play, Pollock saw this as a wise move. Reporters were happy to have the Clowns in the league because they hoped the steady stream of information Pollock provided would set an example for other owners. The *People's Voice* reported:

> Spring can't be too far off. The barrage from the Cincinnati Clowns has started already...It will be a fine thing if some of the other league clubs take a lesson or two from the Clowns in the matter of publicity.[22]

Although they played their usual schedule and claimed success gathering crowds, the wartime conditions were hard on the Clowns. Playing in the league was not as lucrative as Pollock anticipated, and the Clowns, unlike other teams, had not cut back the schedule to deal with gas rationing.

Although restrictions on wartime travel made things difficult for touring teams like the Clowns, Negro League baseball had its best year financially in 1943. Gottlieb and Saperstein were credited with encouraging the leagues to continue operating, negotiating with the Department of Transportation about gasoline rationing, and arranging schedules that saved on travel. Saperstein continued to receive accolades from the black press. Joe Bostic described him as "the sharpest operator in the Negro baseball ivory market," complimenting his skilled negotiations in tough times. Wendell Smith also had praise for Saperstein's business skills. Saperstein was rewarded with reinstatement as publicity agent for the East-West game, earning $700.[23]

## Gottlieb in Charge

Gottlieb, while maintaining his power, was also working to improve his relationships in the Negro National League. Effa Manley and Gottlieb were making efforts to work together, although difficulties remained. Manley tried to reach out:

> Let's don't quarrel. I still think what I did a few years ago. You have all the ability necessary to put Negro Baseball on a permanent paying basis. But in order to do this Negro Baseball must come first, and Ed Gottlieb second. Is this too much to hope for?

Gottlieb replied that his interest in "Negro Baseball" and his own interests were one and the same. Gottlieb owed the league money from Satchel Paige's appearances in Yankee Stadium, but would not release the funds until the Manleys paid their share. From his perspective, it was their recalcitrance and not his management style that was holding back the financial well-being of the league. He reminded her that they made much more money with Paige there, even after paying his fee, than they would have without him.[24]

Gottlieb also solidified his control of the NNL. At the winter meetings in 1943, Tom Wilson was reelected to the presidency, with the support of New York owners Alex Pompez and Jim Semler. To win them over, Gottlieb had given the New York Cubans and New York Black Yankees more lucrative bookings in Yankee Stadium. Only the Homestead Grays' ownership switched sides and joined the Manleys in opposition to Wilson's election. The Grays would begin to play many of their games in Griffith Stadium, focusing on capturing the audience in Washington, D.C., in order to avoid having to play under Gottlieb's power in New York. Gottlieb's power over four league teams was a virtual monopoly. Joe Bostic called the winter meeting Gottlieb's "annual show," and referred to him as "ringmaster Eddie" and "Boss" Gottlieb. Bostic didn't blame Semler and Pompez, assuming they had no choice but to yield to Gottlieb if they wanted to make money. New York newspapers were all aware of Gottlieb's new powers. The *New York Age* announced that "bankroll man" Gottlieb was going to be making "a very juicy piece of melon" from the opening doubleheader of the season at Yankee Stadium. Unlike Pollock, Gottlieb remained quiet and never answered his critics publicly. But Joe Bostic assumed that he lost his job as the public address announcer in Yankee Stadium in retaliation for his criticisms. Even his detractors agreed that Gottlieb ran the league efficiently and for the most part evenhandedly. But they disliked how much power he exerted.[25]

Gottlieb avoided calling attention to himself as the owner of the Philadelphia Stars, and operated behind the scenes. He practiced the art of skillful scheduling, keeping their travel burdens lighter than many other teams. The Stars rarely toured in the South, avoiding many of the horrendous experiences of Jim

Crow that other teams endured. He also was responsible for making sure that the Stars got select dates at Penmar Park, and later at Philadelphia's major league venue, Shibe Park, when he got the rights to book black teams there. The players saw him only occasionally at games, but regularly when he paid them. They were aware of his power as a promoter on the local scene. "Everybody knew him," said Stanley Glenn, a catcher with the Stars. "If you wanted a game, you had to go through Eddie. If you didn't, you didn't play." Some of the Stars characterized him as fair, but not generous. Yet Webster McDonald, who played for the Stars from 1933–1940, remembered Gottlieb as more of a "hands on" owner who kept him up late at night talking strategy and who occasionally provided bonuses for good play. Gottlieb believed he was providing good work for a number of men who would otherwise be "bell hopping or mopping floors." He also noted that in the early days the players were paid poorly (often on percentage rather than salary) and worked in bad conditions, but in later years that improved as the owners, like himself, began to make some money and were able to be more generous.[26]

## Controversy Continued

Cordial relationships persisted as the 1944 season began. Abe Saperstein also served as the Clowns' representative at NAL winter meetings that year as they requested a move from Cincinnati to Indianapolis. The Clowns rarely played in Cincinnati, and using Crosley Field did not work out as Saperstein had planned. Bowing to the mores of that segregated city, the Reds' management would not allow the players access to the clubhouse to shower or change clothes. In 1944 the team became the Indianapolis Clowns and played at American Association Park, although they did play a few dates in Cincinnati.[27]

Effa Manley decided to use Saperstein to book games for the Eagles in the Midwest in 1944, including at Wrigley Field, another major league stadium where Saperstein made arrangements for Negro League games. Saperstein informed Manley that he could not set up a date with the Clowns, "who would be the real money earners paired with you out here," because they were already booked elsewhere, but in the end was able to arrange a contest for them at Crosley Field. Despite the bad conditions for players there and her continued discomfort with playing against the Clowns, Manley accepted the arrangements for financial reasons.[28]

At midseason, the power that Saperstein was wielding again became a cause for concern, and "the Negro National League went into an undeclared war on Abe Saperstein, white Chicago promoter." The league decided that they would not play any games against teams that he booked, including the Clowns and Black Barons. Once again it was Cum Posey who initiated the complaint based on what he saw as Saperstein's extraordinary profits. Posey calculated that when

Saperstein booked a game, he took a greater percentage of the gross than either club received. Posey used Indianapolis to illustrate his point. To book games there, Saperstein would offer to pay each club 25 percent of the profits. He then would have 50 percent left to pay for park rental, baseballs, umpires, and publicity. Posey figured that Saperstein would pay out half of his portion on expenses, and so pocket the same 25 percent the owners were getting, in addition to the 10 percent booking fee he charged. As Posey saw it, Saperstein was making too much money, and the league would be better off using local promoters who would also help draw bigger crowds.[29]

Dan Burley came to Saperstein's defense. Again comparing Saperstein to Abraham Lincoln, Burley chided Posey and other NNL owners who

> in their zeal to eliminate Saperstein from the picture, are appealing to the public and the sports writers on a basis of race and color, a dangerous procedure which, happily, is finding little or no response from thinking people who look at the results before making decisions.

Burley claimed that Posey's ultimate goal was to drive Saperstein from black baseball. Against Posey's contention that Saperstein was making outlandish profits, Burley argued that teams were in fact getting 30 percent for Sunday games that Saperstein booked. Furthermore, Saperstein spent more money on promotion and achieved greater success than other promoters who didn't advertise adequately. Burley suggested that Saperstein was willing to take risks, and did promotions at a loss when rain or small crowds limited attendance. Finally, he said that Saperstein paid players better than other owners:

> I have yet to find a player who says a bad word about Saperstein. In fact, most of them swear by him and are with him to the man. He has more friends among Negro baseball players than any other man in the game. No player who has a contact with him squawks about not getting paid or mistreated.

He also praised Saperstein for never responding publicly to Posey's attacks on him, which would have caused harm to the reputation of the leagues. Wendell Smith also defended Saperstein, calling him a "sobering influence" and someone who has given the Negro American League important advice to keep them from going under financially. He cautioned the leagues not to underestimate the value of Saperstein's gift for publicity, which kept the leagues financially solvent.[30]

Posey prevailed, however, and a new league agreement was written to prevent promoters from taking excessive booking fees. Saperstein was also not invited to do the publicity for the 1944 East-West game. The owners also decided not to pay Satchel Paige the eight hundred dollars he demanded to play in the game.

With Saperstein's assistance, Paige took his complaint to the Chicago press, telling them he would only play if the profits went to charity, knowing, of course, that the profits from the East-West game were spent on running the League offices. Joe Bostic saw this as Saperstein's revenge. For "shrewd Abraham," Bostic argued, publicizing the fight with Paige was a way of getting even.[31]

Bostic was undoubtedly correct in his assumption that Saperstein handled Paige's publicity and planted those stories. It is likely that he did it to support Paige, and that Paige was happy to help Saperstein exact vengeance. This was a subtle way for Saperstein to make the point that paying Paige and other premier players well, and using them strategically, was the best method of making money for black baseball, and that league play would never gain profits unless the owners were willing to pay players like Paige what they deserved.

Dan Burley again took up Saperstein's cause, and for the first time charged Posey with an "anti-semitic viewpoint." To defend himself against such accusa-

*Figure 3.3* Abe Saperstein joking with Satchel Paige as Walter Dukes of the basketball Globetrotters looks on (UCLA Charles E. Young Research Library, Department of Special Collections, *Los Angeles Times* Photographic Archive, © Regents of the University of California UCLA Library).

tions, Posey asserted that the new joint agreement to control Saperstein's excessive profit taking was composed with the aid of the other Jewish promoter, Ed Gottlieb. The agreement condemned the practices of booking agents who took more than 10 percent and paid out less than 30 percent to the teams. Posey argued that Gottlieb, as "the booking agent for the Eastern NN league clubs for many years, would certainly not have agreed to any parts of it which were unfair to all concerned." According to Posey, all the clubs abided by the agreement with the exception of the Birmingham Black Barons and the Cincinnati Clowns, who were controlled by Saperstein. To emphasize his point, Posey announced that the Homestead Grays would not play against the Birmingham Black Barons in the World Series, boycotting because Saperstein refused to comply with the agreement. Wendell Smith intervened, assuring Posey that T. H. Hayes would handle all the arrangements, and the series went on.[32]

Posey's antipathy to Saperstein in this case derived from an honest concern over booking practices that Posey thought were unfair, although any attack on Jewish financial misdeeds, especially those related to excessive profit for middlemen, ran the risk of stereotyping. Saperstein was making a substantial portion of his money from black baseball, and it's not surprising that men like Posey wanted to limit his power. Saperstein was also not respectful of black baseball. He spoke to the press frequently—generating publicity was one of his greatest gifts—but he did not always speak wisely:

'Colored baseball has done so well this summer, has made so much money, that it scares me,' he told a Vancouver sportswriter in 1944. 'The colored man, coming from cotton picking and menial tasks in the south to work in defense plants, now has money. All he knows is baseball, and he can afford the best seats.'[33]

Saperstein's notion that blacks went to Negro League games because baseball was all they knew was simplistic. It left out the pride that blacks felt watching people who looked like them perform acts of great skill that were widely respected in American society. The exchanges between blacks and Jews in this era reveal a wide gap of understanding.

But Saperstein functioned with great ease in black society, and most of the owners continued to trust and rely on him. The league appointed him to work on insurance matters and to select a statistician as the league finally began responding to demands from the press for information about games and player records. No matter how unaware Saperstein was either of the stereotypes of the avaricious Jewish business owner he was conforming to or the stereotypes of the ignorant black man he was perpetuating, what he did for individual players and for publicizing the Negro Leagues made him welcome in the world of black baseball.[34]

In 1944, Pollock began to participate in meetings of the leagues. Pollock was "overheard" in the Hotel Theresa lobby trying to explain that bad publicity is better than no publicity, the motto he had stood by for years. Pollock understood that the Clowns were popular "possibly due to the favorable as well as the unfavorable publicity given them in the past." The other owners became increasingly comfortable working with Pollock despite his theatrical methods, and needed them to sustain profits as the war ended and a new era of integrated baseball, which posed the greatest threat to the Negro Leagues, was about to begin. At their 1945 winter meetings, the NAL supported Pollock by rejecting a request from a group who wanted to bring another team to Indianapolis, making that city (and Cincinnati) exclusively Clowns territory. But changes were coming to Indianapolis. Gus Greenlee was returning to black baseball with plans for a new United States League (USL) and also planning an Indianapolis entry that would compete with the Clowns.[35]

Wendell Smith took this opportunity to go after Pollock again, announcing that fans in Indianapolis would surely support the USL team rather than the Clowns, who rarely played there whether or not they called Indianapolis home. He added that the Clowns would not be welcomed in Detroit, either, because the local promoter with rights to book Briggs Stadium objected to their clowning. He also reported that some Chicago teams would refuse to play against the Clowns for the same reasons. Smith applauded them, and urged others to follow suit. He called Pollock "baseball's Silas Green," another allusion to the minstrel tradition that Smith understood to be at the roots of comedy baseball. Of all the contentious business practices the Jewish entrepreneurs in black baseball were involved with, baseball comedy would be the most disturbing.[36]

# 4

# The Conflict over Baseball Comedy

Professional sports are part of the entertainment industry. Spectators pay admission fees with the expectation that they will derive satisfaction from watching a skillfully played game. Although the main focus is on the contest itself, sporting events often provide added attractions, from concession stands to cheerleaders, to attract crowds. Comedy and novelty performances, like those of costumed mascots today, are part of a long and contested history of incorporating amusements into the serious game of baseball.

Baseball clowning and novelty teams were commonplace in the late nineteenth and early twentieth century. Independent teams did clowning routines, played in costumes, or claimed "exotic" origins in order to amuse fans and increase attendance. Professional players would light firecrackers, turn somersaults, insult the other team, and joke with fans.[1] By 1920, however, clowning was relegated to the sidelines or to pregame festivities as part of major league baseball's effort to transform its image from a rowdy game that attracted gamblers and other unsavory characters into a serious and dignified form of entertainment for a "better class" of men and women.

But comedy would remain an important source of revenue for independent teams that struggled to succeed. Jewish and black entrepreneurs operated many of these independent comedy and novelty teams. Black and Jewish performers were the "clown princes of baseball" from the 1920s to the 1950s. For Syd Pollock and Abe Saperstein, clowning was first and foremost a way to attract fans, no different from other areas of the entertainment industry in which Jews were active. Some black players and commentators saw clowning as a highly skilled art that added a poetic dimension to the game of baseball. But for many blacks, clowning represented an embarrassing reminder of the degrading legacy of minstrelsy. Pollock and Saperstein carried out that legacy and found themselves in the middle of controversy.

## The Legacy of Minstrelsy

Black baseball and minstrelsy were intimately connected. The skits, comic routines, dancing, and use of blackface—basic elements of minstrel tradition—found their way into black baseball by a circuitous route. In the late nineteenth century, black teams incorporated elements of African aesthetic and comedic traditions into their play. Their innovations were most likely the origins of all baseball clowning.[2]

Although early baseball historians often credit the turn of the century Cuban Giants as the first team to perform pantomime and clowning, Henry Bridgewater's St. Louis Black Stockings team played in blackface, adopting routines from the Callender and Georgia Minstrel troupes, as early as 1880. But these routines were not meant to entertain. Instead, they were used for strategic advantage. They would catch and run with great theatrical flair in an attempt to confuse and rattle the other team. The Black Stocking team also invented "comical coaching." A player, designated to be the "boss yeller," would stand on the sidelines and engage in verbal contests with the opposing team, in the tradition of the "dozens," another method to shake the opponents' concentration. Team uniforms with bright colors and elegant styles were part of a "sartorial dandyism" that transformed the players into aesthetic objects and distanced them from poverty.[3] Without understanding the nuances of these traditions, white sportswriters observing their games would reduce them to "clowning."[4] Players dressed in top hats and morning coats, moving theatrically and making verbal jests would be associated by white audiences with what they would have observed in minstrel theater.

Minstrelsy arose in the United States in the early nineteenth century. White men in blackface makeup would perform a "variety show" that included singing, dancing, juggling, acrobatics, and novelty acts in a parody of what they imagined to be African American styles. "Jim Crow" (the ignorant slave) and "Zip Coon" (the dandified city slicker, eccentrically and elaborately dressed) were the main characters in these shows by the 1830s. Enterprising white entertainers made blackface minstrel shows the most popular type of variety entertainment in the United States by midcentury. Minstrelsy was responsible for many of the dehumanizing images of blacks and the rumors of their contentment with slavery that circulated in the North before the Civil War.

The blackface minstrel show was invented by whites who were both threatened and enthralled by the descendents of Africans. Whites dealt with their fascination and fear by creating a form of entertainment that provided an outlet for their emotions. Minstrel traditions were probably based on naive or malicious interpretations of black aesthetic and cultural styles of humor and music.[5] Many of the racially demeaning "Sambo" stereotypes of the happy-go-lucky slave, for example, had African roots in the storytelling, verbal jesting, and punning that is central to oral culture. Enslaved Africans relied on humor to maintain balance in the face of adversity and mitigate the effects of oppression. Wit was a weapon to use against the dominant culture. The laughter and joking of slaves was a medium both to conceal anger and an outlet to express pent-up aggression without outwardly displaying hostility. To insiders, it revealed the absurdity of the racial system in the United States.[6] Minstrelsy pulled this out of context, making it a parody of itself and becoming the main lens through which white people saw and interpreted the African American culture. The white sports-writers who observed the Black Stockings and New York Cubans repeated that pattern.

However pernicious blackface minstrel traditions were in the hands of whites, black performers and entrepreneurs developed their own traditions of min-strelsy, as the story of Henry Bridgewater's St. Louis Black Stockings suggests. Black performers founded minstrel troupes, entertaining in traveling road and tent shows, mostly in small towns in the South. The humor traded on images of the black buffoon. It also showcased performers' gifts for telling stories and verbal play, leading to careers on the stage for gifted comedians like Billy Kersands and Bert Williams, who served as models for black baseball comedians.[7]

Blacks themselves were the main audience for black road shows. In these venues they could be less inhibited, not worrying what whites might think. They understood that these stereotypes did not represent their rich and varied black culture. They could affirm minstrel humor for what it was—an exaggerated por-trayal of characteristics that they recognized in themselves and for that reason found funny.[8]

But black minstrelsy was controversial within the black community—especially for middle-class blacks in the North in the early twentieth century. To many, black comedic traditions were an embarrassment. Aspiring to assimi-late to mainstream society, and believing it possible, they worried that these shows would perpetuate stereotypes and impede this process. They saw working-class black approval of this type of performance as troubling and feared that it would not help advance the race. Later generations have come to appreciate the irony of the performances, and see them as a way for the per-formers to flaunt their differences and play the trickster outwitting the master.[9]

The concerns were justified, however. The meaning of black humor was missed entirely by white audiences. Jokes about stealing, lying, and drinking reinforced stereotypes. Playing the fool could provide a slave with respite from work and protection from mistreatment (you can't mistreat a "jolly guy"), but would also reinforce white images of blacks as the "carefree, laughing Sambo." As Mel Watkins put it:

> No matter how ironic the wit or how aggressive the underlying implica-tion, blacks were aware it was invisible to most whites. Slave tricked master, Bert Williams infused the slow talking stage darky with intelli-gence and humanity, Stepin Fetchit made money, but to white America they were still minstrel sambos.[10]

It is likely that, depending on the context and circumstances, performances like these could be either destructive or positive, and possibly both simultaneously.[11]

At the end of the nineteenth century, entertainment venues—movie theaters, amusement parks, baseball parks, vaudeville theaters—replaced minstrel shows as the sites of commercial culture. Like the changes made in baseball to appeal to a middle-class audience, shows in these venues were meant to be inoffensive in order to attract women and children. Vaudeville's more polite style dominated in the period 1880–1920, until competition from radio and film edged it out. Vaudeville broadened the audience for variety shows that included musical, comedy, and novelty performances. The shift from minstrel shows to vaudeville did not mean an end to Jim Crow entertainment, however. Audiences were still segregated. While black entertainers performed, they were always limited to one act per show, and only the most talented had opportunities to work. Black stereotypes of dandies, lazy fools, and slick operators were present and pervasive. So were exhibits of "darkest Africa" at festivals and fairs where Africans were represented as "repulsive savages."[12]

## Jews and the Entertainment Industry

Jews were no strangers to this kind of prejudice. They had also been the targets of demeaning stereotypes in nineteenth-century variety shows. Jews were characterized as swarthy, with prominent noses, ill-fitting clothing, and sing-song Yiddish-accented speech. They were depicted as clannish and cunning, especially in business transactions. But unlike representations of blacks in vaudeville, by the beginning of the twentieth century negative characterizations of Jews on the stage had diminished, although they remained in the public consciousness. The shift occurred because Jews were welcomed as theater patrons and performers, and because Jewish groups protested against these characterizations. In contrast to black experience, vaudeville provided, as Michael Rogin has eloquently argued, a vehicle for Jewish immigrant performers to take on a racialized white identity in minstrel roles. "Blacking up" created a unique opportunity for immigrant Jews to reinforce the racial hierarchy and to shift from their positions as outsiders.[13]

Vaudeville attracted Eastern European Jews with backgrounds in cantorial singing and the Yiddish theater. In vaudeville they were able to move beyond Jewish cultural spaces onto a national platform—unlike blacks, whose opportunities were limited. Music for vaudeville was produced on Tin Pan Alley, which was another venue for Jewish talent in the early twentieth century. Jews changed the music business through publishing and selling minstrel sheet music, songbooks, joke books, makeup, and costumes. Al Jolson, George Gershwin, and Irving Berlin began their careers not only as blackface performers but as interpreters and purveyors of black music, making money through the appropriation of black culture. Through their music, Gershwin and Berlin transformed Jews into translators of blackness, providing another opportunity for Jews to be welcomed into the American cultural mainstream.[14]

The world of comedy baseball was another aspect of the entertainment industry where Jews would exercise power that would put them in conflict with the black community. It was part of the business side of the entertainment industry where second-generation Jews found a place, creating theatrical syndicates and working as booking agents and producers. They were able to operate theaters and sporting enterprises because these businesses required minimal capital. Because this industry itself was suspect, it lacked the social taboos that prohibited Jews from entry into more highly respected businesses. Small entrepreneurs might acquire real wealth in these behind-the-scenes positions.[15]

## Perpetuating Stereotypes

Vaudeville lost its popularity at the end of the 1920s, but stereotypical portrayals of blacks found renewed popularity in radio and film and in black baseball. The tensions within the black community over these portrayals are exemplified by the controversy about the radio program *Amos 'n' Andy*. The original radio show was about black migrants from the South seeking a better life in Chicago. It was created and voiced by two white actors, Freeman Gosden and Charles Correll, who were quite familiar with minstrel traditions, and this was reflected in the program they produced. When the show began in the late 1920s, it followed the minstrel tradition of white fascination with and fear of African Americans. Yet the show was most popular among black audiences, who were pleased to have any representations of black life on the radio.

But the black community itself was divided. In 1931 the *Pittsburgh Courier* began a campaign to have the show taken off the air because of the demeaning stereotypes it fostered. Despite a largely positive response from readers, the *Courier* could not sustain the campaign. At the time, the *Chicago Defender* supported the show, and other black organizations remained silent.

The argument focused on whether stereotypic representations of blacks in public life were harmful to the race. Those who believed they were pointed to the Irish and Jewish efforts to put an end to jokes about their groups, and encouraged African Americans to follow their model. Others argued that the show was good-humored, and showed blacks as "humans" and part of the American fabric. Opponents also disagreed about whom to hold responsible, the whites who starred in and produced it or the blacks who made up much of the listening audience. By contrast, in 1951, when a television version of *Amos 'n' Andy* began, cultural awareness about stereotypes and their pernicious nature had changed dramatically. The NAACP organized a successful campaign to get the show canceled. Stereotypes were no longer contentious, they were simply unacceptable.[16] This shift in sensibilities could be observed in black baseball as well, although comedy baseball found support in the black press long after the stereotypes on which it was based had become taboo.

Black stereotypes in films, particularly the "lazy, inept, crap-shooting, watermelon-eating, chicken-stealing, docile servant," also prevailed in the 1930s and 1940s. This caricature dominated the work of Lincoln Perry, better known by his stage name, Stepin Fetchit. He perfected the character of the "laziest man in the world" and was the most popular and best-known black actor in America until criticism of his act derailed his career in the late 1930s. Recent scholarship has suggested that Perry's "playing the fool" was in fact a form of resistance that gave the outward appearance of accommodation. Perry made a fortune tricking white people into paying to see his skilled performance, and getting his audience to believe he was something he was not while hiding his true self.[17] Similar arguments would be made about black baseball's greatest showman, Satchel Paige.

The self-deprecating humor that Perry performed is common to both African Americans and Jews in the United States, and to any outsider group that seeks to guard itself against the hostility of the majority culture. This humor, with all its troubling aspects, lived on in comedy baseball.

# Comedy Baseball

## *Major League Clowns: Al Schacht and Max Patkin*

In the world of independent baseball, the traditions of black comedy and aesthetics came together with Jewish vaudeville humor and entrepreneurship. As organized baseball adopted a more serious style of play and was recreating itself as family entertainment, unabashedly humorous (and ribald) behavior by players became less acceptable. The clowning tradition was continued primarily by two Jewish performers, Al Schacht and Max Patkin, the "clown princes of baseball." They did routines in the major and minor league white circuits similar to the comedy acts in black baseball, but limited to pregame or sideline performances. Over the years, influences flowed in both directions as baseball comedians, like other comics, borrowed freely from one another.

Al Schacht was the first self-anointed "clown prince of baseball." Schacht grew up in an Orthodox Jewish family in New York City. In his autobiography he recalled loving baseball and loving to clown. As a child, in an effort to raise money to buy uniforms for his team, he simply "whipped up a minstrel show" and in blackface played the standard parts of interlocutor and featured soloist. He did his first professional baseball clowning for an independent team in Walton, New

*Figure 4.1* Al Schacht, "The Clown Prince of Baseball" (1892–1984) (National Baseball Hall of Fame Library, Cooperstown, N.Y.).

York, doing a pantomime impression of a pitcher who would not leave the game. His comedy career was inspired by "the great [Jewish] minstrel man Eddie Leonard." Schacht used Leonard's trademark song "Rolly Bolly Eyes" as part of a baseball comedy routine that he performed at a Newark burlesque house. It is not surprising that Schacht's developing artistic style was based on minstrelsy. Like other young Jewish boys, Schacht would adapt the humor and routines he found in minstrel tradition as a way of becoming American.[18]

Schacht's professional baseball career began when he was recruited by John McGraw of the Giants, who was always looking for Jewish players to lure Jewish fans to watch his team at the Polo Grounds. Schacht met another baseball clown, Nick Altrock, in Washington in the early 1920s. Altrock coached first base for the Washington Senators, using routines that were popular in baseball's early era but were beginning to fall out of fashion. Altrock clowned from the coaching box during infield practice, juggling baseballs and heckling umpires. He always wore his cap sideways and kept a big wad of chewing tobacco in his cheek. In 1924 Schacht became Washington's third base coach, and he and Altrock formed a team.[19]

Working together, Schacht and Altrock did three pregame comedy routines: a prize fight, a pantomime tightrope walk, and a concert. Schacht wore an old top hat and tailcoat over a uniform in the Zip Coon sartorial dandy tradition. Later,

Schacht and Altrock added other routines that Schacht took credit for inventing. In 1925 they introduced a fishing routine, swimming with water spouting from their mouths and high diving off the mound. This would become a staple in black baseball comedy in the 1930s. Schacht and Altrock achieved much attention for their performances, which resulted in an off-season tour of the vaudeville circuit in the late 1920s, and they even invested in a Chicago theater together. Their act was popular in vaudeville houses, but was out of step with trends in baseball. However, it lasted until 1935, when the Senators traded Schacht to the Boston Red Sox. Although Altrock and Schacht had worked together for a decade, they had a difficult personal relationship. Schacht claimed that Altrock was an anti-Semite who called him a "Jew kike bastard" when he got drunk.[20]

On his own in Boston, Schacht developed a solo career. He took his act to the grandstands, kissing women, exchanging men's hats, and bringing kids onto the field between innings. Although this was low comedy of the burlesque tradition, he was always mindful that baseball preferred "family entertainment" and "kept his act clean." He did pantomime mocking players, including his favorite, the "swell-headed pitcher." He took great pride in his pantomime work as art, but also thought it his job to engage the fans, especially when he was the only one out on the field before the game or between innings. He disdained the work of his successors, including the costumed mascots of today who "don't get the laughs...throw an imaginary ball...do a one-man prizefight with imaginary opponents...you can't teach a guy to do pantomime."[21]

Comedy baseball in the major leagues had limited appeal and was confined to the periphery. Although Schacht was invited to appear at the annual All-Star Game beginning in 1934, his act was relegated to pregame entertainment. He took center stage for a brief time, but fans were not all that interested in his performances. At the 1942 All-Star Game, Schacht performed at length during a rain delay, but got little response. Newspapers reported that the fans seemed only to be waiting for the game to begin.[22]

Schacht's immediate successor as "clown prince" was Max Patkin. Patkin grew up the son of Russian Jewish immigrants in Philadelphia. He began his career with the Cleveland Indians sometime after 1946, when he was hired by their new owner Bill Veeck. Veeck was the exception to just about every rule in major league baseball, including his stance on clowning. As an owner, he believed in flouting baseball traditionalism when and where he could. He was a good friend of Abe Saperstein, and quite familiar with clowning traditions in black baseball. His most famous stunt was borrowed from the Indianapolis Clowns. As owner of the St. Louis Browns in 1951, Veeck signed a midget, Eddie Gaedel, to play for the team. Hiring Patkin was not at all out of character.

Although Patkin claimed to have inherited the "crown" to a "small kingdom" from Al Schacht, Schacht disapproved of Patkin's brand of comedy. Patkin's acts were based on broad, physical humor, similar to those seen in the Negro Leagues

*Figure 4.2* Max Patkin (1920–1999) (National Baseball Hall of Fame Library, Cooperstown, N.Y.).

in later years. He smelled his own shoe and pretended to faint from the odor. He also went into the stands to kiss women and snatch purses. His best-known routine was filling his mouth with a vast amount of water and spraying it out for an extended time. For most of his career, Patkin worked primarily in the minor leagues, as growing disdain for baseball comedy kept him out of major league baseball entirely. He was bitter that, other than Veeck, there were too many "baseball purists" who disliked clowning, tried to make baseball a "religious experience," and couldn't laugh at the game.[23]

## Clowning in Black Baseball

Players on independent touring teams, black and white, continued to perform humorous routines. They also relied on novelty teams to attract fans. Novelty teams sometimes included comedy, but also drew people because of some unusual or "exotic" dimension of the players' identities. Players sported outlandish costumes and were identified as "foreign" in some way. All-Nations teams brought together players of different ethnic and racial origins. Bloomer Girl teams were mostly composed of women (with men pitching and catching, often in drag costumes). Black American teams claimed to be Cuban, and spoke "gibberish" to mystify and entertain. Actual teams from Cuba were also considered novelties. Even African American teams were advertised as a "novelty" when playing in the North and Midwest, where some white residents had never seen a black person before, and black teams were sought after as much for the curiosity they engendered as for the quality of their play. They sometimes clowned to ease the tensions created by interracial play, especially when the black team was winning by too great a margin and embarrassing its opponents.

One of the most prevalent and highly skilled clowning routines was shadow ball. In shadow ball, players went through the motions of fielding and hitting, but without the ball. Their pantomime, which was based on expert timing and communication, convinced observers that they were actually playing with a real ball. Nick Altrock did a shadow ball routine for the Washington Senators in the early 1920s, and the black New York Lincoln Giants were known to do the routine as early as 1911, along with pregame juggling and acrobatics. The Philadelphia Colored Giants and the Kansas City Monarchs also featured shadow ball routines in that era.[24]

Black players from the early days remembered other comedy routines reminiscent of the pioneering efforts of the St. Louis Black Stockings. Arthur Hardy recalled members of the Topeka Giants hitting from their knees or running the bases backwards as early as 1907.[25] Carter Wilson also remembered observing clowning on the Gilkerson Union Giants. An outfielder, Willis Jones, would read a newspaper with a hole cut through it, and Bingo Bingham would do a running commentary from the first base coaching lines. The Gilkerson Union Giants continued to clown through the 1930s. An article about them in a local white newspaper from Oregon described their show, alluding to the similarities to Altrock's performances:

> The (Gilkerson Union) Giants bring along their own private side show.... [T]hey have a comedian billed as the Nick Altrock of colored baseball, Charles Akers.... [W]arm up... is said to be a three-ring circus all in itself, the way the boys whip the ball around and clown for the grandstand.[26]

Although black baseball player, owner, and historian Sol White assumed that clowning would die out in black baseball when it became unpopular in the major leagues, each team continued to carry some player noted for showmanship. In the 1920s and 1930s, Harry Howlett's Bellevue Clowns (also called the Detroit Clowns) wore clown suits, but advertised themselves as playing to win first and to entertain second. Buck Leonard told stories about minstrel troupes with their own baseball teams. He also related the tale of a Brooklyn Royal Giants player named Country Brown who played third base and clowned in the 1920s. Brown would arrange with the other teams in advance to do a crap-shooting routine with a pair of oversized dice. He would also pretend to be on the telephone with a girlfriend who was cheating on him. And the Black Yankees had "Thomas, the clowning center gardener [fielder]" on their team during this era. The Negro Leagues maintained their aesthetic traditions as well. They did not abandon speed and trick pitches when the major leagues changed their style of play in the 1920s, favoring power and outlawing the spitball and other pitches. Negro League star Newt Allen commented that while white baseball sought to be "squeaky clean" and play by boxing's "Queensbury" rules, black baseball maintained the "coonsbury rules."[27]

## *The House of David*

A few independent white teams also clowned and relied on novelty to gain bookings. The best known of these was the House of David. The team originated in 1916 within the Israelite House of David messianic Christian group based in Benton Harbor, Michigan. Like the Belleville Grays, the team began as a recreational activity for the community. They played well, and began to send out a touring team in 1919. The colony split in the 1930s, and both groups continued to promote traveling baseball teams, one of which continued through the 1950s. Many members of the community played, but they also welcomed outsiders, including major league baseball stars like Grover Cleveland Alexander and the female star Babe Didrikson, who was a well-known athlete in golf, basketball, and track and field. There were also many imitation House of David teams, including the Havana Cuban House of David organized by Syd Pollock. The original House of David once tried to take the imposters to court to protect their name, but there were simply too many imitators.

The House of David was a novelty team because the community's religious practice of wearing extremely long beards made their appearance exotic. All the players were required to grow beards, even those outsiders who played as "ringers" and were not members of the colony (although sometimes the beards were fakes). The House of David also entertained, and the team is credited with inventing pepper ball, a game that became a staple of comedy baseball. Doc Talley of the Benton Harbor community claimed that they developed the game in 1923. In pepper ball, players throw or bat the ball back and forth to one another at close range and great speed. While this activity was also used as a standard warm-up drill by many teams, the House of David teams perfected it to entertain the fans and show off their skill and agility. Although they are not frequently associated with other types of clowning, they did occasionally dress the first baseman, Kenny, in a clown's outfit and have him perform a juggling act.[28]

The beards and the name Israelite House of David led many people to assume it was a Jewish group. Although they were not Jewish, they were vegetarians, so the colony's guest house provided an option for religious Jews who observed the dietary laws. For that reason many Jews from Detroit and Chicago vacationed at the Benton Harbor headquarters on Lake Michigan. In the 1930s, functioning as a Jewish resort was one of the main ways the House of David sustained itself. They even built a synagogue on the grounds for a group of Rumanian Jews from Chicago who became regular customers.[29]

In the film *The Bingo Long Traveling All-Stars & Motor Kings* (1976),[30] the assumption that the House of David was a Jewish team led to a farcical conclusion. In one scene, Bingo Long's barnstorming black comedy team played against the House of David, as if a team of Hasidic Jews were playing against African Americans. Instead of the long beards and old-style uniforms that the House of David was known for, the team sported six-pointed Jewish stars on their uniforms and wore traditional Hasidic garb—long black coats, hats (*shtreimels*), side curls (*payis*), and the familiar long beards. The vendors in the stands for that game sold food in containers marked "going out of business" and making reference to shoddy Jewish business practices. Producer Rob Cohen was responsible for the Jewish touch. He also took a cameo role as the second baseman on the House of David team. Jewish comedic actor David Warfield actually clowned at baseball games by dressing up as a Hebrew peddler in "scraggly beard, baggy pants, and hat pulled down tightly over his ears who wandered through the crowd clowning and selling souvenirs" in the early twentieth century. Both routines fall into the category of self-deprecating Jewish humor that plays on stereotypes about Jewish business practices.[31]

The imagined connection between Jews and the House of David was also referenced in the 2001 graphic novel, *The Golem's Mighty Swing*. Author James Sturm imagined a Jewish baseball team barnstorming in the late 1920s. Sturm called the team the "Stars of David" and described them as the "bearded wandering wonders." Sturm drew them with Jewish stars on their uniforms and long beards. Although Sturm borrowed the idea from the Israelite House of David, he knew that the original team wasn't Jewish. But he drew the parallel intentionally to introduce the struggles of immigrant Jews—and how they connected to the racism experienced by blacks—in the world of independent touring baseball.[32]

In *The Golem's Mighty Swing*, the team captain, Noah Straus, preferred traveling on the road to working in sweatshops like his father. The star of the team, along with Straus and his brother, is Hershl Bloom, a powerful African American hitter, described as a "member of the lost tribe," an allusion to the possible ancient connection between Hershl and his teammates. He is not, however, a black Jew. His true identity as Henry Bell, who played in the Negro Leagues for over twenty years before joining the Stars of David, is eventually revealed. A promoter (interestingly, not drawn with any Jewish characteristics) comes up with the suggestion that Hershl dress up in costume as "The Golem." Noah doesn't want to add comedy to baseball, but Henry says he got used to it, playing pepper and pitching two balls to two batters: "Against the Top Hats I hit one that knocked the hats off three of them."[33]

But in contrast to the major leagues, Jews in black baseball were the promoters, not the comedians. Jewish entrepreneurs Syd Pollock and Abe Saperstein saw baseball comedy teams in the context of the entertainment business. They built comedy teams in the world of black sport beginning in the late 1920s as vaudeville was dying. They never questioned the minstrel origins of the comedy they produced, and never responded to the controversy that it created in the black world. To them, including comedy was simply a smart business decision because it attracted crowds and paid the bills.

## Jewish Promoters of Black Baseball

### *Getting Started*

Like many Jews of his generation, Syd Pollock grew up in the theater business, working from a young age managing the vaudeville and film theaters owned by his family in North Tarrytown, New York. Pollock also played and loved baseball, and he built a career that combined his interests. From the beginning, Pollock's baseball promotions involved novelty and comedy. He started his career by booking novelty Bloomer Girls teams in the early 1920s. When he took over the Havana Red Sox in 1928, Pollock promoted them as a novelty team. In a feature article in the *Pittsburgh Courier* about an upcoming game between the Red Sox and the Homestead Grays, Pollock announced that the Red Sox would "feature shadow play before the game. This is done while they are warming up and the stunt has never failed to go over in big style." The article also declared that "the chatter of the Cubans" kept the games "livened up." Similar descriptions would be repeated in press releases that Pollock wrote and the black press frequently published.[34]

Early in 1929 Pollock continued to advertise the Red Sox team he was putting together. He went into great detail about the uniforms: "blue suits . . . long peak caps . . . socks of red, white and blue design used by the New York Giants in 1927." But the emphasis on fancy dress was also an aspect of the black comedy aesthetic that Pollock sought to exploit.[35]

Pollock often inserted information about himself when discussing his teams, noting that he

> is connected personally with a large theatrical organization in NYC, and
> his plans are to combine his experience from this source with his

knowledge of the baseball game and offer a combination of both that will prove a sensation wherever his club appears.[36]

With that statement, Pollock announced the path he would follow for the rest of his career. He continued to work in the family business, owning and operating the Strand Theater in Tarrytown, which featured movies and vaudeville shows. Pollock understood baseball as an entertainment business, and it was his desire and genius to synthesize his interests in comedy baseball. He seemed for the most part unperturbed that to achieve that goal he would have to operate in a world that was predicated on segregation.

Abe Saperstein also claimed to have begun his career in sports comedy when he became the owner and promoter of the Harlem Globetrotters basketball team in 1928.[37] Although Saperstein achieved his fame as the owner of the Globetrotters, they were but one part of the sports empire he built from his small office in Chicago. Much of Saperstein's income would be derived from promoting and booking black baseball comedy and novelty teams.

Saperstein was part of the Chicago sports scene in the 1920s and was friends with many former Negro League players who sponsored touring teams throughout the Midwest. Saperstein's first recorded venture into sponsoring novelty baseball was as owner of the Cleveland All-Nations team in 1933. He was also the Midwest promoter for Pollock and other comedy teams beginning in the 1930s. In the 1940s, Saperstein had the Globetrotters play baseball in an effort to keep members of his basketball team fully employed and their names in the news.

Saperstein's successes with the basketball Globetrotters made him the best-known sports comedy entrepreneur. But Syd Pollock was the dominant figure in comedy baseball. Pollock did not invent any of the routines that his team used; he borrowed them either from the House of David or from earlier black comedy tradition. His key contribution was popularizing and defending the genre. He followed up his experiment with the Havana Red Sox by working with baseball clown Ed Hamman to form a white Canadian Clowns team in 1930. Hamman had been a "ringer" on the House of David team, where he excelled at pepper ball and other ball-handling tricks. Influenced by the success of the House of David team and his work with Hamman, Pollock changed the name of the Havana Red Sox to the Cuban House of David in 1931. They used the same routines the Havana Red Sox had been performing, but grew their beards "to an unusual length" and placed more emphasis on "shadow-baseball and other comedy entertainment."[38]

## The Impact of the Depression

While other black baseball teams suffered the effects of the depression at the gate, comedy and novelty baseball was a growing industry. Charlie Henry's Zulu Jungle (sometimes Cannibal) Giants, who played in war paint, grass skirts, and under assumed "African" names, began to gain attention in the black press. Henry had been a pitcher for Hilldale and the Harrisburg Giants in the 1920s. The Zulu team was based in Louisville. Newspapers described their costumes as "picturesque garb of primitive Africans" with names borrowed from chiefs and rulers from the Congo regions. Henry claimed to have come up with the idea after seeing the House of David, the Detroit Clowns, and the Kentucky Colonels. Even the *Atlanta Daily World* reporters, who did not generally object to comedy baseball, called them a "zoo aggregation" and assumed they were entertainers and not players. Pollock became their booking agent in the Northeast. Abe Saperstein was booking them in the Midwest. Henry owned the Zulu team until 1937, when he sold it to Colonel Charles B. Franklin. According to Pollock's son Alan, Henry also sold the team to Pollock and Saperstein, collecting cash from each. Although rarely mentioned in the sports pages in later years, the team survived through the 1950s.[39]

Seeing the financial success of teams like the House of David and the Zulus, and having given up on the expense of fielding Cuban teams, Pollock looked for a new opportunity to own and operate his own comedy baseball team. In May 1936 he announced that he was handling the tour of the Ethiopian Clowns, "winners of 31 consecutive games," who were training in Florida. It is likely that Pollock made that record up to attract attention, since there is no record of Ethiopian or Miami Clowns in 1935. Pollock's biography claims that the team was created from another touring team, the Miami Giants, in the winter of 1936. It is not known whether the Giants did comedy acts. But one comedian from the Zulu team, Richard King (King Tut) began playing for the Clowns in 1937 and probably brought some of the routines with him.[40]

Although clowning was not featured in Pollock's press releases in the team's early years, he drew attention to their "antics," such as doing a "Corrigan Double Play" by running the bases backwards. Pollock's release described a game against a team called the St. Louis Clowns Colored Giants, during which the Ethiopian Clowns, winning by a wide margin, began running to the wrong bases. "The crowd of over 5,000 fans were in an uproar as one of the Ethiopian Clowns players ran into the pitcher's box and started to adjust a pair of shin guards on the pitcher's leg," Pollock wrote.[41]

The *Atlanta Daily World* called attention to "clown stuff" that was on the rise in baseball. It suggested that the "vaudeville element" was amusing. The author credited the House of David, with its "bewhiskered" ballplayers, with being the first vaudevillian team. The article described how the Ethiopian Clowns, Zulu Cannibal Giants, and Grover Alexander's Whiskered Wizards were all trying to outdo one another with "bizarre outfits." "With baseball partially in the doldrums," such dress and comportment were seen as wise methods of bringing fans to ballparks. Significantly, the article noted, these teams played good ball, even in their costumes. The Southern press would remain sympathetic to comedy baseball and rarely critique the racial politics of this genre in the years to come.[42]

## Combining Comedy and Athleticism

Beginning in 1939, Pollock developed a new advertising strategy to call attention both to the players' athletic prowess and their skills as entertainers. He began sending press releases describing the Clowns as "the strongest and most sensational aggregation of colored stars in baseball today, ranking on par with the best of Major League white teams." But the accompanying photographs depicted a team of circus clowns in white face paint wearing clown uniforms.[43] This tactic would begin to draw criticism from the black press. They didn't object to comedy baseball but wanted to make sure it wouldn't be associated with the Negro League teams that were playing a serious professional brand of baseball. Pollock wanted it both ways.

Black sportswriters were also uncomfortable with a white man running a black comedy team. In the first of many battles fought in print, A. E. White wrote about white promoters expecting their black players "to be clowns . . . dress in grass skirts . . . adopt fictitious and phoney names and put on a show." *Chicago Defender* sports editor Frank (Fay) Young took White to task, arguing that black-owned and white-owned clubs played under the same conditions and most of them were neither clowning nor in costume. Young noted:

> It is true that there is a club booked by Syd Pollock [of] NY state, a white man, which is known as the Ethiopian Clowns, but it has been told me that this idea was taken from the Negro-owned Ethiopian Clowns even to some of the players names being the same.

Apparently Young was not aware that Pollock was the driving force behind the Clowns from their inception. Some of Pollock's press releases drew attention to his role, but at other times he stayed behind the scenes, aware that his white identity would have an impact on how the team was perceived. Young defended Pollock's right to put players in costumes because black owners did the same. He accused White of acting like a "booger in the woodpile," putting out harmful and inaccurate information just at a time when white newspapers were taking some interest in black baseball, a business in which black and white owners and bookers worked cooperatively and well. Young was probably referring to Abe Saperstein's work in Chicago, which was gaining wider attention due to the phenomenal pitching of Satchel Paige.[44]

It is likely that the "white promoters" White referred to were Pollock and Saperstein, as the two were working together to promote comedy baseball. Pollock and Saperstein had been acquainted for years, and Pollock's Cuban

All-Stars had played against Saperstein's All-Nations team in 1933. They divided territories for booking the Zulu Giants in the mid-1930s, and Saperstein later became Pollock's Midwest booking agent for the Clowns. Saperstein and Pollock combined forces in 1939, organizing a tour starring the Clowns and Jesse Owens, whom Saperstein promoted. Owens was featured as a pregame attraction, racing against a runner from each team. Owens would do this "novelty base running act" again in 1940.[45]

Saperstein sought out famous athletes like Owens, helping them capitalize on their earning potential. He provided access to publicity and they lent their names and talents to attract crowds to comedy baseball. With the help of Saperstein and other promoters, Owens used his track talents in comedy venues and earned his living in this way for many years. Soon after his heralded victories at the Berlin Olympics in August 1936, Owens found himself back in the United States without a job. In December 1936, Owens ran against a horse at the Cuban National Sports Carnival in Havana. P. T. Barnum invented this stunt and commonly used it in his shows, and it was performed at major league baseball games as early as 1916. Owens did running exhibitions at major league and Negro League baseball games as well, and once ran against Joe Louis in a staged race at a game between the Birmingham Black Barons and the Chicago American Giants. In his autobiography, Owens recalled making "a few bucks" in Negro baseball, but in fact these promotions paid quite well. Owens claimed to have despised and resented this work and to have done it for only a year, but newspaper reports suggest that he continued to run as an attraction at independent and Negro League games for many years, often with teams owned by Saperstein. The conflict between making a good living and the debasing nature of the work would cause much hardship and ambivalence for the black athletes employed by Pollock and Saperstein.[46]

Thanks to Saperstein's connections, the Clowns also played against Satchel Paige. Paige credited Saperstein with helping him restore his reputation after an arm injury threatened his career in 1940. Saperstein, with the assistance of Broadway entrepreneurs George Kaufman and Moss Hart, got Paige coverage in the *New York Times* and other New York dailies for several guest appearances with the New York Black Yankees in which he announced his triumphant return to form. In return, Saperstein became Paige's personal manager and got first crack at promoting his services.[47]

Paige was in demand because of the quality of his pitching, but he was also known as an entertainer and did not shy away from comedic performance. Newt Allen noted that Satchel Paige reminded him of Stepin Fetchit:

> He talks and sounds just like him…And he's a solid comedian, he's another Bob Hope. He can keep you laughing all the time. Quite a character. All the ballplayers were crazy about him, because he was a showman, he was really a showman.[48]

Like Owens, Paige was a famous and gifted athlete who was able to use his superior comedic skills for financial gain. Unlike Owens, he carried the image without complaint, knowing the advantages that accrued to him because of his willingness to perform the role. Like Lincoln Perry, Paige permitted the press to depict him as a shuffling, lazy black man. He also put on a show when he pitched in the tradition of black comedy. He paid the price for doing so, as white journalists assumed that Paige's tendency to "act the fool" was both what kept him in demand and also what kept him from becoming the first black man in the major leagues. As black baseball's most gifted player, he was the most likely candidate.

Lester Rodney, the sports editor for *The Daily Worker*, who had interviewed Paige extensively, thought this view of Paige was a misleading stereotype. In his experience, Paige was a thoughtful and serious man, and black audiences knew that he was merely performing a role. "They loved it," and were willing to pay to see him. Saperstein, Pollock, and also Ed Gottlieb knew that an appearance by Satchel Paige would bring crowds. Although other players in the Negro Leagues may have been as talented as Paige, his combination of skill and showmanship made him the greatest draw in black baseball. Other owners were less interested

*Figure 4.3* Satchel Paige exhibits his showmanship and skill for the Harlem Globetrotters (National Baseball Hall of Fame Library, Cooperstown, N.Y.).

in highlighting individual players, fearing that their salary demands would cut into profits and undermine team cohesion. The black press called the "merchandising" of Paige one of Saperstein's "hustles." But these Jewish owners and promoters had a different perspective, believing that entertainers like Paige should be showcased for their individual skills and allowed to play for whatever team would draw the biggest crowd in the best location.[49]

## Gaining Public Attention

Saperstein's promotions brought attention to the Clowns, and they made their first appearance in New York City in 1939 at Dexter Park against the Bushwicks. New York had no tradition of comedy baseball, and reporters were curious. The *New York Amsterdam News* described them as a "weirdly garbed but talented baseball club" wearing "costumes resembling those of African natives" but with "pompoms on their caps" to resemble clowns, and "paint on their faces as if preparing for a war dance." The article illustrated the level of discomfort with the comportment of the Clowns. Playing against white teams and before predominantly white audiences like those in Dexter Park left blacks open to ridicule, and the costumes in particular would meet with strong resistance as the years went on.[50]

Despite these concerns, Pollock became more open about his ownership of the Clowns. His press releases for the 1940 season indicated that he would be the financial backer of the club that coming year, and "personally guide the 1940 destiny of the Clowns," working in partnership with Hunter Campbell. He had also purchased "a new streamlined 21 passenger bus with reclining seats" to prove that he was concerned with the needs and comforts of the players. Saperstein continued to book the team and give them high priority for good venues, since they drew crowds and made money. When the Clowns toured with Owens again in 1940, Pollock's press release for the tour dubbed Saperstein "the Joe Jacobs of Negro Sports" and named him as the man who "directed" the Clowns' road tours.[51]

Unlike their northern counterparts, the black press in the South appreciated the aesthetics and humor of the Clowns' routines. Lucius Jones of the *Atlanta Daily World* wrote a feature on the Clowns' first baseman, revealing only his pseudonym, Blue Gerolubi. Jones said Gerolubi reminded him of another player, Ted Gillam, who played in a similar "nasty" style in the early days of black baseball, catching everything that came his way with broad, joking gestures. He argued that Gerolubi's play was equal to that of the great Buck Leonard and Dave "Showboat" Thomas. Jones went on to explain that players with that kind of talent were called "sloppy" first basemen in the early days. He concluded, "Blue Gerolubi is one of the sloppy boys," placing him and the game the Clowns played in the lineage of black comedy traditions. E. B. Rea of the Norfolk *Journal and*

*Guide* also wrote positively about the Clowns and lamented that although their comedy compared favorably to "Nick Altrock or Al Schatz [Schacht]," the white entertainers drew bigger audiences. It would continue to be difficult for black baseball to gain the attention it deserved, although Pollock and Saperstein worked hard at it.[52]

Pollock was not afraid to use comparisons to both white and black comedy performers when advertising his players. Ed Davis, who performed under the name "Peanuts Nyasses," was not only a star pitcher, but also a comic performer. Davis pitched brilliantly and was compared by sportswriters to Satchel Paige. He also did sideline humor while "coaching" when he wasn't pitching. Pollock described him as

> a combination of Stepin Fetchit, Nick Altrock and Al Schacht with a touch of Bert Williams thrown in...funny as the proverbial barrel of monkeys, a real "Clown Prince of Negro Baseball" all right, and a whole lot more than that...on the mound and throwing his fast one by the opposing batters.[53]

Pollock did not have other black baseball players to compare Davis to, since by 1940 the Clowns were the only comedy team on the national scene in black baseball. By this time Altrock and Schacht were no longer working in the major leagues, and Bert Williams and Stepin Fetchit were being criticized by blacks. Although Pollock tried to ignore cultural shifts and cling to the past, he was beginning to get criticisms that compelled him to make some changes.

He responded halfheartedly to critiques in the black press about degrading Ethiopia by referring to the team as the Miami Clowns, although references to "the Ethiopians" or "Ethiops" lingered in some of his press releases. Pollock also began to occasionally use players' given names, although the pseudo-African nicknames still appeared in box scores. Pollock replaced the team's pompom clown hats with helmets. He claimed it was to protect them from being hit by pitches, but he was probably also bowing to pressure to make the team less vulnerable to ridicule.[54]

To replace "Gerolubi," Pollock hired Dave "Showboat" Thomas, a Negro League veteran who would manage and play first base. Known, as his nickname suggests, for his "showboating" at first, Thomas was also an outstanding player who would fit right in with Pollock's team. Pollock announced that Thomas would work on a new infield routine, the "Lightnin' 2-Ball Infield exhibition," which involved having two batters hit two balls simultaneously while the fielders kept them both in motion. The team was doing so well at the box office that Pollock announced that he was going to pay the players salaries rather than percentages of the gate.

The *Indianapolis Recorder* quoted Abe Saperstein comparing the Clowns to the Harlem Globetrotters, praising them, in colorful language similar to Pollock's own, as "a diamond studded attraction that for sheer entertainment comical diamond antics and a daily display of fast, aggressive baseball, cannot be surpassed." This was one of the rare times that Saperstein was quoted in the press praising the Clowns. Although he booked and promoted them for many years, and was often assumed to be their owner, he distanced himself from Pollock's outfit in public, sensitive to the criticism from sportswriters and Negro League owners with whom he needed to work. Saperstein could not resist the financial rewards of booking the Clowns, however. He continued to call on Satchel Paige to pitch against them, backed up by his all-star team. Paige was under contract with the Monarchs, and using Paige to draw crowds evoked the ire of the other owners.[55]

The Clowns and Paige's All-Stars split a doubleheader before a reported crowd of 12,000 in Cincinnati in 1941. But the most important development for Pollock's team was the endorsement of Fay Young, who attended the game and wrote a news report and a column, both enthusiastically praising the Clowns. While fans came to see Paige, he suggested that the majority, including a substantial number of white patrons, came out to see the Clowns. Ed Davis pitched brilliantly. Young described him as "the elongated pitcher who resembles Stepin Fetchit." Young also described Davis' pitching in a "cutaway frock coat" and doing a fishing routine during which one of the players (called Mofike, possibly Thaddeus Christopher) spouted water on the mound. Max Patkin would do the same routines in the same costume at major and minor league games a few years later.[56]

Young went on to retract his earlier criticisms of Pollock's team. He had only positive words for Ed "Peanuts" Davis, who excelled by winning the first game and then clowning brilliantly in the second. He wrote that whether or not everyone liked how they painted their faces with "white chalk...the Clowns prove, from the crowds they draw, that they have something the public wants." As with the controversy over *Amos 'n' Andy* a few years earlier, the more conservative *Defender* columnist saw nothing wrong with the minstrel-based humor, while the civil rights–oriented *Courier* criticized Young's report and saw clowning as an obstacle to racial progress. The *Courier* also insinuated that Young wrote the column because he was on Saperstein's payroll. Young and Saperstein were indeed close and he may have been paid by Saperstein, but he was not the only reporter who consistently gave Saperstein good press. *New York Amsterdam News* reporter Dan Burley and the *Courier*'s Wendell Smith would also become Saperstein supporters (and rumored employees) in future years.[57]

The touring combination of the Clowns, the Monarchs, Paige's All-Stars, and the Havana Cubans (a team Pollock pulled together to tour with the Clowns) had drawn record crowds throughout the West, Midwest, and Canada during July of 1940. The Clowns' financial success encouraged Saperstein and Pollock to try to gain a legitimate place for them in the Negro Leagues. Cincinnati was a logical place to make their home, since Saperstein had recently negotiated for the use of

Crosley Field, Cincinnati's major league ballpark, and the Clowns drew well there in their debut in June. Cum Posey wrote a column exposing what he believed were Saperstein's true motivations. Instead of booking legitimate league clubs, he kept those clubs idle so that he could force Pollock's novelty teams, the Ethiopian Clowns and Havana Cubans, and Satchel Paige's All-Stars on fans in Cincinnati instead. Posey claimed that H. G. Hall (of the Chicago American Giants) and J. L. Wilkinson (of the Monarchs) voted for Saperstein in league meetings because they wanted good dates with the Clowns and Saperstein could help them make money. Supporting comedy baseball made Saperstein's business plans seem even more suspect.[58]

## Drawing Ire

Pollock and Saperstein found themselves in trouble with other Negro League owners. The comedy they were producing ignored the growing displeasure in the black community over degrading stereotypes. Some of the owners and writers were sincerely troubled by the Clowns' demeanor and Pollock and Saperstein's lack of regard for black sensibilities. But others saw this as part of a struggle for economic control of the leagues.

In June 1941, Saperstein attended the joint meeting of the Negro American and National Leagues in New York where he was reappointed the Leagues' publicity agent for white newspapers and radio stations for the East-West game. Two owners, Cum Posey and Alex Pompez, objected. Posey and Pompez didn't want Saperstein involved in black baseball, deeming him a "bad influence" because he was booking the Ethiopian Clowns. An article in the *Pittsburgh Courier* described the Clowns as "a group of colored players who travel over the US with their faces painted to represent the mythical natives of the African jungles," and made it clear that the author found their performance degrading and unbecoming of a professional team. While the other owners voted down Posey's proposal to avoid clubs and promoters (the unnamed Saperstein and Pollock) "who aid in ridiculing Negro baseball," the issue was finally on the table. The early 1940s found much dissension among African American owners about the role of Jewish promoters. Pollock and Saperstein would be tolerated because their publicity methods worked and their promotions were making money for the teams. But not all the owners were pleased with the clowning that was behind their financial success.[59]

Emory Jackson, who wrote a syndicated column that originated in the *Atlanta Daily World*, presented a contrasting Southern perspective. He argued that Posey and Pompez were themselves only seeking financial gain. He assumed that their arguments against Saperstein were about business, not the Clowns' style of dress or play. Jackson asserted that Posey and Pompez were themselves responsible for destroying the Negro Southern League "so that they can have a monopoly."

Although Jackson did not deny that clowning baseball was a detriment to the race, he saw "cutting the fool" as no worse than "cutting throats," which, he claimed, the Negro League owners now wanted to do to independent clubs, because they, and in particular the clowning teams, were competition. He also reminded his readers that the Clowns were not the only team to be involved in ridiculing Africa. He praised the Clowns for admitting that they were clowns and criticized the other owners for refusing to call themselves "racketeers and frauds."[60]

## The Clowns Struggle for Legitimacy

In order to prove they were a legitimate team, the Clowns returned to the *Denver Post* Tournament for the third time in 1941, and won. The *Denver Post* highlighted the Clowns' impressive play, but also focused on their clowning. They particularly complimented Ed Davis, who was still playing as "Nyasses," for winning easily while engaging in "clownish gyrations." The *Post* also wrote glowingly about the two-ball infield practice, pepper ball, and the rowboat stunt. Buster Haywood, former star of the Belleville Grays and now playing as "Khora," was named the tournament's Most Valuable Player. Haywood contributed to the clowning by going to bat in his catcher's equipment.[61]

But this very public event raised larger racial issues. When the Clowns won the tournament, Jack Carberry, *Denver Post* reporter, told Dave Thomas, "You boy, Showboat, are a credit to your race." The team was also praised for not arguing calls or responding to taunts from players or fans. His comment on their comportment revealed that the white reporter needed to reassure himself about black participation in the event. Black teams had often resorted to clowning in order to make it easier for the white observers to handle the black winners. Carberry's comment makes it clear that the clowning also made it possible for whites to create distance between themselves and these black men with strange costumes and names.[62]

As a result of these successes, Pollock and Saperstein came up with a plan to legitimize the Clowns. Assuming the Negro League owners wouldn't accept them in league play, they would build a league of their own, with the Clowns as the main drawing card. The league would be called the Negro Major Baseball League of America and the Clowns would finally have a home base, in Cincinnati, where they had drawn big crowds the summer before and where Saperstein had access to the major league ballpark, Crosley Field. This was an audacious move by Saperstein and Pollock. It was based on their belief that black baseball was different from the major league game and that clowning was an important component that would draw crowds and attention.

The idea of the vaudevillian clowns in a serious organized league caused concern in the black press. Lem Graves of the *Journal and Guide* saw the Clowns as an attraction to please a predominantly white audience, similar to Bert Williams.

"They really enjoy seeing a Negro act the fool and large numbers of them really believe that Negroes are capable of nothing but clowning," Graves commented. "That style of play should be kept out of organized baseball." The Clowns playing league ball was "a serious blow to the earnest efforts of our people to earn for capable Negro players places on the roster of big league teams," which was their ultimate goal.[63]

Wendell Smith of the *Pittsburgh Courier* was the greatest critic of the Clowns. He agreed with Graves that their comedy routines were designed for "entertaining whites...with their slap face comedy antics." He countered Pollock's claim that their comedy was "Broadway caliber," and compared them to minstrels and "Mississippi showboats." Newspaper reporters began to raise the possibility of boycotting the Clowns. Samuel Haynes, a bureau manager for the *Journal and Guide*, urged Lem Graves to "crack down" on the Clowns for their makeup and antics, which both offended black people and made them objects of ridicule for whites. Graves acknowledged his own discomfort with the way the Clowns dressed and with the idea of having them in league play. But he also argued that not only did the Clowns play a decent brand of baseball ("about as good as any in Negro baseball when they really wanted to play") they also attracted large crowds, especially in the South. As an independent team, as long as they stopped using face paint, he could support them. Graves also didn't see this as a race issue. He compared the Clowns to the House of David; both teams played "unorthodox baseball." Arguing for a color-blind approach, he thought the Clowns had a role to play as long as it was not in an organized league. In their proper place they were not a detriment to the black race any more than the House of David was to whites.[64]

As criticism intensified, Pollock changed tactics, believing he could defuse the tension in the press. He wrote to Wendell Smith to deny that he was the owner of the Clowns, and claimed that Smith's comments were "founded in filth and untruths." Pollock went on to say that he was only the general manager and the team was owned by a black man, Hunter Campbell. Smith was not fooled by Pollock's ruse, but used his lie to advance the argument. He turned his criticism to Campbell, who as a member of the race, should surely have known better. He used the opportunity to lecture Campbell on race politics, reminding him that

> every Negro performing in public life stands for something more than the role he is portraying; that every Negro in the theatrical and sports world is somewhat of an ambassador for the Negro race, and that whether he likes it or not, is responsible to 13,000,000 people for his actions.[65]

According to Smith, the Clowns were a detriment to the race, and Campbell was even guiltier than Pollock who, as an outsider to the black world, was not expected to understand. Smith certainly did not believe that because Pollock and Saperstein were Jewish they would have a view that separated them from other whites or provide him with any insight on racial politics. And Smith was correct. Pollock believed that comedy baseball was an honest profession that provided financial gain for him and the blacks who worked for him, not a political or racial matter.

Ignoring the criticisms, Pollock and Saperstein continued with their plan to include the Clowns in an organized league. Throughout June and July the Clowns played some games against other teams in the Negro Major Baseball League of America and some independent games against white teams, including the House of David and Dizzy Dean's All-Stars. Pollock sent out press releases that emphasized their clowning, especially the verbal jests of pitcher Ed "Peanuts" Davis, the fishing routine, pepper ball, and shadow ball. Pollock also advertised their new acquisition, Lloyd "Pepper" Bassett, a solid veteran catcher who was well known in Negro League baseball for catching while seated in a rocking chair. The team continued to use pseudonyms, and several new players took on old names like Aussa, Sardo, Askari, and Khora. Pollock hired college football star Lou Montgomery to play the outfield, and created a new football stunt for him. Saperstein also placed articles about Ed Davis in white dailies, including the *Sporting News*, the baseball "bible," which rarely paid attention to black baseball. An article about Davis and the Clowns in *Liberty* magazine capped the successful hunt for publicity in the wider world and further alienated the black press and black entrepreneurs.[66]

But comedy baseball would not be enough to sustain the new league, which failed before the season ended. Saperstein and Pollock were not dissuaded from their goal to bring the Clowns into organized black baseball, however. Playing the Clowns (and pleasing Abe Saperstein) provided great financial rewards for most of the other owners, and they could not resist. In 1943, Negro American League owners finally voted to permit the Clowns to join the league, with the understanding that they would stop painting their faces and, according to some reports, end their comedy routines. The Negro National League did not approve when their owners met in the winter. Cum Posey remained angry that the American League did not honor the boycott of the Clowns, to which he claimed all the owners had agreed in 1942, and Wendell Smith kept up his attacks. The Clowns did as promised, dropping the term "Ethiopian," and ending the use of white face paint. But Pollock had no intention of ending the entertainment aspect of their game, and was making plans for new routines that winter.[67]

## King Tut and Goose Tatum: A Contrast in Styles

According to Alan Pollock, in order to enter the league the Clowns did drop some of their more offensive routines, which were thought to be "unfit for children." Those routines were mostly performed by Richard King "Tut." Tut played on the

Zulu Cannibal team and had been with the Clowns since their inception. While Ed Davis's routines were in keeping with the old "boss yeller" tradition of black baseball verbal comedy, Tut's routines were derived from the world of burlesque and minstrelsy. Tut shot craps in pantomime, first winning and then losing not only his shirt, but stripping down to his "huge flowered boxer shorts." Another routine, that was "unfit for women," had Tut dressed in drag, mockingly adjusting his bra straps, checking his stocking seams, and excessively powdering his nose, armpits, and shoes.[68]

Joining the league did not stop Tut's performances; his off-color routines continued through the 1950s. Joe Bostic reported that Tut was engaging in

*Figure 4.4* Richard King "Tut" (1905–1959) (National Baseball Hall of Fame Library, Cooperstown, N.Y.).

comedy in 1954 that "would have been a bit risqué even in a bordello." Tut was best characterized as a "low comedy specialist of the black face, minstrel school." Some of his material was daring, as it involved going into the stands and provoking confrontations with spectators. Negro League umpire Bob Motley said Tut frequently grabbed white babies in the stands, courting danger in the South.[69]

Although Tut's routines were objectionable, the new attraction for the Clowns in the 1940s, Reece "Goose" Tatum, was, like Ed Davis, a gifted pantomime artist and comedian. Ted "Double Duty" Radcliffe claimed to have discovered Tatum in Arkansas and brought him to the attention of Abe Saperstein. Saperstein was impressed with Tatum and sent him to play outfield and then first base for the Birmingham Black Barons in 1941. For most of the 1942 season, Tatum played for the Minneapolis-St. Paul Gophers, a Negro Major League team that also toured with the Clowns and was booked by Saperstein. It was clear to Saperstein and Pollock that Tatum's skills were right for the Clowns, and he joined the team in early September. Tatum had been called "the King of showmen" since his days with the Barons. His talents made him a perfect fit not only for the Clowns but, Saperstein realized, also for comedy basketball, and Tatum joined the Harlem Globetrotters. Tatum blossomed in both sports. Except for his time in the Army during World War II, Tatum was the Clowns' first baseman from 1942 to 1949 while he played for the Trotters in the winter. He was probably the finest comedian to play baseball, as well as a good fielder and hitter. His long frame and arms allowed him to move with great grace at first base and on the basketball court, where he is credited with inventing the hook shot. White sportswriter Dick Freeman called Tatum "the best showman I have ever seen on the diamond, and that included Nick Altrock, Al Schacht, Dizzy Dean, Babe Ruth, and the rest." Max Patkin agreed: "I have to say that Goose Tatum is the funniest man I've ever seen. He had those long arms, and a unique gait and a voice that made people laugh."[70]

Although Tatum did individual routines at first base, he also teamed up with Tut and "Peanuts" Davis. Rare footage from 1946 of the Clowns playing against the Monarchs features Tatum playing a "sloppy" first base, catching balls while reading the newspaper, using his long arms and incredible footwork to make catches that would be out of anyone else's reach. He did a Stepin Fetchit–like slow walk, but also performed lighting-fast play. His pepper game is reminiscent of the way he handled the basketball as a Globetrotter. The footage also captured Tatum's "down-on-knees prayer" pantomime and a shadow ball sequence with Peanuts Davis and King Tut, who is dressed in his standard tailcoat and crooked baseball cap. The clip closes with the routine using Tatum's foot as smelling salt to revive Tut. All of these routines were standard in baseball comedy, but the Clowns perfected them and made them their trademark.[71]

Negro League veteran Othello Renfroe talked about how players as well as fans enjoyed watching the Clowns' elaborate comedy routines and fancy infield practice. His favorite was the dentist routine, in which Tut would fill his mouth

*Figure 4.5* Reece "Goose" Tatum (1922–1967) (John Mosley Photographic Collection, Charles L. Blockson Afro-American Collection, Temple University Libraries, Philadelphia, Pa.).

with corn. Tatum would pretend to try to pull Tut's teeth, to no avail. The problem was solved by Tatum lighting a firecracker, prompting Tut to spew the corn from his mouth. Even though they did the same act every night, he and the other players would still be laughing.[72] To Pollock's critics, those routines were reminders of minstrel comedy and had no place in organized black baseball. But others saw no difference between the Clowns' slapstick humor and routines white performers did in variety shows and circuses. The multiple views about clowning in black baseball put Pollock in an interesting position. As a Jew and an outsider who was encouraging controversial entertainment practices as a way to make money, he was on dangerous ground. But he had support from within the black baseball community, and he made enough money for himself and other owners that he was able to continue and build his team.

Goose Tatum became a great draw, and Pollock traded the Clowns' regular first baseman so that Tatum could play all the time. That did not please everyone. Manager Bunny Downs fought with Pollock about the move. But Tatum's value at drawing fans outweighed considerations about winning games. Pollock also felt obliged to please Abe Saperstein, who wanted as much exposure for his future Globetrotter star as possible.[73]

Both Tatum and Ed Davis were in the Army in 1944, so to ensure the comedy continued Pollock added "Pinsy" Davis and his trick horse Pluto. Ed Hamman, the white clown with whom Pollock had worked in the 1930s, also joined the team, coaching along with Tut. After the war Tatum resumed his clowning. He drew attention when he was selected to play first base at the East-West All-Star game in 1947. Tut was also on the team as a "special comedian."[74] Sports reporter Ric Roberts was surprised that Tatum could both clown and play strong baseball. He described Tatum's show-stealing role at the East-West game:

> He dug scatter-gut heaves out of the dirt with scoops, backhands and traps; his sensitive bag-thumping foot played tick-tag, hot foot or gave out with the Pavlova…a one-man riot of color, clowning, and cold efficiency, and what was more he's a solid hitter from either side of the plate.[75]

As major league baseball began to integrate after World War II, rumors circulated that teams were interested in Tatum for his playing ability, not his clowning. Ric Roberts thought that Tatum might have to limit his antics if he made it into the majors, but saw no reason why he couldn't follow in the tradition of Rube Waddell and Dizzy Dean, major league pitchers who were known for their odd behavior. But this proved to be unrealistic. The black players who were selected were not the comedians but those like Jackie Robinson who were familiar with white culture and mores and who would be more able to blend in. Tatum, like most other Negro League veterans, would also not get serious consideration for the major leagues because of his age. The few teams who showed interest in integrating wanted young talent that they could train in the minor leagues.[76]

After the 1948 season, Saperstein's relationship with Pollock began to deteriorate. The tension would have a major impact on Tatum and the Clowns. In 1948, Tatum began to miss games. Pollock learned that he was playing in Chicago on local teams "closely associated with Abe Saperstein" instead of traveling with the Clowns, to whom he was under contract. Tatum drew crowds, and Pollock grew angry at Saperstein for keeping him away. Although Saperstein and Pollock were business partners, and outsiders saw them as Jews who colluded with one another, Saperstein's first allegiance was to building the Harlem Globetrotters and supporting those who worked for and with him. He and Pollock were never personally close, and Saperstein began to see the Clowns and Pollock as a liability. To symbolize the end of their relationship, Pollock crossed out Saperstein's address on the Clowns' letterhead.[77]

Pollock's only recourse was to ask the league to suspend Tatum for leaving the team. Tatum returned to the Clowns at the end of the season, signed a contract for the following year, and even organized his own all-star team to tour against the Clowns during the winter. Pollock, in his usual fashion, issued a press release to

*Figure 4.6* : Ed Gottlieb (left) with Goose Tatum (center, misidentified as Goose Goslin, who played in the major leagues) at a benefit for a Jewish camp in Philadelphia (Philadelphia Jewish Archives Center in Urban Archives of Temple University Libraries, Philadelphia, Pa.).

announce Tatum's return. In it, he included speculation that the Boston Braves were interested in signing Tatum. The release also included a warning, really addressed to Tatum and not the general public, that the Braves would be watching not only his abilities as a showman and a fielder, but also his "general behavior."[78]

In response, Saperstein told the *Chicago Defender* that he was encouraging his friend Bill Veeck to sign Goose Tatum to play for the Cleveland Indians. In fact, Saperstein was encouraging Tatum to play year-round for the basketball Globetrotters, which he began to do in 1950. In 1952, many of the major black newspapers carried an interview with Tatum as part of the Globetrotters' publicity campaign. In it, Tatum suggests that he got an offer from Veeck in 1945 (possibly to play for the American Association team he owned, since Veeck had not yet purchased the Indians). Tatum wanted to be clear that his choice was between a major league career and playing year-round for the Globetrotters, although it is not likely that his baseball talents would have been sufficient for the major leagues. Tatum credited hours of conversations with Veeck and Saperstein for the decision. Tatum's interview with Wendell Smith the following year recast the story:

> the highest paid basketball player in the world...said, wistfully: 'Yes, I like basketball. That's how I make my living. But, you know, if I had it to do all over again, I'd try to be a big league baseball player. Baseball is my first love.' [79]

According to this version of the story, Tatum was convinced by Saperstein to make the choice that would provide him with a better salary, and that was true. Tatum credited Saperstein with taking good care of him. "'I can't complain. Mr. Saperstein has been very good to me. He picked me up when I hardly knew what a basketball was and taught me all I know about the game.'" But Saperstein was also looking out for his own interests, as Tatum was a brilliant basketball comedian and would go on to be the Globetrotters' star player and greatest attraction. The relationship between Saperstein and Tatum would end bitterly in 1955, although Tatum never publicly criticized Saperstein. Pollock and Saperstein were running an entertainment business that depended on the labor of talented African Americans, and they did not always treat them with the respect they deserved. Tatum was the finest sports comedian ever to play, and neither the Trotters nor the Clowns would ever regain their brilliance after he left.[80]

## Clowning in the Negro American League

As the Clowns began to play Negro League teams regularly in 1943, the debate over clowning intensified in the black press. Wendell Smith once again attacked Pollock for using black men as "hired hands" doing a "song and dance" and using "bandana placards," reminiscent of advertisements for minstrel shows. He called the comedy "Uncle Tom antics" and questioned Pollock's "obscene sales methods," suggesting that Pollock couldn't distinguish between "baseball salesmanship and old-fashioned minstrel shows." With thinly veiled anti-Semitism, Smith contended that Pollock's theater and movie industry background was the driving force behind his way of doing business, and urged the league to make him change his practices. It was unlikely, however, that the league would be able to assert power over him, since the Clowns provided an important source of revenue for all the owners.[81]

Reporters like Dan Burley, sports editor for the *New York Amsterdam News*, had always been skeptical about the Clowns. Burley had spoken out early against using Ethiopia in the team's name. Most of his sophisticated New York readership would dismiss a team called the Clowns because they took their baseball seriously. But when the team made its league debut in New York in June 1944, playing the Black Yankees at Yankee Stadium before a crowd of 8,000, Burley came to a surprising conclusion. He credited the Clowns with a "clever, well-played victory" and a "burlesque that surpassed even that of the celebrated Al Schacht of the big leagues." Burley concluded that "they made the grade." He had already written several columns supporting Abe Saperstein, and it's possible that his reaction was based on loyalty as much as his own observation, but he may also have appreciated the Clowns' routines and seen no difference between the work of King Tut and Al Schacht.[82]

## Comedy Baseball in the Era of Jackie Robinson

Comedy baseball had long been an important source of revenue, but after Jackie Robinson signed with the Dodgers in 1945, it was the only lucrative option for black baseball. Integration posed a major challenge to the viability of the Negro Leagues. Black sportswriters took the occasion of Robinson's signing to highlight the contributions blacks and the Negro Leagues had already made to baseball. Columnist Lucius Harper reminded readers of the *Chicago Defender* that comedy, which blacks introduced and developed, had been an important part of black baseball since the early years. Blacks brought artfulness to first and third base coaching, giving the coaches license to banter in order to entertain the spectators. Players did pantomimes, and the catcher indulged in razzing the batter with humor. The style never caught on in white ball, and most of the players who tried it, with a few exceptions, "appeared foolish rather than funny." The Zulu Cannibal Giants and the Clowns revived the "art of baseball buffoonery" in the 1930s. Harper disdained the "dignified and grim" performance in white baseball and considered black baseball, with its looser approach, a better game.

Robinson would bring the elements of daring and speed to major league base-ball, but comedy would be left behind.[83]

Syd Pollock believed that comedy would help black baseball continue to attract an audience. Abe Saperstein assumed that Negro League ball was doomed. He began to experiment with adding comedy baseball teams to his sports empire as a temporary measure. By 1946 Saperstein and Pollock had created four traveling teams that played against the Clowns and each other, creating their own comedy baseball tours that were independent of the leagues. The Cincinnati Crescents (managed by one of Saperstein's longstanding business associates, Winfield Welch) and the Harlem Globetrotters (managed by Double Duty Radcliffe) were Saperstein's comedy teams. Saperstein also maintained an interest in the independent Chicago Brown Bombers. He started a Pacific League, thinking that black baseball might survive in the Northwest, far from the major leagues. Jesse Owens was vice president of the Seattle Steelheads, who were financed by Saperstein.

Pollock went back to organizing novelty Cuban teams to play against the Clowns. The Havana La Palomas were now the Clowns' traveling partners. The La Palomas team was managed by Cuban American Ramiro Ramirez, the former manager of the Havana Red Sox, who returned to work with Pollock for the first time in many years. White comedian Ed Hamman did the clowning. Pollock signed four new players from Latin America for the Clowns and several for the La Palomas. The La Palomas played comedy baseball, and Pollock had them speaking "Spanish" for humorous effect, as he had in years past, as if nothing had changed since the 1920s:

> Their constant running fire of chatter in their native tongue delights the fans no end, but the way they play ball has many of the American teams facing them plenty anxious to know what they're saying. One or two clubs…believe the LaPalomas' signals are mixed up in their incessant chatter.[84]

The Clowns and their touring partners had a very successful year in 1946. Most of the players who had been in the armed services returned. The Manleys were interested in setting up games for the Eagles against the Clowns in Florida in the spring. A newsreel featuring the Clowns' comedians was playing in theaters. The team began the season in the South playing before large crowds, often over 10,000. The largest attendance was 23,000 against Satchel Paige in St. Louis. In 1947 Pollock again fielded a La Palomas team, which traveled with Saperstein's Globetrotters and the Crescents when they weren't touring with the Clowns. The NNL also began to do benefits for organizations like the National Negro College Fund, the National Council of Negro Women, and the Urban League, and the Clowns often participated.[85]

## The Demise of Black Baseball

By 1948 the world of black baseball had changed drastically. Although only two major league teams had signed black players, it was becoming clear that the best young Negro League prospects would be going to organized baseball's major and minor leagues and black baseball would survive only by scouting players for the major leagues or doing comedy. The story of former Belleville Gray and Birmingham Black Baron Tommy Sampson is representative. Abe Saperstein provided financial backing for Sampson to assemble his own traveling comedy team, the Birmingham Clowns. While he was scouting players, Sampson claims, he discovered one of baseball's great players, Willie Mays. As Sampson tells the story, he took Mays on the road with the Clowns, but could not keep him. When the team played the Chattanooga Choo-Choos, the owner bought out most of Sampson's players, including Mays. Sampson continued to manage the remnant of the team, taking them to Texas and Canada, where Saperstein had booked them. In the middle of the season, he sent his players back to Birmingham and he played the rest of the season for the New York Cubans.[86]

Although he would remain connected to black baseball as a financial backer, Saperstein's primary focus was the Harlem Globetrotters. The fact that Saperstein's comedy basketball team continued to thrive when comedy baseball was collapsing is a puzzling matter, but it may have only been a question of timing and the difference between the less established business of basketball and the old baseball establishment. Basketball as a professional game was in its beginnings, and the Globetrotters, who achieved their fame playing and winning consistently against college teams, were a well-known attraction that brought out crowds for the nascent professional league. Before the National Basketball Association integrated in the early 1950s, the Globetrotters had a monopoly on black basketball talent. Saperstein tried to stop integration because it would destroy his team. Rather than try to compete, the Globetrotters began to concentrate exclusively on comedy. As the Cold War began, Saperstein took the Globetrotters on international tours and publicized them as ambassadors of good will. Unlike the Clowns, the fame of the Globetrotters was so great that they were able to continue attracting crowds, as they still do today as a successful black-owned business.

The Clowns focused more and more on clowning in 1948, adding Juggling Joe Taylor to their comedy team. During the season Pollock made another controversial move. He brought Ralph Bell, a little person who would be incorporated into comedy routines as "Spec Bebop," to play for the Clowns. Cal Jacox of the *Journal and Guide* expressed consternation. Like other sportswriters and African Americans in general, he thought the Negro Leagues should become training grounds for individual players to join the major leagues. He claimed the fans would be looking for "good games, not clowning." But clowning would soon be all that was left. And clowning would not sustain the Negro Leagues as a viable business.[87]

By 1949 most teams could no longer make a profit, and the Negro National League dissolved. The four remaining teams, the New York Cubans, the Baltimore Elite Giants, the Houston (formerly Newark) Eagles, and the Philadelphia Stars, merged into the Negro American League. Abe Saperstein was not committed to keeping the league going, and the working relationship between Saperstein and Pollock, strained over Goose Tatum, came to a bitter end. In prior years, Saperstein had made it possible for the Clowns to use ballparks in Cincinnati and Indianapolis as their base. In 1949 Saperstein changed the conditions of the agreement for Indianapolis, and Pollock would not accept them. Saperstein leased the Indianapolis field to the now independent Homestead Grays and used it for his own Harlem Globetrotters comedy baseball team instead. The disagreement between Pollock and Saperstein became public at a league meeting where the "differences between owners and promoter who held franchise at Victory Field" were resolved, and the Clowns did play a few games at Victory Field in the later part of the season.[88]

In 1950 Pollock's difficulties negotiating with Saperstein resumed, and the Clowns moved their nominal home base to Buffalo, although they retained Indianapolis as their official name. Following the 1950 season, Wendell Smith, representing Saperstein, publicly criticized Pollock for his unwillingness to play in Indianapolis and accept Saperstein's terms for Victory Field, and for running the team as a "barnstorming aggregation." According to Alan Pollock, the dispute between Pollock and Saperstein started over a $10,000 loan Pollock made to Saperstein that was never repaid. Whatever the reason, the difficult financial circumstances these entrepreneurs faced provoked a conflict, and the two never spoke again. In later years, Pollock would claim to have been Saperstein's mentor in comedy sports, while Saperstein simply never mentioned Pollock.[89]

## Pollock Stays in the Game

Despite the many problems faced by Negro League baseball, Pollock remained upbeat. In an interview, Fay Young asked "Is Negro Baseball doomed?" Pollock responded with a resounding no. Ignoring what was happening around him, Pollock blithely asserted that the league should be looking forward to its best season yet. Publicity, Pollock's favorite weapon, would save them. Bowing to the cultural support for moving players to the white leagues, Pollock said his team would feature "carefully selected potential major league stars." The Clowns continued to make money and could still draw crowds in New York and Philadelphia, where they enjoyed the support of sportswriters who still printed Pollock's press releases. Some even believed, like Pollock, that once the novelty of having black players in the big leagues was over, teams like the Clowns would provide an important dimension to black life and the leagues would rebound. Not surprisingly, the Clowns remained popular in the South, filling an important role for black patrons who were not welcome to attend games at segregated minor league stadiums.[90]

The Clowns continued to draw at the box office in 1950 and ended their season on tour with an all-star team organized by Jackie Robinson. They traveled through thirteen states, drawing 125,000 fans and making over $200,000. Although Robinson often criticized black baseball, he and the other major league players on the tour benefited from the Clowns' drawing power. In 1950, the team's clowning was still balanced with good play, but the clowning occasionally took over. Louis Clarizio, one of the white players who signed with the Chicago American Giants in a failed effort to integrate the Negro Leagues, remembered the Clowns as a good team, but also commented that it wasn't easy to play against them because of the clowning. "If you took a swing at a ball and missed, they would bring out a bat that was like eight feet tall, real big and fat, and they would hand it to you. They'd light firecrackers behind you while you were batting."[91]

By 1951 clowning was the main feature of the game. Satchel Paige, back from his first major league experience with the Cleveland Indians, was pitching for the Chicago American Giants and barnstorming along with the Monarchs and Clowns. The tour did poorly in Philadelphia, although they drew over 7,000 in Washington, D.C. A game at Comiskey Park, honoring Negro National League founder Rube Foster, drew 10,000. Again the Clowns toured with Jackie Robinson's All-Stars at the end of the season, while Tut and Spec provided the pregame comedy. Pollock added more clowning acts, including Paul Blackman, who played as "Boogie Woogie Paul," a one-man band. The Clowns also added acrobatic acts, jugglers, musicians, and other variety-oriented entertainment, including Pollock's daughter Estelle doing "Afro-Cuban acrobatics" along with her husband, Alfonso Carol.[92]

Sportswriters like Joe Bostic still encouraged fans to go see the Clowns, whose "harmless antics" were "a pretty good buy." He saw an obligation to support the Negro Leagues both for sentimental reasons and because they were the source of all the black talent then playing in the major leagues. By the end of the summer, Bostic concluded that the Clowns would be better off staying away from large metropolitan centers, however, as their "low grade comedy and worn out routines" would no longer be accepted by audiences except in the "boondocks." Despite their inability to draw in New York or Philadelphia, the Clowns claimed to draw 22,000 to a game in Detroit as Pollock was able to secure Briggs Stadium, the home of the Detroit Tigers, for the first time.[93]

In 1953 only three teams (Kansas City, Memphis, and Birmingham) remained in the Negro American League along with the Clowns. Other teams folded as

*Figure 4.7* The Indianapolis Clowns of the 1950s (National Baseball Hall of Fame Library, Cooperstown, N.Y.).

black fans deserted the Negro Leagues and were absorbed in following the hand-ful of black players in the majors. They preferred to watch stars like Jackie Robinson, Roy Campanella, Monte Irvin, Larry Doby, and Willie Mays on the few teams that had welcomed them, in hope that their acceptance in "America's game" foreshadowed equal rights in other dimensions of life.

But Syd Pollock did not give up. Trying a new approach, he returned to another brand of novelty baseball he had promoted in the 1920s. He invited Toni Stone to play for the Clowns, making her the first woman to play in a men's professional league just as the race- and gender-segregated All-American Girls Professional Baseball League was coming to its end. Stone played second base for the first few innings of each game. Pollock promoted the move by saying "this is no publicity stunt." Of course the goal was publicity, and people did come to the Clowns games in greater numbers that year. According to the box office data Pollock sent to black newspapers, Stone attracted crowds, although the figures were likely exaggerated. They reported attendance of 18,000 in Kansas City for the opener, 21,000 in Detroit, 9,500 in Philadelphia, and 13,500 in St. Louis for Stone's debut in each town. To draw even more attention, Pollock claimed that he was paying Stone $12,000, a high salary even for the major leagues at that time. Stone denied that she ever received such a sum.[94]

Clowns' manager Buster Haywood had made his peace with whiteface and grass skirts, clowning routines and their temperamental performers, and the evils and hardships of Jim Crow. He defended comedy by saying:

> The Negro leagues weren't drawing. The Monarchs were. The Grays and Elite Giants did okay. But the Clowns outdrew every team in both leagues. We brought money and good baseball into the league, and that was our purpose, and the critics can say whatever they want about that.[95]

In the early years, Haywood participated in comedy as a catcher, going to bat with his catching equipment on. In later years, he developed a routine of his own with umpire Bob Motley. Motley wrote that it happened quite by accident. Once, in the middle of an argument, "Haywood lurched at me, just inches from my face and said, 'Motley, can't you see how much these people are loving this?'" He encour-aged Motley to pretend they were still fighting. "Haywood could have kept it going for hours." From that time on, they began a "regular shouting routine much to the delight of fans all across the country." Fans assumed they were bitter enemies, but Motley declared his respect for Haywood, "even though his antics sometimes overshadowed his genius for managing the game. He was an extremely knowledgeable skipper and knew exactly how to get the best from his players."[96]

But Haywood could not accept the idea that a woman could play for the team he managed:

That was the only year I was ever angry... I had to play Toni Stone at second the first three innings every game. She wasn't a ballplayer, and I'm playing to win.... It was the worst season of my life; made me sick.[97]

For the first time in several seasons, the Clowns were not league champions, and Haywood held Stone responsible. He decided to leave the Clowns after the 1953 season. He did not reveal his reason for leaving publicly, although later he suggested that he signed to manage the Memphis Red Sox in 1954 instead because there "men were men and women were spectators."[98]

In 1954, following Pollock's lead, Monarchs owner T. Y. Baird began to employ circus acts to travel with his team, and also hired Toni Stone to play for the Monarchs. Pollock brought two new women athletes, Mamie Johnson and Connie Morgan, to pitch and play second base. While one woman was tolerated as a novelty, having three in the league began to cause serious problems. Sportswriter A. S. "Doc" Young reported that playing with women was demoralizing for the men. Although the women had great athletic ability, it was not easy to integrate them either on the field or when they traveled. What today would appear to be an effort at gender equality was then a deep insult to the pride of the Negro League veterans. Morgan survived the whole season, but Mamie Johnson quit in August. Malcolm Poindexter wrote that it was the "life of poor pay, filthy accommodations and nerve-wracking schedules" that ended the women's brief careers. He criticized Pollock, who "lives in luxury in Tarrytown, NY while Connie packs 'em in through the Southland." This was the first indication that Pollock was beginning to cut corners on the team's accommodations as the Clowns were not making the kind of money they had in the past. Reporters were beginning to pay attention to the disparity between Pollock's social status and that of his employees.[99]

In 1954 Emmett Ashford, the first African American to umpire in organized baseball, gained public attention when he was promoted to the prestigious Pacific Coast League. Ashford's dramatic (some said flamboyant) style reignited the controversy over clowning in the black press. A few writers were critical and found Ashford's behavior embarrassing and not appropriate for major league baseball. But other African American commentators expressed their comfort with the black comedy aesthetic and came to Ashford's defense. Comparing him to Goose Tatum, Satchel Paige, and the Indianapolis Clowns, one writer noted that like them Ashford was demonstrating the skill and talent required to be funny. Clowning was only bad when it ridiculed the clown, and the art of the Clowns is to ridicule the fans who want to be entertained in that way.[100]

Attendance was reduced dramatically, and 1954 was the last year that the Clowns played in the league. They were able to make more money playing independently. Pollock could still get publicity for the team, although the league owners tried to convince the press not to cover the Clowns, fearing the competition. During the 1955 season, Syd had a heart attack, and his family relocated to Florida. He sold the Clowns to his old friend Ed Hamman, but stayed on as general manager, claiming that he was still in the game, "planning the biggest and best baseball circus we've ever had."[101]

It was a circus indeed. Baseball hardly mattered; the Clowns were now a variety and burlesque show. They did skits with animals and traveled with a circus act, The Flying Nesbits. Hamman, Tut, and Bebop were joined by Jim "Natureboy" Williams and Prince Joe Henry to clown. Shifting back to the old ways, "Natureboy" played in bare feet and grass skirt. Even supportive sportswriter Marion Jackson decried the risqué nature of Tut's act, commenting that "the bawdy house stench is in the routines but you take the attitude it ain't necessarily so." Pollock had purchased the New York Black Yankees to accompany the Clowns on tour, so there wasn't even a competitive aspect to the games they played. Malcolm Poindexter wrote a scathing article, accusing Hamman of rigging games and producing sloppy, "sandlot" play. The players, poorly paid ($125 per month), were not being taught skills and had no hopes of ever getting major league contracts. But mostly the team was just ignored.[102]

The Clowns carried on. They added other entertainers, including Steve Anderson, a one-armed pitcher; a second little person, Billy Vaughn; and another gifted comedian, Birmingham Sam Brison. Max Patkin and Satchel Paige performed with the Clowns on occasion in the 1960s. Pollock died in 1972, and that same year Hamman sold the team to George Long of Muscatine, Iowa, who kept it going into the 1980s touring in small towns.[103]

## Looking Back at Black Comedy Baseball

In 1976 Rob Cohen and Berry Gordy collaborated to produce the first popular film that told the story of the Negro Leagues, *The Bingo Long Traveling All-Stars & Motor Kings*. The Negro Leagues had been forgotten and the film helped bring them to public attention. The film and the novel on which it was based were the result of early research into the Negro Leagues. They touched on critical issues related to segregated baseball: poor treatment of the players by the owners, financial and social hardships under Jim Crow, the difficulties of travel, the accomplishments of outstanding players like Satchel Paige and Josh Gibson, the role of Latin American baseball leagues, and the "discovery" of Jackie Robinson by major league scouts. The film starred Billy Dee Williams, James Earl Jones, and Richard Pryor and received generally appreciative reviews. But the film focused disproportionately on clowning, and some reviewers pointed out that, not unlike the subject it depicted, the film would not have succeeded without the comic dimension.

Director John Badham highlighted the clowning because it was all that remained of the Negro Leagues. Ed Hamman was a technical advisor, and Indianapolis Clown team members were used both for the baseball scenes and the comedy routines. The players included the one-armed Steve Anderson, Birmingham Sam Brison in oversized mitt and tail coat, and small person Dero Austin catching. The film showed scenes of players performing shadow ball and pepper ball routines, setting off firecrackers, and doing the rowing routine. Badham said that he included these scenes to document an aspect of Negro League ball that he believed had never been captured on film.

The film ignited the controversy over clowning one more time. Although the film made it clear that clowning was controversial during the Negro League era, suggesting that it was done only to make money and out of necessity, many Negro League veterans found the portrayals offensive and not representative of their experiences. William Brashler's revised preface to the 1993 edition of the book on which the film was based indicated that many former players were "irked" at the depiction of the comedy, when they remembered "serious, high-level competition" as the main focus of black baseball.[104]

Lester Rodney got to know many of the players well through his coverage of the Negro League games. He commented on their "tenacity and patience." While they expressed "disgust and frustration" they also exuded "extraordinary elan" and "high spirits." He appreciated the "looser feeling" and the "fooling around and showmanship" that were both necessary to draw fans but sometimes negatively affected the caliber of play. Rodney thought the movie actually portrayed this complex reality well. Althea Fonville of the *New Pittsburgh Courier* questioned whether clowning was a central dimension of black baseball, and provided evidence to support the claim that it was not. When she interviewed Buster Haywood and Chet Brewer, they agreed that not all teams included comedy routines, but that they and their teammates also "experienced both physical and mental pain before they switched to comedian ball playing," noting that comedy was necessary to pay the bills.[105]

The film was also a catalyst for Negro League researchers to denounce the association between clowning and black baseball. Neil Lanctot had nothing positive to say about Pollock and the Clowns, or clowning in general. He was mostly concerned that white America didn't take black life and culture seriously, and the clowning and relaxed style of Negro League teams provided evidence to confirm that prejudice. While he understood that clowning kept the leagues in business, Lanctot argued that, especially in the 1950s, clowning teams were detrimental to the image of the Negro Leagues and were part of the reason that black fans preferred to support individual black major league players.[106]

The strong reaction against comedy in black baseball by some Negro League researchers may be understood in the context of the guilt that whites experience when we look back at the effects of Jim Crow. In their own embarrassment at the comedic element, the researchers have shown Saperstein and Pollock only in a negative light. Alan Pollock defended his father against these claims:

> Although in the entire 35-year history of Dad's black comedy teams, there was never a moment of fan protest over entertainment at a Clowns game, Clowns players were aware of the greater tolerance given white comedians...no white sportswriter had ever called the House of David a parody of...the European heritage.

But Pollock is overstating the case. Baseball comedy was maligned in general, and white comics were also disdained in the major leagues. But black comedy bore an additional burden. Pollock could not acknowledge that the history of minstrelsy and the inequalities faced by African Americans made the comedy that Pollock's teams performed different from the comedy whites performed.[107]

Historian Raymond Mohl, in a well-researched article about Pollock, concluded that the controversy around the Clowns was not only about clowning, but also "a more focused set of disputes between Blacks and Jews over economic control of baseball."[108] Saperstein and Pollock were motivated by economic goals, and also understood themselves to be entrepreneurs in an entertainment business. They believed that the segregated game of black baseball would only be financially successful if it offered the attraction of comedy. They chose to ignore the complaints of critics who thought comedy baseball was a throwback to minstrel traditions and detrimental to the race. They believed they were making a contribution by providing employment (and entertainment) for the black community, and they knew the comedy games provided added revenue to the other teams. Some black writers and owners welcomed these outsiders and their ideas, others did not. Men like Cumberland Posey disliked the comedy and novelty baseball both because it traded on stereotypes and because Saperstein and Pollock were his economic rivals.

Although Abe Saperstein concentrated his efforts on comedy basketball, Syd Pollock stayed in baseball, believing in its innocence until the bitter end. After Pollock died the team remained in white hands, while the players remained predominantly black. The Clowns still played small towns through the 1980s. Given Pollock's commitment to a segregated institution, it is surprising that he argued for the integration of organized baseball as far back as the 1930s. When the major leagues finally did integrate, Jews were central to the effort.

# The Jewish Contribution to Ending Jim Crow Baseball

Jackie Robinson's debut with the Brooklyn Dodgers in 1947 is the pivotal event through which the story of baseball's integration is told. But the process of ending the color line didn't begin with Robinson, nor did it end with him. The focus on his dramatic saga has obscured the long history of activism that made it possible, and the decade-long process of fully integrating major league baseball that followed.

The black press was the driving force behind the push for integration, and had been since the 1920s. But white journalists, politicians, and team owners played strategic roles, and Jews were prominent among them. As in the business and entertainment aspects of black baseball, the interests of blacks and Jews in integration were sometimes compatible but at other times antagonistic. Both made important contributions to what they understood to be a simple matter of justice, but neither group ultimately had the power to determine how the story would unfold.

## Challenging Baseball's Color Line

Blacks and whites occasionally played on the same baseball teams through the 1880s, and independent baseball created some opportunities for interracial play in the 1930s. But from 1889 to 1946, major league baseball teams and their minor league affiliates drew a color line based on the prevailing racial ideology of the time. Organized baseball made room for anyone who did not seem to be or was not discovered to be of African descent, including lighter-skinned Latin Americans, Indians, and white ethnics. There was no official rule against including blacks on baseball teams, making this "unwritten law" difficult to challenge.[1]

The black press had long called attention to the absurdity of the color line in baseball, speculating as early as 1926 about the possibility of ending the "unwritten ban." Some black journalists believed that the Commissioner of

Baseball, Judge Kenesaw Mountain Landis, would do so. But Landis would remain neutral at best until his death in 1944. John Heydler, National League President from 1918 to 1934, spoke for the baseball establishment in support of the ban in 1926, suggesting that there was a difference between blacks and whites in terms of their "character" and style of play, and arguing that segregated baseball was necessary because the "public" rejected interracial mixing.[2]

The first sustained effort to call attention to the ban began in 1933 when two white columnists for New York daily newspapers, Heywood Broun and Jimmy Powers, raised the issue at the Baseball Writers Dinner and in the editorial pages of the *New York Daily News*. Their words created the opportunity for Chester Washington, sports editor of the *Pittsburgh Courier*, to begin an open discussion in the black press. He solicited comments from prominent major league managers and players, including Lou Gehrig, Branch Rickey, Frank Frisch, Jacob Ruppert, and John McGraw; only McGraw did not profess to have an open mind on the subject.[3]

Washington and others took the opportunity to challenge Heydler's presumptions: "If Negroes had the chance, they would act just like the white players ... except they might play better ball." The *Chicago Defender* quoted Henry Farrell of the (white) *Chicago Daily News*, who attended the inaugural Negro League East-West All-Star game in 1933 and observed that the losing East team could easily replace the major league teams in Cincinnati or Boston. The *Defender* took Farrell's comment as an opportunity to point out that "Every known nationality, including Indians, Cubans, Filipinos, Jews, Italians, Greeks," is welcome in baseball, "with the lone exception of the American black man." This evocation of ethnic inclusion would become a common refrain but would not translate into a successful argument. To those who perpetuated segregated baseball, excluding African Americans from major league baseball was simply an expression of the unwritten rule of a society where black and white defined racial difference, and ethnics and even other "races" were acceptable provided they were not noticeably of African descent.[4]

The *Chicago Defender* singled out the case of Jewish inclusion for comparison:

No Hitler movement [was] created in America when John McGraw [manager of the New York Giants] put Andy Cohen, a Jew, on second base. It was up to Cohen to make good or go.

The example of the inclusion of Jews would be used frequently in the efforts to end segregation in the major leagues. Anti-Semitism was growing as Hitler was coming to power and Jews were also the objects of racial hatred in both Europe and America. Logically, if the Jews were accepted based on their ability, the same should have been true for blacks. But the difference between the treatment of Jews and blacks in baseball was dramatic. Jews were not only accepted, but by the 1920s they were sought after as a way to lure Jewish fans. John McGraw, who spoke out against bringing blacks into the major leagues, was often looking for a "Jewish star" for his New York team. Andy Cohen's debut in 1926 was heralded and heavily publicized in the press to that end.[5]

The Jewish case served as an example, and the Jews who were involved in black baseball made contributions to the struggle. Chester Washington compiled a long list of other "Nordic writers" who would support an end to the ban. The one Jew among them was Syd Pollock. Pollock sent to the black press a copy of an unsolicited letter he had written, which Washington chose for his series. The letter was addressed to William Veeck, Sr., owner of the Chicago Cubs. The Cubs were looking for strategies to bring fans to the ballpark during the Depression, and Pollock thought he had the answer: "lift the ban on Colored ball clubs."[6]

Pollock used the letter as an opportunity to advertise the achievements of his team (then called the Cuban Stars), which was playing in thirty-two states and defeating all opposition, including white minor league clubs. He was not making an argument on moral grounds, and didn't raise comparisons to the acceptance of other ethnic groups. He argued that baseball was a business, and in business "social pride and prejudice must be overlooked" rather than overcome. Pollock turned John Heydler's comment that blacks and whites had incompatible styles into an asset, asserting that the way the black game was played was more exciting and therefore likely to meet Veeck's goal of drawing fans. Pollock imagined that replacing some of the mediocre major league clubs with a "colored aggregation" (echoing Henry Farrell's idea) would stimulate interest. He went beyond Farrell to wager that not only an all-star team but teams like his own Stars, the Homestead Grays, the Pittsburgh Crawfords, or the Kansas City Monarchs could compete well even against some of the better major league teams. Finally, Pollock suggested that he would be happy to field such a club in the majors in 1934.[7]

Neither Pollock nor any of the Negro League teams would ever be invited to become part of organized baseball. Pollock's strategy of selecting a club rather than bringing individual players into the majors was not pursued. While such a strategy would have been less threatening because it would avoid "interracial mixing" on teams, it also would have been more radical in opening the door for black and Jewish owners of Negro League teams to become part of what was by the 1930s a very exclusive group. The idea of inviting a whole club of black players into the major leagues was ignored until Satchel Paige raised it speculatively in a newspaper article in 1942. Paige's suggestion was the source for the legendary tales of the never-completed 1943 sale of the Philadelphia Phillies to the son of the man to whom Pollock originally suggested the idea, Bill Veeck, Jr., and his partner Abe Saperstein, which would have involved filling the team with black players.

Although the black press continued to draw attention to baseball's color line, their efforts did not attract notice from outside the black community again until

Jesse Owens triumphed at the Berlin Olympics in 1936 and Joe Louis won the world heavyweight boxing championship in 1937. These men put blacks, and the race question, back on the sports page as well as in the headlines, challenging social assumptions that black men lacked the physical and mental abilities to compete as athletes. Owens won four gold medals in the Olympics in Berlin, where Adolf Hitler, presumably embarrassed, refused to shake his hand. Louis was the second black heavyweight champion. The first was Jack Johnson, who held the title from 1908 to 1915. Johnson challenged racial boundaries in that era, and was subjected to virulent antiblack racism. In contrast, Louis' mild-mannered and cautious approach made him a national hero when he beat the German heavyweight boxer Max Schmeling before a crowd of 70,000 in Yankee Stadium in 1938. Both Louis and Owens were perceived as gaining symbolic triumphs for America over Hitler's pro-Aryan racism.[8]

Owens and Louis made national headlines and were proclaimed heroes. If blacks were the nation's sports heroes, then all the more reason they should be included in baseball, the game that claimed to represent American ideals of fair play and social inclusion. And if America wanted to distinguish itself from Nazi Germany, this country had better look at its own racism. To the black sportswriters, the triumphs of Joe Louis and Jesse Owens made baseball's Jim Crow policies a travesty. The *Chicago Defender* proclaimed that unless the ban was ended baseball should no longer be called the national pastime. But integrating baseball would take another decade. During that time the black press took the lead in pressing for change. Although credit is often given primarily to the young reporter from the *Pittsburgh Courier*, Wendell Smith, and his counterpart at the *Washington Afro-American*, Sam Lacy, virtually every black sportswriter in the nation made frequent and powerful moral arguments that challenged baseball's power structures. They had occasional support from a few white sportswriters and politicians, and they solicited the opinions of players, managers, and even some owners and league executives who were willing to speak out.[9]

Their most ardent and consistent comrades in this struggle were a group of young Jews who had found an outlet for their antiracist values in the official newspaper of the American Communist Party, *The Daily Worker*. The contributions of these writers, in the context of the virulent anti-communism that began to take hold in America in the second half of the twentieth century, were ignored (and even assumed to be detrimental) until researchers in the 1990s restored them to their rightful place. Some have argued that *The Worker*'s small circulation and ideological focus severely limited their influence, but that does not tell the whole story. Although the actual circulation of *The Worker* was small, its impact went beyond its readership. These sportswriters introduced the story in 1936 and followed its progress weekly or monthly until the last teams integrated in the mid-1950s. They communicated regularly with black sportswriters and Negro League players to keep the question in the public eye and worked to arrange major league tryouts for individual players. Using their access as members of the Baseball Writers Association, they continued to raise the issue with major league baseball officials, owners, managers, and players. They used their contacts in the communist and union movements and with elected officials to send petitions, picket ballparks, and organize rallies. Their ideological focus brought out the moral dimension of the story, which they explored from every conceivable angle.[10]

The three *Daily Worker* sports editors—Lester Rodney, Nat Low, and Bill Mardo—came from Jewish backgrounds. Many American Jews found communism to be an attractive philosophy, and a good number joined the Party in the 1920s and 1930s. Communism was compatible with the Jewish vision of social justice, including beliefs in human equality and dignity, and the rights of laborers to fair wages and decent working conditions. The communist belief that blacks were entitled to the same rights as whites, their work on behalf of civil rights, and the public stands they took against antiblack racism and anti-Semitism attracted Jews as well. As anticommunist forces became more powerful in the 1940s and right-wing groups began spreading the idea that communism was a Jewish plot, many Jews left the Party, and liberal Jewish organizations distanced themselves. Blacks were also affiliated with the Party and served in leadership positions because of communists' early and outspoken support for racial equality. But communism assumed that class, not race, was the main social problem, and expected that solving the problem of class would make racial issues disappear. The privileging of class over race, combined with the strong anticommunist rhetoric in the wider society, eventually turned many blacks away from communism as well.[11]

Although the sportswriters at *The Worker* were employed by the Communist Party, they were allowed a fair amount of latitude in the opinions they expressed and the issues they raised. Because the goal of the sports page was to attract those outside the Party to read *The Worker*, their mission was not narrowly ideological. To be sure, they looked at sports as a set of economic institutions, frequently reporting on the need to improve athletes' pay and labor conditions through unionization. But they also wrote about sports for their own sake. Their fight to end baseball's color line both fulfilled and went beyond the Party philosophy. The communist leadership was enthusiastic about exposing the failure of America's national pastime (and its wealthy owners) to live up to democratic values. But *The Worker* sportswriters had their own agenda. They went to great lengths to support any measure that would bring an end to racial segregation in baseball, even if those measures supported capitalism.

Lester Rodney, the first sports editor of *The Worker*, was a third-generation American Jew. His grandparents had come to the United States from Britain and Vienna in the 1860s. His father was a businessman in New Jersey, a lifelong Republican who lost his wealth in the 1929 stock market crash. Rodney strongly identified as a Jew, and claimed to have pride in a heritage that has an "historic tradition of peace, justice and empathy." While he was most clearly aligned with the communists because they "DID something about (the good parts of) their beliefs," he also noted that many of those who were involved in communist efforts were Jewish. Jewishness was compatible with communist values, or, as he phrased it, "As my grandmother might have said: 'It didn't HURT that you were Jewish.'"[12]

Rodney, Mardo, and Low believed that the campaign to bring blacks into the major leagues was a moral imperative born out of their communist and Jewish values of social justice. They saw themselves as partners in the struggle with black journalists and players. Their dramatic strategies and their identity as communists also put them in conflict with the black sportswriters and players they intended to support. Their relationship with the black journalists, team owners, and players was as complicated as those of the Jewish businessmen in the world of black baseball.

## The Communist Effort

Although a high percentage of Communist Party members were immigrants who themselves followed and participated in sports in Europe, the Party initially viewed sports, like religion, as a distraction from the important task of social change. *The Daily Worker* did comment on the absence of blacks in organized baseball when the topic was raised in 1933, but there was no initial interest in taking up this cause, and there was little coverage of sports in the paper. *Worker* columnist Mike Gold argued for a change in editorial policy. He pointed out that since Americans loved baseball, providing baseball news would attract readers. By 1936 the communists had launched the Popular Front, an effort to encourage engagement with mainstream liberal trends and groups in society. And a focus on American sports would help the party capture the attention of the children of immigrants who were interested in becoming more American.[13]

The sports section of *The Worker* first appeared in the Sunday edition in 1936. The initial issues were devoted to the victorious exploits of Jesse Owens at the Berlin Olympics. Owens' prominence opened the question of the treatment of black athletes in American sports. In August, the *Sunday Worker*'s front-page banner declared "Jim-Crow Baseball Must End." The campaign began with testimonies from fans, athletes, and the press. *The Worker* published stories of Negro League stars' accomplishments and described their exciting style of play, calling Satchel Paige "another Dizzy Dean" and Josh Gibson "the equal of Lou Gehrig." To find out why major league baseball was not open to black players, *The Worker* spoke to the president of the National League, Ford Frick. Frick claimed that no one was barred from baseball based on race; players needed only "unique ability and good character and habits." Hiring decisions were strictly in the hands of team owners, not the leagues. *The Worker* then followed up with several owners who either refused to comment or were unavailable. These various approaches to the story would become regular features of the sports page for many years.[14]

Lester Rodney, who was then a young journalism student at New York University but not a Party member, talked himself into a job as sports editor by pointing out that while writing social critique through the lens of sports was important, attracting a regular readership of sports fans would require writing in a way that conveyed the joy and beauty of sport. Rodney convinced *The Worker* editors that they would have to publish the sports page daily and really cover sports stories, and that he was the man for the job. Although Rodney was a sports fan first, he was also deeply committed to the political goals and especially the fight to integrate baseball. Rodney's first column appeared in the *Sunday Worker* at the end of August. In it, he encouraged fans to inform team owners that they wanted baseball to be integrated:

> Some pressure is already being brought upon them, but much more is needed. It won't take much, sports fans. The performance abroad of our stellar Negro athletes in the Olympics has brought the question of baseball's short-sighted discrimination squarely to the fore.[15]

At first Rodney did not have a plan for the "end Jim Crow" campaign, but he developed a strategy as the effort progressed. The goal was to keep the problem in the public eye. To accomplish that, the sports page would familiarize readers with Negro League stars and provide coverage of Negro League games played in New York. Writers would interview major league players, managers, executives, and owners who were willing to go on record to denounce the status quo. And because communists believed in taking action on their principled stands, the campaign would include regular letter-writing and petition-signing drives, rallies, and demonstrations, so fans could register their discontent with the baseball teams and their owners. From time to time, the campaign would also target a specific goal. The first was an effort to persuade the Brooklyn Dodgers to sign Satchel Paige.

## *The Daily Worker* Campaign for Satchel Paige

When the subject of integrating the major leagues was discussed, Paige was always the first name mentioned. There was no question that he had the talent to be an excellent major league pitcher. He had played against white teams and beaten them frequently. Some considered him the best pitcher alive. The Dodgers, on the other hand, were a team that had not had much success over the years. Rodney was a long-time Dodger fan. He was excited both about the possibility that his team would be the first to integrate and that adding Paige would help them win. This effort would be the first targeted campaign that was ever attempted. *Worker* reporter Ted Benson brought the suggestion to one of the owners of the Dodgers, Judge Stephen McKeever, who responded enthusiastically. But McKeever claimed it wouldn't be his decision; the manager, Burleigh Grimes, would be the one to decide. Grimes declined to comment. Benson wrote bitterly about it, noting that Grimes was a Southerner and "Satchel Paige, I forgot to mention, is a Negro." Although Benson was disappointed with the answer, Rodney saw the conversation with McKeever as a first step. To follow up, as the lead sports article a few days later Rodney printed a letter written to Grimes by *Worker* subscribers Martha Berman and Jack Walter, urging him to "take the lead in the fight against Negro discrimination." Rodney praised them, and used the opportunity to encourage other fans to create their own campaign to supplement the one the newspaper was undertaking.[16]

The campaign to get Grimes to sign Paige continued for several months in the winter of 1937 with weekly headlines, the letter-writing campaign, editorial cartoons, and a visit to deliver a petition to the Dodger office. Rodney did not miss an opportunity, when reporting on Dodger games, to point out that since the Dodgers were dreadful it would only make sense to sign up Paige and other "Negro stars." Although he made arguments on the basis of justice and democracy, and often pointed out that other sports like boxing and track were already integrated, his main argument was that integration would be in the Dodgers' self-interest. The Dodgers needed better players of any background. Not only did he argue that they could use the help, but, in opposition to communist principles, Rodney often appealed to the financial interests of the wealthy owners by suggesting that Negro players would "sign up for a song." *Worker* columnist Mark O'Hara also appealed to the economic interests of owners, noting that sixty-four thousand people came to the Negro League doubleheader that he had attended the week before, and that they would be willing to spend money to see their heroes the same way Italians and Jews supported Joe DiMaggio and Hank Greenberg.[17]

Joe DiMaggio had played against Satchel Paige in California winter baseball, and he told a *Worker* reporter that Paige was the greatest pitcher he had ever faced. This endorsement was used strategically in the campaign. It led Rodney to conclude that the players were not the impediment to change, so the campaign should be targeting the owners. And it made him hopeful. Since Ford Frick had already admitted there were no written rules barring black participation, Rodney concluded that DiMaggio would be "playing against Paige for real" in the near future. Rodney, and his successors, would express this dogged optimism many times during the next eight years.[18]

A few days later Rodney interviewed Paige, who was in New York with a team from the Dominican Republic to play against a National Negro League All-Star team at the Polo Grounds. With pride, Rodney wrote that Paige was familiar with *The Worker*'s campaign and that he even had a copy of the Monday edition with the quote from DiMaggio in his hotel room. Paige showed his eagerness to play in the major leagues, outlining a proposition that Rodney published on his behalf. "Let the winners of the World Series play us just one game at the Yankee Stadium," Paige asserted. If the major league team won, Paige would not ask to be paid. But if his black all-star team won, then he would agree to join any major league club for the 1938 season at his own expense until he'd proven his worth based on a vote by the fans.[19]

During the winter months, Rodney kept up his campaign with the Dodgers and their general manager, Larry MacPhail. MacPhail didn't respond, even when Rodney threatened action by organized labor against the team. *The Worker* organized volunteers to demonstrate at Ebbets Field, handing out leaflets for fans to send back to the Dodgers. They read:

> I am in favor of ending un-American discrimination in big league baseball. I would like to see the Brooklyn Dodgers, who could use added strength, break the ice and hire Satchell Paige.[20]

Rodney incorporated references to the campaign in many of the articles he wrote on other subjects. When reporting that night games would become a regular feature of play at Ebbets Field, Rodney remarked that he favored innovation, and that this one should be accompanied by other changes like bringing in black players, lowering prices, and getting rid of Judge Landis as commissioner because he was unwilling to force the owners to desegregate. *The Worker* campaigned for other social issues through the lens of sports, and Rodney fought bitterly against Branch Rickey's St. Louis–based "farm system," which restricted players at all minor league levels to one organization and built a monopoly on young white talent for Rickey's Cardinals. Rodney attacked Rickey with a vengeance. "Branch Rickey has been getting away with murder in the chain-gang, coolie wage farm system he's built up for the St. Louis Cardinals," he wrote. Rodney also frequently critiqued the Yankees' dominance, and argued that the answer to the problem was obvious: other teams (not only the Dodgers) should bring in Negro stars to create more competition for the Yankees and thereby increase interest in baseball.[21]

## Comparing Blacks and Jews

*The Worker* continued to compare blacks with other ethnics, and especially Jews, who also experienced discrimination. Writer Charlie Dexter underscored that the explanations for black exclusion were merely excuses. One common argument against integration, for example, was that white Southern players would refuse to play with blacks, and spring training venues would refuse to accommodate them. Since many hotels in the South also barred Jews, and if the ban on blacks was the result of white southern discomfort, it could have logically been applied to Jews as well. But Dexter pointed out that popular Jewish stars Hank Greenberg, Harry Danning, Moe Berg, Buddy Myers, and Morrie Arnovich were able to play in the majors and train in the South without problems.[22]

*Pittsburgh Courier* reporter Wendell Smith also compared Jews and blacks, but in a very different way. Major league owners had made a public statement criticizing Adolf Hitler in the aftermath of *Kristallnacht*, the night in November 1938 on which Jewish stores in Germany were vandalized with state sanction. Smith was outraged that the owners could righteously protest against Hitler, when "they discriminate, segregate, and hold down a minor race, just as he does." Although he agreed that Hitler was wrong in his hatred, at least he acted openly rather than hiding his prejudices. "Hitler Landis" on the other hand, "when asked about the inclusion of the black 'jews' never gives a straight answer." Smith then added his own observation about American Jews who "do the very same thing to black folks that he is doing to them over there." Unaware of the full implications of Hitler's racial policies, Smith singled out Jews as part of the power structure in America that oppressed blacks. Experiences with the Jewish booking agents and owners of black baseball teams no doubt contributed to his impression. His reaction was not uncommon among blacks whose exposure to white Jews was as landlords and merchants in their neighborhoods.[23]

Although Rodney might not have agreed with Wendell Smith's assessment of Jewish power, he followed his campaign for baseball integration closely. Smith interviewed National League President Ford Frick, who this time blamed the ban on public opinion. Rodney wrote about Smith's interview, noting that Frick had come a long way since the interview he had done with *The Worker* two years earlier. Rodney was pleased that Frick did not single out the "character" of the Negro League players as the problem. And while Frick told *The Worker* that integration would come in the distant future, this time he indicated that the "constant crusading by the presses of both races" would bring it about "soon." For Rodney, this meant the campaign was being noticed by league powers, which he took as a good indication of progress.[24]

Rodney also took it as a hopeful sign that Frick compared the situation of black players to the experiences of Jewish players at the turn of the century. Rodney quoted Frick as saying, "There was a time when Jewish players were not wanted . . . Johnny Kling was one of the first Jewish boys in baseball and he was treated very poorly at first. Now the Jewish players are just as popular as any of the others." Rodney interpreted this to mean that soon black players would also be welcome. He pointed to Frick's statement "when people ask for the inclusion of Negro players we will use them" as an opportunity to encourage his readers to write to Frick and to the New York owners and managers.[25]

In the spring of 1938, Smith conducted a series of interviews with forty National League players and managers to find out whether they would support integration. Like all other African American sports reporters, Smith was denied membership in the Baseball Writers of America. Without credentials, he did not have access to players in locker rooms or on the field, so he did these interviews in the street and at hotels. Smith got positive responses from all the managers except Bill Terry of the Giants, and the *Courier* published the results during the summer.[26]

Rodney followed the series closely, believing this would be the weapon that would "bust Jim Crow right out of American baseball." *The Worker* reprinted Smith's whole series, with the *Courier*'s permission. Both Smith and Rodney highlighted Cincinnati manager Bill McKechnie's statement that he "knew of at least twenty-five Negro League players who could play in the majors." This was a central piece of evidence that demonstrated an awareness of the quality of the Negro Leaguers. Smith also interviewed Morrie Arnovich, the "slugging Jewish star" of the Philadelphia Phillies, who was leading the National League in hitting. Both Rodney and Smith suggested that Arnovich's presence in the majors was a hopeful sign, assuming erroneously that there was a time when Jews were also barred.[27]

For *The Worker*, the most important interview in the series was the conversation with Leo Durocher, manager of the Brooklyn Dodgers. Durocher talked about playing against Josh Gibson and named other Negro League players of major league caliber: Oscar Charleston, Martin Dihigo, Satchel Paige, and Mule Suttles. Rodney keyed in on Durocher's statement that he would use such players if he could get permission from ownership. The year before the Dodgers' owners had said they would hire Satchel Paige if the manager (then Burleigh Grimes) would agree. Rodney took Durocher's agreement as the necessary assent, and used it as evidence in several of his subsequent columns. Judge Landis would subsequently chastise Durocher for his statement, calling attention to Rodney's role in publicizing it.[28]

Wendell Smith wrote privately to Rodney to express his appreciation both for publishing the series and for Rodney's past efforts, suggesting that they might work together in the future. But there would be no further communication between them. Smith did not acknowledge *The Worker*'s contribution publicly, nor did the *Courier* reprint any of Rodney's stories. During the course of this long fight Smith acknowledged other white sportswriters, and other black newspapers often reprinted Rodney's stories and credited *The Worker* for its tireless role in the struggle. Smith's antipathy to *The Worker*, like his antipathy towards Jews, would have a powerful effect on the way the story of baseball's integration would later be told.[29]

# Bill Benswanger and the Pittsburgh Pirates

Believing that the team owners were the ones who could bring about change, in 1939 Rodney wrote to all of them, but received only a few responses. The most positive was from William Benswanger, owner of the Pittsburgh Pirates. Benswanger was at the time the only Jewish owner of a major league team. He had succeeded his father-in-law, Barney Dreyfuss, as president of the Pirates after Dreyfuss' death, serving as chief executive from 1932 to 1946. While in earlier periods of baseball history Jewish owners were common, the baseball establishment had become more socially conservative. Benswanger, a second-generation owner of German Jewish ancestry, was accepted, but his Jewishness still set him apart from other owners. As the only major league owner to publicly support integration before World War II, Benswanger made an important symbolic contribution. Like his father-in-law before him, Benswanger had a close relationship with the *Pittsburgh Courier* and Cumberland Posey, whose Homestead Grays leased Forbes Field when the Pirates were out of town. That relationship probably contributed to his willingness to speak out. But as the only Jewish owner, Benswanger lacked the power to persuade the other owners and the courage to single-handedly end the color line in baseball.

Benswanger made a strong statement in response to Rodney's inquiry. He indicated that he would be in favor of admitting blacks into the majors, because "the Negro people" were entitled to opportunities in all endeavors. Benswanger also told Rodney that he'd already gone on record with his support in the *Courier* the year before, and still stood by his statement. Although Benswanger did not respond either to the *Defender* or *The Worker* when both papers surveyed the owners in 1936, in 1938 the *Courier* published a long interview with him. Benswanger displayed his thorough knowledge of Negro League baseball. He rated Josh Gibson ready to enter the majors. He suggested that the whole league might come into baseball in Class B of the minor leagues and players could move up from there. As a way of suggesting that he wasn't prejudiced, he noted that the Pirates employed a black trainer, George Asten, who had been traveling with the team since 1910.[30]

The following year the *Courier* published a letter to Benswanger from a Pittsburgh fan, Alan Meyers, urging the Pirates to make good on their intentions, using the familiar comparison to the situation of the Jews. Meyers identified himself as white, although he pointed out that he would "not be classed as an Aryan in Germany." He argued that blacks have been included in other sports and entertainment endeavors as equals, and that their presence on the Pirates would not only improve the team but "win the applause of liberals" and be fair to a race that has been subject to discrimination "even more than the Jews in Germany."[31]

Benswanger had not acted on his 1938 statement, but Rodney interpreted Benswanger's comment that he would support integration "if the question becomes an issue" as a pledge to take a stand at the upcoming meeting of Major League owners. Other black newspapers reported on Rodney's conversation with Benswanger as a hopeful sign. Benswanger's statement was the most positive and public response that an owner would make for many years. But he would not act on it. Benswanger saw himself in a position to take a stand only if others took the initiative. Although he would not be the one to bring an end to baseball segregation, he would continue to be involved in events leading up to baseball's integration.[32]

## The Campaign Intensifies

*The Worker* changed strategy in 1940. Rather than targeting the Dodgers and Satchel Paige, they focused on Judge Landis, who, Rodney reasoned, could simply make a broad and final decision to end the ban. *The Worker* organized a petition drive targeted at Landis. The Young Communist League carried out the effort. They collected many signatures at Negro League games and became friendly with the players, including Josh Gibson, who both signed the petitions and introduced them to African American fans who were eager to sign. They claimed to have collected fifty thousand signatures, and they presented the petition to Landis, Ford Frick, and Will Harridge, president of the American League. Their hope that the petition and Benswanger's support would force the owners to discuss the issue at the 1939 winter meetings was not realistic. Integration was not on the agenda.[33]

*The Worker* continued to broaden the coalition, enlisting fifty-five unions and establishing a committee to "End Jim Crow in 1940." The union constituency was predominantly Jewish, as were the readers who wrote urging an end to the ban. Students from DeWitt Clinton High School (in the Bronx) who were members of the Frederick Douglass Club, the American Students Union, and the Shofar Society all sent petitions. Thirteen college newspaper sportswriters got involved. *The Worker* printed a letter from Dick Goldberg of City College of New York, who compared the ban to "restrictions and racial persecutions in Europe." Like Wendell Smith, he considered it ironic that the magnates would speak out against Nazism, but fail to do something at home to "do their own little part" in making such evils disappear. But he stopped short of comparing Landis to Hitler, or the American Jews to the Nazis, as Smith had done. Nonetheless, the comparison between Nazi racism and American Jim Crow was becoming a dominant theme of this campaign.[34]

The war in Europe complicated *The Worker*'s role in other ways as well. After the Nazi-Soviet nonaggression pact of 1939, communists, now associated with enemy

*Figure 5.1* Communist protest against segregated baseball (Communist Party of the United States Photographs Collection, Tamiment Library, New York University).

forces, were under attack. *The Worker's* involvement in the fight to integrate base-ball was already being shunned by the *Courier*, where Lester Rodney's name was never mentioned. But the rival *Chicago Defender* again praised *The Worker's* campaign, and was critical of the rest of the black press for remaining silent. The *Defender* writer assumed that the other editors were holding back because the fight to end the ban was being associated with *The Worker*, and "condemned as 'Red.'" But the *Defender* was not cowed, pointing out that "everything that systematically and consistently tends to better conditions among our people is now challenged along the 'Red scare' line." The *Defender* urged colleagues to keep up the fight. That the struggle to integrate baseball was so closely associated with *The Worker* puts to rest arguments that the communist newspaper had little influence.[35]

The *Worker's* sports page continued to include regular coverage of Negro league games, feature articles about black players, and reports on the work of the trade unions and the committee to lift the ban as they gathered signatures and made plans for an "End Discrimination Day" at the New York World's Fair. Rodney was delighted to see articles about Satchel Paige in *Collier's* and the *Saturday Evening Post*, assuming they were efforts to prepare the public for integration. Actually, they were Abe Saperstein's efforts to gain publicity for Paige. And while it is unlikely that Saperstein's goal was to get Paige into the major leagues, the publicity campaign did call white America's attention to the absurdity of the color line.[36]

Rodney admitted to being discouraged in the winter of 1941, "after five years of campaign." But he took stock of what had been accomplished so far. The campaign had brought the issue to public attention, made it clear that there were a significant number of blacks who could play at a major league level, and pushed other newspapers and magazines to get involved. He hadn't anticipated that the war in Europe would galvanize "anti-democratic forces," including the "Jim Crow magnates" who again refused to discuss the question at their winter meetings. Rodney acknowledged that he was proud to have started the campaign and intended to keep it going.[37]

The next effort was a leaflet to distribute at major league games featuring the quote from Joe DiMaggio about Satchel Paige. *The Worker* also continued to target Judge Landis. They criticized his refusal to postpone a World Series game that was to be played on Yom Kippur. They viewed this as another example of Landis's "race or religious prejudice," linking his lack of sympathy for Jewish fans whose religious holiday would keep them from attending the World Series game with his obstructionist role in the anti–Jim Crow campaign. If he had the power to make the decision to play on Yom Kippur, surely he had the power to end segregation in baseball.[38]

The following winter the United States was at war. President Roosevelt contemplated canceling the baseball season as part of the plan to restrict all but essential transportation, but decided that baseball, America's national pastime, was important to morale. *The Worker* responded by reminding baseball owners that with this important role came the obligation to respond to another presidential mandate: to end racial discrimination. The war would provide the perfect opportunity to integrate, since many major leaguers would be called to serve in the military and the teams would need talented substitutes. Negro Leaguers would also serve in the military, albeit in smaller numbers and mostly in segregated units. Yet if they could die for their country in the war, how could they not be allowed to play major league baseball? Rodney and others would continue to link the fight to integrate baseball with the fight against Hitler and for democracy. He took note of the first Southern white newspaper to go on record in favor of ending the ban, the *Louisville Courier-Journal,* and was pleased that the Louisville paper also linked the ban to the war effort.[39]

Rodney's own opportunity to fight against Hitler came a few months later when he was drafted. Before he left for the service he began his famous "Can You Read, Judge Landis?" campaign in a monthlong series of articles. On June 5 Rodney wrote his farewell column. He reflected with pride on the campaign he had conducted and his accomplishments:

> It's almost six years since the *Daily Worker* sports page was born with an interview [with] National League president Ford Frick... We followed

with the story of Satchell Paige and Joe DiMaggio . . . This year it's rolling downhill on old Judge Landis . . . I guess that's the main thing the page has accomplished.[40]

## Nat Low Takes Over

With Rodney fighting overseas, Nat Low took over as editor of the sports page. From 1942 to 1945, he made a critical and unrecognized contribution to *The Worker* campaign. Low, a working-class Jew from the Brownsville neighborhood in Brooklyn, had joined *The Worker*'s sports department as a volunteer in 1940. He later wrote for *People's World*, a communist newspaper in Los Angeles, where he had moved after the war for health reasons. His career was short; he died of heart disease in 1951 at the age of thirty-four. Rodney believed that Low was motivated by a sympathetic understanding of the "fighting spirit and militancy of the Negro people."[41]

Low didn't waste any time in pursuing the campaign. His column, "The Low Down," featured frequent stories about Negro League games in New York. He met and interviewed Terris McDuffie, the Philadelphia Stars pitcher, about his interest in being in the major leagues, and began a series highlighting the skills and abilities of twenty-five Negro League players who could enter the major leagues without further preparation. The series started with a feature on Roy Campanella, who had told Low that he was being scouted by the Phillies. Although the Phillies would never follow through, Low interpreted their interest as another hopeful sign.[42]

Low also reported on new developments in the "Can You Read, Judge Landis?" campaign that Rodney had initiated. A Chicago committee, headed by Catholic Bishop Bernard Sheil, was meeting with Landis. The leaders of the predominantly Jewish communist fraternal group the International Workers Order sent Landis a letter condemning segregated baseball. Low began to work with a communist member of New York City Council, Peter Cacchione, to plan new strategies, while the Young Fraternalists were handing out leaflets, this time featuring Lou Gehrig, and selling buttons at games. And Low became active in the CIO's "Citizens Committee to Get Negroes in the Big Leagues," where he made contacts with black leaders like Max Yergan and Walter White and black sportswriters Dan Burley and Joe Bostic. This activism was a major part of Low's strategy, broadening his contacts in the worlds of black baseball and communist and interracial politics.[43]

Low got to know Effa Manley through the Citizens Committee, and interviewed her to get her thoughts on how bringing blacks into the majors would affect the Negro Leagues. She praised *The Worker*'s campaign, and said that she did not fear the impact of major league integration on her team. "If our men made good in the majors fans…would want to see the teams that they came from." She thought that having the majors as an outlet would encourage more young black athletes to take up baseball, and heighten interest in the game. Manley was a complicated figure and an astute businesswoman. She thought that taking some black players into the major leagues might even enhance the future of the Negro Leagues. Had the Negro League owners worked together towards that goal, and had the Major Leagues been willing to incorporate them into their farm system as Benswanger suggested, at least some of the teams might have survived.[44]

The pressure the activists put on Landis paid off. In a widely covered statement in the summer of 1942, Landis repeated what Ford Frick had said several years before, that there was no written or unwritten ban. But he went further to clarify that it was the responsibility of the owners to sign players and not something that the league could mandate. He did not, however, call into question the ability of black players to play in the major leagues, or discuss any possible negative reaction from the public, as Frick had done.[45]

At the same time, Landis called Brooklyn Dodgers manager Leo Durocher to his office to criticize him for telling *The Daily Worker* that he'd be willing to take black players if the Dodgers' owners approved. Durocher later apologized, but also denied having made the statement. Of course, he hadn't made the statement to *The Worker*, but to Wendell Smith of the *Courier*. Lester Rodney repeated it frequently in his columns, which tied Durocher's statement to *The Worker*. Landis's own statement was similar to the one Durocher had made. Both men denied they had power to do anything about accepting black players and placed responsibility on the owners. It remains unclear why Landis singled out Durocher or mentioned *The Worker*, since other managers also said they would use black players if permitted to do so and the black press was responsible for gathering the managers' statements.

Nat Low, however, was more than willing to take credit for Landis's statement, and declared a premature victory. He even took out an advertisement for *The Daily Worker* sports page in the *New York Amsterdam News*, emphasizing their "complete" coverage of Negro National League games and noting that "only one newspaper fights every day, all year, to end Jim Crow in baseball." Response to Landis's statement in the black press was mixed. The *Pittsburgh Courier* and *Chicago Defender* were not so impressed, and called the statement hypocritical and empty. But Lucius "Melancholy" Jones, sports editor of the *Atlanta Daily World*, called it "the most significant declaration that has ever been voiced." Dan Burley of the *Amsterdam News* took the statement as an opportunity to review the history of efforts to lift the ban. He noted that the black press had been agitating on the issue since 1929, mentioning the eleven "old school" writers and ten of the "current crop" who had been hard at work. The daily press also wrote occasionally, but it was Lester Rodney and Nat Low, according to Burley, who deserved the most credit, because they used the power of their organizations to get up circulars, petitions, and to call mass meetings on the issue. Results are seen in the "smoking out" of the hitherto silent Judge Kenesaw Mountain Landis, supreme ruler of organized baseball, whose statement last week made sports history.[46]

## The Pittsburgh Tryouts

Emboldened by the victory with Landis, Low took another daring step. Taking Landis at his word that the owners would be the source for change, Low went to talk to the most receptive owner, William Benswanger. When Benswanger said the Pirates could use a catcher, pitcher, and second baseman to replace players in the service, Low gave him the names of Negro League players Roy Campanella, Sam Hughes, and Dave Barnhill. Low reported that Benswanger agreed to give them tryouts at Forbes Field on August 4. Following on the heels of Landis's statement, Benswanger's willingness to explore integration was indeed newsworthy, and the item was picked up by the Associated Press and national publications, including *Life* magazine. Low pursued the story, contacting the three players. He met Campanella at the Woodside Hotel in Harlem to inform him that he had made arrangements for a tryout with the Pirates, and told him he'd be getting a letter from William Benswanger to confirm it. Campanella, who had been disappointed with his contacts with the Phillies, was open to the proposition. He described the conversation with Low in his autobiography:

> ...the fellow sounded sincere and he seemed legitimate enough. He said he was a newspaperman and the trials were being arranged by his newspaper, the *Daily Worker*. I had no idea at the time that it was a Communist paper.

By the 1950s, when Campanella was writing about this event, the fact that he was willing to talk to a communist reporter required explanation, but in 1942 it would not have.[47]

The plan Low made with Benswanger, combined with Landis's statement, had drawn the attention of some the owners who really were opposed to bringing blacks into major league baseball. Dodger executive Larry MacPhail called Landis a liar, claiming that there was indeed an "unwritten law" against admitting black players and saying that he would do everything in his power to maintain the status quo. In an effort to share the blame, he claimed that the Negro League owners agreed with him, and didn't want their teams "raided" for talent by the major leagues.

Effa Manley had already gone on the record favoring integration. Dan Burley asked other Negro League owners for their feelings. Abe Saperstein claimed that he was too busy with basketball to reply to Burley's request, but then named eight

Negro League players, including Barnhill and Campanella, who he believed could play major league baseball. Burley contacted Benswanger, and assumed from his response that Benswanger would stand up to MacPhail. Benswanger said:

> Colored men are American citizens with American rights. I know there are many problems connected with the question, but after all, somebody has to make the first move. Some paper [*The Daily Worker*] called me up and asked if I'd allow certain members of the Colored National League to try for my team. I agreed. I guess the players will come down at their own or the paper's expense.

Emory Jackson hailed Benswanger's statement as "an American move to make an American sport truly American." Benswanger's comment gave the impression that he was ready to be the first owner to break the color line.[48]

While the other African-American newspapers were reporting that Nat Low had set up the tryouts and named the players, Wendell Smith took action to make sure that *The Worker* did not receive the credit, especially in his home community of Pittsburgh. Smith persuaded Benswanger to permit the *Courier*, not *The Daily Worker*, to name the players for the tryout. Smith reinterpreted the summer's events as "climaxing this paper's long campaign for the integration of Negro ball players into the major leagues, recently adopted by *the Daily Worker* and leading dailies throughout the country." Smith reported that the Pirates' president, "obviously irked" with *The Worker* story, "denied with emphasis" that he had ever made a commitment about a specific date or players:

> The sports editor of the *Daily Worker* put words in my mouth...I told him I was all for it, and suggested he contact the *Pittsburgh Courier* whom I granted a story four years ago on this particular question...and I still stood behind my statement made at that time.[49]

Benswanger seemed to be referring to the conversation he had with Lester Rodney in 1939, as his statement did not reflect the conversation with Low about the upcoming tryouts. According to Smith, it was Benswanger's suggestion that the *Courier* come up with names of players for the tryout, but it is likely that Smith persuaded him to change his plans. It was important for the *Courier* to claim credit.

While it appeared to some that Low had truly created an opportunity, the leading black journalists like Smith experienced his help as disrespectful. Atlanta University professor William H. Dean, in a letter to the *Atlanta Daily World*, also argued that while the support of allies like Jimmy Powers, Westbrook Pegler, the CIO Maritime Union, *The Daily Worker*, and *PM* was important, "NEGROES THEMSELVES" should be leading the fight. Fay Young also gave "white citizens," unions, and newspapers credit, but added, "We, Negroes have the job to do." Smith's intervention was critical for racial pride.[50]

Low may have been upset at Benswanger's change of plans and disturbed by the *Courier*'s strategy, but he did not take issue with Smith or refute the accuracy of the *Courier*'s report. Instead he focused on the Negro League games in New York that weekend. He described the large crowd (31,000) and extensive press presence at the doubleheader that Sunday at Yankee Stadium, featuring the Baltimore Elite Giants, Philadelphia Stars, New York Cubans, and Kansas City Monarchs, teams for which the tryout prospects played. Low interviewed Satchel Paige about his reaction to the sudden fuss over the games that weekend as newsreel cameras, photo syndicates, and others "used up a couple of thousand negatives" on photos of Paige, Barnhill, Campanella, and Hughes. He reminded readers that they would soon get tryouts "as a result of the DAILY WORKER interview with President William E. Benswanger," although the article was published on August 4, the day the tryouts were supposed to have taken place.[51]

Cum Posey had a close relationship with Benswanger, and also did not appreciate Low's interference. He underscored Smith's complaints about the "communistic *Daily Worker*" and criticized their "erroneous" and "premature" report, as well as Low's choice of Campanella and Hughes. He thought Benswanger would fulfill his promise and supported his right to choose the time and place as well as the players, concluding, "we know Mr. B. better than anyone connected with Negro baseball and his word is good enough for us on this or any other question."[52]

Posey and Smith convinced members of the black press that Low's announcement was an "unethical slip." Low never offered an explanation. Instead he began to present the *Courier*'s version of the story, and described Benswanger as the "progressive and popular president" who would try out the men the *Courier* had selected: Josh Gibson, Willie Wells, Leon Day, and Sammy Bankhead. Low showered praise on the *Pittsburgh Courier* for "long carrying on the fight" and praised Benswanger for being the "trail-blazer among magnates." He followed up a few days later with an open letter to Benswanger, congratulating him for his courage. To illustrate the courage of the Pirate owner he told readers about a letter he had received from Benswanger "some time ago" detailing the mixed reaction the Pirates had been getting from fans in response to their openness to black players. Low closed the letter by reminding Benswanger how much was at stake in the tryouts. "The eyes of America will be on Pittsburgh and we know Pittsburgh will not fail."[53]

Wendell Smith also still believed that Benswanger would go ahead with the tryouts. He devoted a whole column to Benswanger's promise, calling him the "greatest liberal in baseball history," willing to withstand the criticism of his fellow owners and stand up for his belief in democracy. Smith credited Benswanger's statements in 1937 with renewing the fight to break down baseball's color barrier, praised Benswanger's deep sincerity, and even speculated that this brave stance would hurt his reputation with the other owners and, as Low's comment also suggested, he might be "risking too much for an ideal." But by the end of the season Cum Posey and others realized that Benswanger would never carry out his promise. Posey thought that Benswanger was sincere in his desire, but wouldn't do anything without support of the other owners, and it was clear that he was under pressure from men like MacPhail.[54]

By September, when no tryouts had taken place, the black press began to protest. What had inspired such enthusiasm was now the source of disappointment. Dan Burley criticized the whole concept of tryouts, arguing that all a major league owner would have to do was pick up the phone to find out which Negro League players would be capable of major league play. And he was also extremely critical of Wendell Smith (whom he disparagingly called "Windy") both for undermining the actions of *The Daily Worker* and overestimating the good intentions of Bill Benswanger. Fay Young of the *Defender* credited *The Daily Worker* for forcing the issue with Landis, but criticized Low for naming Campanella and Hughes because, like Posey, he believed they were not ready for major league play. He acknowledged Wendell Smith for putting Benswanger on the spot, but criticized him for picking men like Wells and Gibson, who were too old. Ultimately, he was disappointed that despite all the hopes, another year passed and "the Negro is still out of the picture."[55]

Nat Low had also reluctantly given up hope that Benswanger would offer tryouts to the Negro League players. But he thought the events of the summer would at least encourage other major league teams to scout at Negro League games and arrange tryouts for after the season. Low concluded that Benswanger did not go through with his promise because the pressure from other owners was too great. At the end of the year, Smith hadn't wavered in his confidence in Benswanger, and presumed the offer was "still on the fire." Smith would not express his disappointment publicly until April 1945, when plans for other tryouts were in the works. At that point Smith finally accused Benswanger of breaking trust with him and the *Courier* and costing good candidates for the major leagues the opportunity to have their skills tested. He expressed doubt that Benswanger's explanations—that he was interfered with by other owners or that he objected to something Smith wrote—were worthy reasons to fail to keep his promise. He also suggested that Benswanger's interest in having the revenue from the Homestead Grays in Forbes Field was part of his reluctance.[56]

Although the tryouts never came about, Benswanger did contact Campanella about them. Campanella's autobiography refers to a letter he received from Benswanger as a result of Nat Low's intervention. Campanella described the letter as "discouraging" and full of caveats and warnings about having to spend time in the minor leagues and possibly not making the team at all. He recalled responding to the letter, but never receiving a reply. Campanella's experiences are often used to confirm Benswanger's insincerity, but the fact that he followed up on Low's efforts and contacted Campanella at all is rather startling. It supports the conclusion that Benswanger was sincere but lacked both the power to persuade other owners and the confidence to act on his convictions to defy the "gentleman's agreement." Benswanger sold the team in 1946, and the Pirates did not integrate under his leadership.[57]

Despite these failures, Low remained optimistic. In 1943 the Citizens Committee to End Jim Crow in Baseball would target its campaign on a "certain number of magnates." Wendell Smith was invited to participate, and he was listed among those who joined the effort. Despite pressure from the journalists, unions, and fans, major league baseball's winter meetings again adjourned without discussion of the ban. Low called the meeting "a disgrace" and reminded baseball that it "needs Negro stars to help prove to the conquered peoples that we are fighting for a true people's peace—for real democracy for all people, everywhere!"[58]

## Branch Rickey Comes to Brooklyn

In the fall of 1942 Branch Rickey became the president of the Brooklyn Dodgers. The campaign to encourage him to integrate the team began with an open letter by a new *Daily Worker* sportswriter, Bill Mardo, suggesting that Negro League stars Buck Leonard, Willie Wells, and Ray Brown could help the Dodgers fill in at first base, shortstop, and pitcher, where the Dodgers were weak. Working on Branch Rickey was Mardo's first assignment. Mardo, a Brooklynite, would join Low (and Rodney on his return) as yet another Jewish sportswriter on *The Daily Worker*.[59]

Given Rickey's history as the baseball executive who invented the farm system and general manager of the Cardinals team in segregated St. Louis, *The Worker* staff assumed he would not be open to their suggestions about Satchel Paige. Nor did Rickey reveal any interest, keeping secret any plans he might have been making. Rickey later claimed that he began his search to find "the right" black player to integrate baseball began as soon as he came to Brooklyn. He presented his passion for equal rights as rooted in his Methodist beliefs. Responding to critics who accused Rickey of integrating baseball for economic gain, he frequently told the story of how he came to his belief in racial equality. In 1903, Rickey was coaching the Ohio Wesleyan baseball team, which had a black catcher, Charley Thomas. In their travels, Thomas was denied a hotel room. Rickey shared his room with Thomas, and Thomas shared his despair with Rickey. According to Rickey, this was the moment of his conversion and the root of his plan to integrate the Dodgers.

Nevertheless, Rickey hadn't been an active participant in the campaign to end Jim Crow. He claimed it would have been unrealistic to try anything in segregated St. Louis, but that it was one of the first things he raised (albeit circumspectly) with the Dodgers' directors when he arrived in Brooklyn. As Rickey began to frame the narrative of his "great experiment," he would actively counter any idea that he was influenced by pressure from the outside. Given Rickey's secrecy, it would be several years before *The Worker* staff (or anyone outside the Dodger organization) had any idea what he was up to. In the meantime, Mardo and Low would continue to barrage him with visits, petitions, and suggestions in the form of "open letters" in *The Worker*. Rickey would later deny being aware of any such effort to influence him.

Wartime travel restrictions required that teams move spring training to sites in the North. That gave *The Worker* the opportunity to suggest that since the Dodgers weren't training in the South, they had one less excuse to keep blacks off the team and continue the "nauseating policy [that] serves Hitler." Articles consistently appeared in the press about the player shortage caused by the war, and Branch Rickey solved his problem by signing up two white players over the age of forty. Low wrote Rickey another open letter, reminding him that Josh Gibson was twenty-eight and Sammy Bankhead twenty-nine, and that he'd be happy to supply information about other players. When Pee Wee Reese, the Dodgers' star short-stop, was inducted into the Navy, *The Worker* began a "[Willie] Wells for Reese" campaign. Low supported a boycott of the Dodgers, which had been suggested by black sportswriter Joe Bostic. As the season began, the Young Communist League again brought leaflets and petitions to Brooklyn with the message to Rickey: "For a pennant winning Dodger team in '43 sign up Negro stars now."[60]

## The Philadelphia Phillies

In 1943 Nat Low wrote an open letter to William Cox, the new president of the Philadelphia Phillies, telling him that signing any number of "Negro stars" for that ailing ballclub would make his first year of ownership "a memorable one" and providing a long list of possible candidates. Low was not the only person who entertained the idea that, under new management, the Phillies might become the first team to integrate. This possibility became the subject of two baseball legends involving Abe Saperstein and Ed Gottlieb. While neither story can be verified, these myths provide a link between Jewish Negro League entre-preneurs and the efforts to end Jim Crow in baseball.[61]

Although neither Saperstein nor Gottlieb had played a role in the campaign up until this point, Saperstein had acknowledged that any number of black players could have great success in the major leagues. But, as Syd Pollock and Satchel Paige suggested, bringing in a complete Negro League team would also be an interesting solution, and a way of challenging the major leagues to acknowledge the athletic ability of black baseball players. A team would provide solidarity, and help relieve some of the pressure an individual player would experience trying to negotiate white culture. It also might have given the Negro League owners an option to maintain their businesses. The plan to bring a whole team into the major leagues was a strategy that neither the black press nor *The Daily Worker* considered. For the black and the Jewish communist journalists, the goal of integrating the major leagues was predicated on their belief that segregation was wrong and the racial barrier imposed by the major leagues immoral. Adding a segregated team would not have accomplished what they demanded. But to Saperstein and Gottlieb, black baseball was a business, and one in which they were doing very well financially. While they would have had little incentive to consider integration, the idea of a team of blacks in the majors probably intrigued them both.

For a businessman like Abe Saperstein, who loved publicity, bringing a black team into the majors would have been an appealing scheme. Saperstein did not have the capital to purchase a major league baseball team, but his friend Bill Veeck, Jr. did. In Veeck's 1962 best-selling autobiography, *Veeck as in Wreck*, he claimed that he was going to buy the Phillies in 1943 and assemble a team from the Negro Leagues, and named Abe Saperstein as his partner in this venture. Veeck claimed that he was ready to make an offer to buy the Phillies, but Judge Landis prohibited the sale. The veracity of Veeck's assertion has been questioned by baseball researchers, but there is good evidence to suggest that he and Saperstein did at least entertain the idea. The bankrupt owner of the Phillies, Gerry Nugent, informed the other National League owners that Veeck had expressed interest in 1942, but Nugent didn't think that Veeck was sincere, and Veeck didn't follow up the initial conversation.[62]

The Veeck story first came to light in 1953 when journalist Shirley Povich reported that Veeck and Saperstein had planned to buy the Phillies and replace their players with Negro League stars like Paige, Gibson, Campanella, Buck Leonard, and Oscar Charleston. Saperstein also told the story in an interview in the *Chicago Defender* the following year:

> Do you know what Veeck planned to do? He was going to take the Phils to spring training in Florida and then—on the day the season opened— dispose of the entire team. Meanwhile, with a team composed entirely of Negroes, who would have trained separately, he would have opened the NL season. I don't think there was a team in either league, back in 1943, that could have stopped the team he was going to assemble.

The details of Saperstein's description match comments Satchel Paige made to the *Sporting News* in 1942, lending credence to the possibility that Veeck, Saperstein, and Paige did seriously consider the idea before Veeck approached Nugent. It would have been in keeping with all three men's love of drama and showmanship. Judge Landis, on the other hand, did not share their enthusiasm for spectacle, and would have been likely to prohibit it on those grounds, but it is unlikely that he got the chance to do so.[63]

Eddie Gottlieb also figured in a story about purchasing the Philadelphia Phillies in 1942. The story originated in a *New York Times* column by sportswriter Red Smith shortly after Gottlieb's death in 1979. Smith described a conversation with Bob Paul, a sportswriter for the Philadelphia *Public Ledger*. According to Paul, Gottlieb tried to persuade Dr. Leon Levy, owner of WCAU radio and later the Atlantic City Race Track, to buy the Phillies and make him general manager. Levy wanted assurance that there would be no problem with Jewish ownership of a team. Gottlieb asked Paul to find out from National League commissioner Ford Frick if that would be a problem. Of course, Jewish ownership had not been a problem in the past. The New York Giants, Cincinnati Reds, Chicago Cubs, Pittsburgh Pirates, and Boston Braves all had Jewish owners through the 1930s, and the Pirates were still owned by Benswanger. But anti-Semitism was on the rise during the war years, and Levy did not come from the assimilated German Jewish background that the other owners shared. Nugent also told the National League owners of the Levys' interest, but he rejected them as potential buyers, saying, "I don't like their methods at all." Whether this was coded anti-Semitism or true concern over their business practices is impossible to know. As late as 1949, Lester Rodney would assess Bill Veeck hiring Hank Greenberg as general manager as a "rebuke...to the anti-Semitism high up in baseball's councils." Frick told Paul there was no rule against Jewish ownership, but also declined to meet with the prospective owners, and the idea was forgotten.[64]

Although Red Smith's original story is about Jewish ownership, not racial integration, writers have gone on to assume that had this sale transpired, Gottlieb, like Veeck and Saperstein, would have put black players on the team. In a recent interview, Leon Levy's son Bob confirmed that Gottlieb, his father, and his uncle were interested in buying the Phillies, and "Gottlieb speculated that maybe, just maybe, he could add black players to the Phillies' roster." Given Gottlieb's close association with the Negro National League, the idea is plausible. But it is more likely that Gottlieb was only interested in becoming a general manager of a major league team, not working towards integration. Unlike Saperstein and Pollock, Gottlieb never expressed interest in changing the status quo.[65]

Even if these events never took place, as myths they illustrate how blacks, Jews, and their allies were perceived as outsiders to the baseball establishment. Their racial identities combined with their association with showmanship differentiated them from the conservative owners of baseball teams. These stories, although intended to reveal Saperstein and Gottlieb as farsighted supporters of the integration struggle, only illustrate that while blacks were not welcome as players or owners, Jews were also not welcome in the business of the major leagues during this era and did not have the power to change that situation either for blacks or for themselves.

# 6

# Enter Jackie Robinson

## The Dodger Battle Continues

While Saperstein and Gottlieb may have been entertaining notions of getting involved in major league baseball, Low spent the summer of 1943 urging Branch Rickey to integrate. He and communist New York City Councilman Peter Cacchione paid a visit to Rickey, who declined to meet with them. Low was deeply frustrated that Rickey didn't even acknowledge the visit from an elected official. "The people of Brooklyn are a democratic people," he argued. "They want Negro stars on the Dodgers." He pointed up the contradiction that the first Puerto Rican in the majors, the light-skinned Luis Olmo, was welcome to play on the Dodgers, but his former teammates in Latin American baseball, "brown-skinned people and Negroes," wouldn't be, and he was incensed that the Dodgers ignored the hypocrisy. In addition to arguing on moral grounds, and contrary to what might be expected from a communist perspective, Low continued to question Rickey's business sense. He could not understand why the Dodgers would be willing to lose what he estimated to be "hundreds of thousands of dollars" rather than sign black players. And he also wondered why the Dodgers wouldn't want to win, as he was sure that with Willie Wells at shortstop while Pee Wee Reese was in the Army, the Dodgers would win the pennant.[1]

As the winter meetings approached, Landis decided to allow the topic of integration to be aired, inviting a delegation of the National Negro Publishers Association to make a presentation. Robert Sengstacke of the *Defender* reminded the owners that Judge Landis had said there was no rule against blacks playing in organized baseball. Ira Lewis of the *Courier* countered the argument that the public was not ready and pointed to possible economic gain. Howard Murphy of the *Afro-American* presented a single recommendation for the owners to take immediate steps to bring qualified blacks into organized baseball through the process followed for whites in minor leagues, schools, and sandlots. There was no discussion allowed after the presentations, and many journalists viewed Landis's invitation as an empty gesture.[2]

Landis also invited actor Paul Robeson to address the owners, and his presence brought broader attention to the event. Robeson was at the time the best known and most respected African American celebrity in the country. He was starring as Othello on Broadway. Robeson had also begun to develop associations with American communists as well as with the Soviet Union. Some members of the black press speculated that this was another effort by Landis to associate the effort with communism and discredit it, citing the time a few years before that Landis reprimanded Dodger manager Leo Durocher for speaking to *The Daily Worker*. But others, including Bill Mardo, saw it as a positive step. Either interpretation could have been accurate.[3]

Speaking at the meeting, Robeson reiterated the arguments that *The Worker* and the black press had consistently raised. He spoke of the acceptance and popularity of Joe Louis and other black athletes. He reminded the owners that many white major leaguers had played against black baseball players and had spoken with great respect about their skills and ability. He noted that it would make economic sense for the owners facing a manpower shortage because of the war. And he appealed to their patriotic instincts, reminding the owners that "baseball is…a game of democracy—because its stars come from the people and rise to the top only on their own ability," except for "legions of splendid Negro stars."[4]

Landis died the following year, and was eulogized warmly by Nat Low, who was convinced that Landis wanted to end the ban but didn't have the power to compel the owners. He accepted Landis's statement, and the presentations at the 1943 winter meetings, as real efforts towards change. Landis has frequently been blamed for his unwillingness to end segregation in baseball, which he presumably could have done by using his authority as commissioner. He was known for his strong and authoritarian leadership style, and the fact that he did not exercise it in this case convinced many that he was responsible for the ban.[5]

Black journalists believed that Landis purposely connected the effort to integrate with communism in order to smear the integrationists as un-American. Landis did blame *The Daily Worker* when he publicly reprimanded Leo Durocher, and he might have invited Paul Robeson to speak to the owners because he was associated with communists. But one would have to read deeply into those acts to conclude that Landis employed this as a strategy to avoid integration. In this period anticommunism had subsided somewhat, as Hitler had broken his agreement with the Soviet Union and the Russians were now U. S. allies. It is unlikely that a strategy of blaming the communists, even if Landis intended it, would really have been that successful or even necessary. Nat Low and Bill Mardo did not believe that Landis was using communism to undermine the struggle they, too, were fighting for. But it was becoming clear that baseball's integration would be moved forward by business interests and anticommunists, and not based on the values of social justice that communist blacks and Jews stood for. And if anyone sought to disassociate communism from the battle for integration, it was not Landis but integration's main supporter, Branch Rickey.

In January of 1945 Low wrote that he had learned "from sources placed high in the baseball world" that Branch Rickey "has actually been one of the most adamant magnates in the fight to break the Hitler-like ban on Negro players." The fact that Rickey was also a member of Guideposts, Inc., an anticommunist organization, made this news bittersweet for Low. Rickey was a religious Christian, a staunch Republican, and a firmly committed anticommunist. He did not want this cause associated with communists, and he sought to suppress the role *The Daily Worker* and other radicals played in baseball's integration. His refusal to meet with Low and Cacchione a few years earlier was an indication of his plans to disassociate his "great experiment" from the most passionate forces outside the black press that were agitating for change. When his friend Arthur Mann drafted a statement about the integration process that said Rickey found himself "besieged by telephone calls, telegrams, and letters of petition on behalf of black ballplayers" in 1942 and that "this staggering pile of missives were so inspired to convince him that he and the Dodgers had been selected as a kind of guinea pig," Rickey had him remove these lines. Privately, Rickey often expressed concern that he was targeted by "political pressure groups" and acknowledged to friends that they played a significant role in the effort to end baseball segregation. He wanted to make sure that groups like the "End Jim Crow in Baseball Committee" were kept far away from the spotlight. *The Worker* staff was deeply distressed that their strongest ally in this fight was deeply opposed to their worldview. But, unlike Rickey, they would welcome the efforts of anyone who believed in the cause. These Jewish communists had a vision of what democracy meant based on their cultural and political values, and would overcome their distaste for Rickey as long as he would fight to end discrimination.[6]

It may have comforted Low and Mardo to know that although Rickey would not countenance Jewish communists, he was opposed not only to racial discrimination but also to anti-Semitism. Unlike Landis and Frick, Rickey welcomed Jews into the business end of baseball. He encouraged a Jewish friend, George Trautman, to seek the presidency of the National Association of Professional Baseball Leagues, the governing body of the minor leagues. Trautman's candidacy was being blocked by anti-Semitic owners, and Rickey wanted him to fight them. "Why are you letting a few pettymongers and race-baiters chase you out the back door? You are proud of your Jewish heritage," Rickey reportedly told him.[7]

## Bear Mountain

Although the rumors about Rickey were encouraging, *The Worker* sportswriters continued to pursue other strategies. In February, the New York State Legislature was considering the Ives-Quinn Bill, which aimed to make racial discrimination in employment unlawful. To Mardo and Low, this meant one thing—an end to the color ban for the major and minor league teams in New York. When the bill passed overwhelmingly in March, Low proclaimed that the "final end of the Hitler-like ban on Negro players in our great National Pastime now is only a matter of time—and short time at that." He assumed the next step would have to be taken by Negro League players who would formally apply for jobs with teams in New York to test the law.[8]

One month later, Low planned a scheme to accomplish just that. Although Ives-Quinn would not become law until July 1, Low constructed a test case and invited several black journalists to join him. Only Joe Bostic, a sports editor from the radical black newspaper *The People's Voice*, agreed. The plan was to arrive unannounced at the Dodger training camp at Bear Mountain, New York, with Dave "Showboat" Thomas and Terrie McDuffie, two veteran Negro League players, and demand tryouts for them. Tryouts were still thought to be the means through which Negro League players would be invited to play in the major leagues. They believed that if Rickey refused a tryout it would constitute a failure to grant a "job interview" and an illegal act of employment discrimination.[9]

*Figure 6.1* Nat Low, players Dave Thomas and Terrie McDuffie, and Joe Bostic (Communist Party of the United States Photographs Collection, Tamiment Library, New York University).

Rickey was quite angry when he learned of their scheme. He wanted neither to have his hand forced nor to associate with left-wing journalists. Nonetheless, he treated them cordially. He invited them for a meal, and the following day conducted a tryout. Leo Durocher was still manager of the Dodgers. He was impressed with Bostic and Low's assertive strategy of trying to put Rickey "on the spot." But he was even more impressed with how Rickey managed the situation. For *The Worker*, the event was a triumph, and Mardo asked readers to send Rickey telegrams and letters of thanks. Rickey had kind words for McDuffie and indicated some interest. Thomas, at age thirty-two, was deemed too old. But, as Low pointed out in his next column, Thomas was still three years younger than Dodger star Dixie Walker. *The Worker* reported with pride that the *Sporting News* made the tryout a page-one headline. The fact that the tryouts happened at all was a great improvement over the experience with Benswanger two years earlier. They were making progress.[10]

Describing the event in the *Courier*, Wendell Smith reported that Jimmy Smith, the *Courier*'s New York reporter, had accompanied Bostic and the players. Continuing his policy of ignoring the contributions of *The Worker*, he made no mention of Nat Low's presence. He wrote that it was a "definite first" to have those men in a Dodger uniform trying out, even if they were not the right players, given their age. The tryouts were big news in the dailies as well as in the black press. Rickey biographer Murray Polner credited this experience with pushing Rickey to begin looking for the "right man," although Rickey would only describe it as a distraction and irritation.[11]

## Isadore Muchnick

This tryout was followed by another a few weeks later, organized by Wendell Smith and inspired by the efforts of a Jewish Boston city councilman, Isadore Muchnick. The black press reported that in early April "Councillor Isadore H. Y. Muchnick of Dorchester" submitted letters into the council record demanding that the local teams, the Braves and the Red Sox, create equal opportunity for blacks to play baseball. Muchnick had earlier threatened to block a ruling in favor of Sunday baseball unless the teams agreed to hold tryouts for black players. According to the news report, the council session erupted and several members walked out. The *Courier* quoted Muchnick's speech:

> I cannot understand how baseball, which claims to be the national sport
> and which in my opinion receives special favors and dispensations from
> the Federal Government because of the alleged morale value, can con-
> tinue a pre-Civil War attitude toward fellow American citizens because
> of the color of their skin.

That edition of the *Courier* also featured a strongly worded article by Wendell Smith denouncing baseball for relying on "cripples" and Cubans rather than turning to the Negro Leagues during wartime and also praising Muchnick for his courage. Smith took the initiative to contact Muchnick and began to work on a plan to set up tryouts, "armed with the support of Boston's militant councilman, Isadore Muchnick." Smith himself would pick the players and pay the expenses.[12]

Smith brought Jackie Robinson (Kansas City Monarchs), Sam Jethroe (Cleveland Buckeyes), and Dave Hoskins (Homestead Grays) to Boston, lamenting that he couldn't find Baltimore Elite Giant owner Tom Wilson to get his permission to bring Roy Campanella. At the tryout, Marvin Williams (Philadelphia Stars) replaced Hoskins. Muchnick attended the tryout, and Smith described his participation as "uncompromising and militant." Nat Low greeted the event enthusiastically and lauded Smith and Muchnick for carrying it out. Low was particularly pleased that it took place in Boston and thus without the coercion of the Ives-Quinn law, which he believed had forced Rickey's hand.[13]

Although Wendell Smith appreciated Muchnick's cooperation at the time, when Smith coauthored Jackie Robinson's first autobiography, *My Own Story*, Muchnick went unmentioned. When Lester Rodney reviewed it, he praised the book, but also expressed disappointment that it "yielded to current red hysteria" and left out the part *The Worker* played in the integration story. Smith always omitted the role *The Worker* played, so Rodney should not have been surprised. But leaving out Muchnick indicated not "red hysteria" but Smith's desire to highlight the role of the black press, and particularly himself. As a result, Muchnick and Rodney became forgotten Jewish participants in the fight to end segregation.[14]

As the story was retold, Smith's perspective prevailed over earlier accounts. In Robinson's second autobiography, *Wait Till Next Year*, coauthored by Carl Rowan, Muchnick is described as "a white city councilman … who represented a largely Negro neighborhood." Based on this account, historians concluded that Muchnick acted only to serve his own political ends. Careful writers like Jules Tygiel, who wrote the definitive work on Robinson and baseball integration, represented Muchnick as "a white politician representing a predominantly black district." Robinson biographer Arnold Rampersad also described Muchnick as a city councilman who, "seeing his constituency change from mainly Jewish to mainly black, joined the ragtag band of critics fighting Jim Crow in baseball."[15]

Jewish historians Stephen Norwood and Harold Brackman were disturbed that Muchnick's role as a civil rights pioneer had been written out of the story, and carefully researched the record. They held Wendell Smith responsible for spreading the idea that Muchnick was motivated only by politics. Smith told sportswriters Shirley Povich and Jerome Holtzman that he had called Muchnick and told him that if he wanted to get reelected in a district where the black population was growing that he should push for the tryouts. While self-interest was often a factor in Jewish support of African-American causes, Norwood and Brackman's work showed that, for Muchnick, this was far from the whole story. Muchnick had a record of supporting black causes, including introducing resolutions in 1943 and 1944 to fight racial discrimination in the public schools. They concluded that Muchnick saw this activism as part of his own "deep religious convictions." Norwood and Brackman also found census data to document that Muchnick's district remained almost entirely white until 1950, and that he won reelection during that period twice without opposition. After Norwood and Brackman's intervention, Muchnick began to get credit for his morality-based initiative. African-American sportswriter Howard Bryant wrote:

> The first American politician to disrupt the idea of segregated baseball and emerge with a result was Isadore Muchnick, the former Hebrew school teacher who could have made a fortune in a Yankee law firm if only he had changed his name.[16]

Like Norwood and Brackman, Bryant interviewed Muchnick's children, who described their father as a man who if he saw "something wasn't right, he wanted to fix it. And most times, he paid an unreasonable price for it." They described a close relationship between their father and Robinson, who ate at their parents' home the night of the tryout and who sent Muchnick an autographed copy of *Wait Till Next Year* inscribed:

> To my friend Isadore Muchnick with sincere appreciation for all you meant to my baseball career. I hope you enjoy *Wait Till Next Year*. Much of it was inspired by your attitudes and beliefs.[17]

Muchnick's role, and its basis in Jewish values, was even given a place in American political history when Jewish Congressman from Massachusetts Barney Frank had Bryant's chapter about Muchnick read into the *Congressional Record*.[18]

## The United States League: Branch Rickey and "The Fifteen Percenters"

In June of 1945, Branch Rickey held a press conference to announce that he would be financing a team called the Brooklyn Brown Dodgers, who would play in Gus Greenlee's newly organized United States League. This marked the first time a major league executive would own a black baseball team. Rickey was not really interested in starting a black team, and the USL, like many leagues before it, was short-lived. But this announcement gave Rickey a platform to critique the Negro Leagues and justify his future practice of taking its players without compensating Negro League owners, a practice Eddie Gottlieb, who had worked to get the League on a firm business basis, would be the first to denounce. Rickey dismissed the Negro Leagues as a corrupt business, asserting that a league that operated without contracts and the reserve clause was not really a league. He was not critical of the black owners, but criticized the white booking agents, charging that the leagues were really fronts for a monopolistic game-booking enterprise. He held white "15-percenters" in Chicago, Philadelphia, and New York responsible for controlling the leagues. Rickey had particular disdain for William Leuschner of Nat Strong's Booking Agency, who made arrangements for the few games that had been played at Ebbets Field. Although he didn't name them directly, Saperstein and Gottlieb were no doubt the two Jewish "15-percenters" from Chicago and Philadelphia that Rickey denounced.[19]

Rickey's plan to build a black baseball team confused and angered supporters of integration. Low was incensed by the press conference. He warned Rickey that "discrimination in industry is unlawful and punishable" in New York State. He argued that baseball was not a private business but the national pastime and that the Dodgers belonged to the people of Brooklyn. And he was enraged at Rickey's disparagement of the Negro Leagues, and his "utterly false claim that they are not really leagues and implying they are not run fairly and honestly."[20]

## Continuing the Campaign

Assuming that Rickey was not serious about integration, Low continued with his old campaign tactics. With newspaper deliverymen in New York on strike, *The Worker* attracted attention beyond its regular readership. New reader Daniel Rosethal discovered the campaign to integrate baseball and was delighted:

> We Jews should fight discrimination in our beloved land.... If we do this, possibly we can get our detractors to have more respect and tolerance for us. In other words, let's practice what we preach. Signing on to the fight to get Negroes into the so-called white leagues of organized baseball...

Low remarked on Rosethal's letter with great enthusiasm. Attracting Jewish readers who understood that bigotry against one group was connected to bigotry against all groups was one of *The Worker*'s goals.[21]

Although bringing on new supporters was important, Low's frustration began to mount. The Ives-Quinn Bill had been law for two weeks and the New York owners had done nothing. Low was certain that the only way to force the issue was through a lawsuit. To move things along, *The Worker* started planning a mass demonstration for August 19. At the same time, Mayor LaGuardia had started a committee to study the issue that included Rickey and Larry MacPhail, but only two blacks. For Low, it was not the time for study but for action. Yet when LaGuardia asked *The Worker* to cancel the mass rally because it would interfere with the committee's plans, they complied. MacPhail, now an executive with the Yankees, announced that his team would not sign black players no matter what the Ives-Quinn law required. He supported segregated leagues, and admitted that he did not want to lose the hundred thousand dollars a year in revenue from games in Yankee Stadium and minor league ballparks that the Yankees owned. Recognizing that pressure was mounting, however, he was prepared to think about a plan that would allow a few black players who had been vetted for character and ability to advance to the major leagues at some point in the future. Low's response? "This is tommyrot."[22]

## Rickey Signs Robinson

When anger had reached a fever pitch, Rickey made the historic announcement that he had signed Jackie Robinson to a contract with the Dodgers' minor league team, the Montreal Royals of the International League. Rickey was an instant hero. But *The Daily Worker* sportswriters were not prepared to give up their claim to a role in the story. On the front page, they praised Rickey and Wendell Smith, but also highlighted their own efforts along with those of the Committee to End Jim Crow in Baseball and the Communist Party. Mardo recounted the long history of efforts that brought the story to a close, highlighting the role played by *The Worker*. Nat Low wrote that he had dreamed about writing this column to mark the first time since 1887, when George Stovey pitched in the International League, that a black man would play there again. On the sports page in bold print was a copy of the "Cable to Private Lester Rodney" that Mardo and Low sent off to their comrade serving in the war so that all three of the writers could share in the victory.[23]

*The Worker* staff knew that this was only the beginning of a new stage of the fight, and Low started a campaign to insure that Robinson would be treated fairly and welcomed warmly. He described a broad strategy that included creating Jackie Robinson fan clubs, getting readers to write letters of approval to the Dodger offices, and organizing groups in all the International League cities where Robinson would play. Low also reminded his readers that the fight would not be complete until every team integrated, and promised to keep a watchful eye on how other teams would respond.[24]

As Rickey began to construct the story he would tell of the "great experiment," he denied the influence of outside factors, especially those affiliated with communists. But integration would not have been possible without other actors who paved the way. African Americans, and particularly the black press, carried out an unrelenting campaign that put pressure on baseball. *Daily Worker* sportswriters, other white journalists, a few politicians, unions, youth organizations, and interracial committees also contributed. Jackie Robinson had to be the right person—willing to play the role that Rickey had scripted for him, and able to withstand the inordinate pressures that this strategy dictated. Probably the most important factor was that, in the aftermath of World War II, Rickey could rely on public sentiment to end the "Hitler-like" ban. But Robinson's signing was only one step, and the Dodgers were only one team. Antiblack racism is deeply ingrained in American culture. Changing it would be a long and slow process that still goes on today.

## Bill Mardo and Jackie Robinson

In February, Bill Mardo took over the sports editorship of *The Daily Worker* from Nat Low. He thanked Low for the encouragement he gave him when he joined the sports department four years earlier, and credited him for his "hard hitting job on jimcrow moguls." Mardo began to attend to the question of why the other New York owners did not follow Rickey's lead, and praised Rickey for continuing to sign other African American players so that Robinson would not have to deal with the burden of entering the white leagues alone. Mardo, despite his deep political differences with Rickey, would give Rickey praise and credit, although he was less kind fifty years later. After anticommunists like Rickey had destroyed his reputation, Mardo was bitter. He ridiculed Rickey's story about getting his passion to integrate from Charley Thomas as a "bubbameise" [a Yiddish expression for an old wives' tale], wondering why it then took Rickey from 1903 to 1945 even to raise the topic in public, or do anything about segregated seating in St. Louis from 1919 to 1942.[25]

Rickey could not keep the communists completely out of the picture, and *The Worker* sportswriters continued to use the Robinson story as an opportunity to raise larger questions of civil rights. Robinson, although he would often acquiesce to Rickey's demands, was an independent thinker. He opposed communism, but would not shy away from working with anyone to further the cause of civil rights. While he was still at home in California, he granted an interview to *People's World* in Los Angeles, the Communist Party newspaper Nat Low would later work for. Drawing attention to larger racial issues that were on the communist agenda, the article focused on Robinson's experience in the Army and college sports at UCLA, emphasizing the role of those institutions in breaking down barriers. When Robinson went to Florida for spring training, Rickey hired Wendell Smith to accompany him. Bill Mardo was the only white reporter who also went to spring training, sending back daily reports on Robinson's progress. The Robinson story called attention to the need to challenge Jim Crow laws in the South, which *The Worker* called "as dangerous to American democracy as anti-Semitism was to French and German democracy."[26]

In September, Rodney returned to the sports page after four years away in the Army and a brief interlude at the city desk. He joined forces with Mardo and kept up the campaign to push other owners to integrate. *The Worker* again contacted baseball owners to find out if they were going to comply with the efforts to end Jim Crow in baseball, but only got affirmative responses from Pittsburgh and Detroit. Josh Gibson's death that winter provided Mardo with an opportunity to lament the loss of Gibson and the absence of Paige, who "might have gone down as the battery supreme of baseball history." He also pointed out that fifteen out of sixteen teams still hadn't complied with the wishes of "the democratic fans of America," so the task had only begun.[27]

*The Worker* continued to report on the Negro Leagues, focusing on Satchel Paige. When Bob Feller announced that he'd have a team of all-stars touring with Paige again, *The Worker* noted:

> It's the *Daily Workers*' opinion that Feller's scheduled tour, would be of far greater value were the teams to be mixed—thus indicating the progress made in ending Jimcrow in baseball.

The practice of barnstorming black teams playing against white teams would remain popular for several more years. But the attraction of pitting blacks against whites that fueled barnstorming baseball and supported the Negro Leagues would fade as postwar America began to accept the idea that contests of blacks against whites were more suited to an era that had passed. As a consequence, all-black teams would become an artifact of the past, and the Negro Leagues would no longer sustain themselves. Although they attracted a few white players, and comedy baseball would continue for many years, the black and Jewish businessmen who ran the leagues would no longer be able to attract an audience.[28]

## Ed Gottlieb and Integration

Ed Gottlieb was among the first in organized black baseball to be openly critical of Branch Rickey signing Jackie Robinson without paying the Monarchs for his services, so it is not surprising that Rickey paid Gottlieb a thousand dollars for Roy Partlow, whose contract he acquired from Gottlieb's Philadelphia Stars in 1945. After this public exposure, Ed Gottlieb could no longer remain the "silent partner" of the Philadelphia Stars, and the significant role he continued to play in the Negro National League gained attention. As someone who was profiting from the Negro Leagues, Gottlieb would have to answer criticisms about why his "lily white" basketball team didn't integrate.[29]

Gottlieb could have been a pioneer in integrating professional basketball, but he was not. Now that baseball had taken steps to integrate, the newly reorganized American Basketball League would be expected to follow. When Gottlieb was named the general manager of the new Philadelphia team in 1946, Wendell Smith challenged him to integrate his team. Gottlieb failed to respond and Smith began a campaign against him in the black press. Smith argued that since Gottlieb had been making significant money in the Negro Leagues (an estimated fifty thousand dollars over the previous five years), it was time that "Brother Eddie" did the right thing. It was not right, he argued, to make money off black players in the Negro Leagues and then not to sign black players to professional contracts on his basketball team, as Abe Saperstein had done routinely.[30]

Gottlieb's response, published in the *Afro-American,* claimed that all the good black basketball players were already signed up for the Harlem Renaissance (the Rens) and Saperstein's Harlem Globetrotters. Gottlieb was protecting Abe Saperstein, who wanted to keep black basketball players out of the new professional leagues so that the Globetrotters could retain their near-monopoly on black talent. Taking this position put Gottlieb in a compromised position and revealed his lack of interest in integration as a moral concern.[31]

Smith raised good questions to "Brother Eddie." Why, Smith asked, should Gottlieb, "who practices discrimination so avidly," not only own a Negro League team but also have a conspicuous and strategic role in league meetings and decisions? Why should he "rake in your dough" in the summer, but then not provide opportunities for you in the winter? "Is there not," he concluded, "a stranger among us?" Smith threatened to lead a boycott of the Stars by "Negroes in Philadelphia and vicinity [who] are supposed to be highly racial conscious people." Despite Gottlieb's intimate connections with black baseball, he was indeed a stranger in that world who provoked the anger of the black press because his business interests took precedence.[32]

Smith was not alone. Franklin Bower, writing in the *Afro-American,* chastised Gottlieb for refusing to integrate his basketball team even as he "line[d] his pockets with shekels" from promoting and owning black baseball teams. Dan Burley suggested that Gottlieb turned down black players for the Warriors because he feared interracial dating. "There is dancing before and after games and Eddie didn't want to see any brown-skinned rug cutters cheek to cheeking it with the rosy cheeked chicks with blue, blue, eyes."[33]

Gottlieb had long stayed out of the public eye regarding his deep involvements in the Negro Leagues. But now that his role was out in the open, he was vulnerable to attacks on his integrity. His refusal to integrate the Warriors exposed him as an unprincipled businessman, not committed to advancing the black race. But the criticisms had no impact on Gottlieb. Six years later he had yet to change his position. By then, almost all the clubs in the renamed National Basketball Association had signed black players. The Warriors were losing money and games and could have used black players. When Gottlieb finally spoke out, he told *Philadelphia Tribune* reporter Malcolm Poindexter that he signed players based on ability not on color. Then he revealed his real reason. The NBA was not doing well financially. Their only income was from fans coming to games to see the Globetrotters exhibitions that preceded them. Gottlieb was not about to take players from Saperstein's team, given the financial support the Globetrotters were then providing. Gottlieb always saw himself as running a business, and his decisions were all predicated on maintaining the success of his business.[34]

## Robinson in Brooklyn

As the 1947 season began, Mardo and Rodney waited with great anticipation for Rickey's announcement that Robinson would be moving up from the minor league team in Montreal and playing for the Brooklyn Dodgers. When word came on April 11, it was *The Worker*'s front page story. The event was so important that Mardo noted the exact time, 3:13 on the Ebbets Field scoreboard clock, when he got the news. Mardo acknowledged Nat Low's role in the fight, and hoped the news would improve his failing health. He praised Branch Rickey, who "has earned the respect of decent citizens everywhere." The following day Rodney wrote that he was looking forward to a time when there would be nothing special about a black player on the Dodgers. This moment was the culmination of his dream that sports and social justice could be joined. He could now "remain an integrated personality, a Dodger fan and a Communist." Although *The Worker* was often accused of being overly optimistic about Robinson's reception, they provided balanced coverage of Robinson's experiences in various cities that summer, both the good treatment by fans in Cincinnati and negative attitudes from sportswriters there, the problems in Philadelphia with housing and heckling as well as a threatened St. Louis player strike.[35]

## Robinson and Hank Greenberg

Although *The Worker* covered Robinson's experiences almost daily, and always paid close attention to Jewish players, they did not take note of the encounter between Hank Greenberg and Robinson in May of 1947. Greenberg was nearing the end of his career and had been traded to the Pittsburgh Pirates, for whom he played first base. He was in the field when Robinson got a hit, and they collided at the bag. After the game, an article appeared in the *New York Times* with the headline "Hank Greenberg a Hero to Dodgers' Negro Star" in which Robinson quoted Greenberg as saying to him after the collision, "Stick in there. You're doing fine. Keep your chin up." "Class tells," Robinson said. "It sticks out all over Mr. Greenberg."[36]

Wendell Smith was traveling with Robinson, writing his own column and ghostwriting a *Pittsburgh Courier* column for Robinson. Smith described the collision and the ensuing conversation between Robinson and Greenberg in both columns in great detail. He noted that those who opposed integration thought that such a confrontation between two players would cause a riot, but instead it demonstrated support for Robinson. Smith reported the dialogue: "'Hope I didn't hurt you, Jackie,' the famous home-run hitter said. 'I was trying to get that wild throw. When I stretched out to get the ball you crossed the bag at the same time. I tried to keep out of your way but it was impossible.'" Robinson, pleased and surprised at Greenberg's explanation, said: "'No, Hank, I didn't get hurt. I was just knocked off balance and couldn't stay on my feet.'" Once that was clarified, Smith described a conversation in which they compared their experiences of bigotry and insults from opposing teams. Smith also reported on Robinson's comments after the game about how helpful talking to Greenberg had been. "He helped me a lot by saying the things he did. I found out that not all the guys on the other teams are bad heels. I think Greenberg, for instance, is pulling for me to make good."[37]

Greenberg also used the story to draw connections between racism and anti-Semitism. In his autobiography he wrote:

> Jackie had it tough, tougher than any ballplayer who ever lived. I happened to be a Jew, one of the few in baseball, but I was white and I didn't have horns like some thought I did...But I identified with Jackie Robinson.[38]

As Greenberg later recalled the conversation, he encouraged Robinson to ignore the ignorant comments of Greenberg's Southern teammates, who had been riding Robinson during the game. When Robinson thanked him, Greenberg asked if he'd like to join him for dinner, and Robinson declined because he thought it would put Greenberg "on the spot." Greenberg and Robinson both saw the event as an opportunity for a relatively secure player who had known bigotry in his time to provide support for another who was facing similar trials. This dual role of the Jew, as one who identified with the oppression of blacks based on his own experience and who saw an opportunity to counter this oppression became paradigmatic of the way Jews recounted their role in the Robinson story. Although the reality was much more complex, the memory of this one encounter between Robinson and Greenberg remained central to the myth of black-Jewish relationships as seen through the lens of baseball.[39]

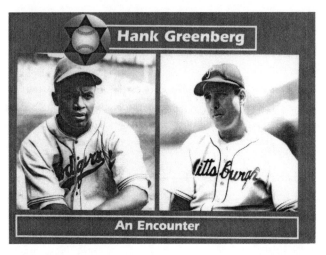

*Figure 6.2* Jewish Major Leaguers baseball card commemorates the meeting between Robinson and Greenberg (courtesy of Jewish Major Leaguers, Inc.; Major League Baseball trademarks and copyrights used with permission of Major League Baseball Properties, Inc.).

In Robinson's 1948 autobiography, Wendell Smith again highlighted the incident. Robinson called Greenberg's words to him "the first real words of encouragement I received from a player on an opposing team," suggesting that Greenberg was "sincere because I heard he had experienced some racial trouble when he came up. I felt sure that he understood my problems." Baseball historian Jules Tygiel saw Smith's interest in highlighting the experience with Greenberg as part of Rickey's campaign to make Robinson seem personable and friendly. But Robinson, like many blacks of his generation, did have a "special relationship" with Jews that exposed another dimension of the story of Jews in black baseball and their role in ending Jim Crow. After World War II, Jewish and black organizations began to work cooperatively to bring an end to discrimination. Their alliance was based on a "unitary theory of bigotry," reasoning that anti-Semitism and antiblack racism were aspects of the same prejudice and could be changed through education and legal remedies. Robinson's relationship with the Jews was emblematic of that effort.[40]

## Jackie Robinson and the Jews

More than any other baseball player, and more than many other African American leaders, Robinson both appreciated Jewish support and was a champion of Jewish causes, not only during his career but throughout his life. Jackie Robinson grew up in an integrated environment in California. Jews did not live in his neighborhood in Pasadena, but he met some as a student at UCLA. As Robinson's biographer Arnold Rampersad noted, "Jewish students also knew a degree of ostracism; Shatford [a black friend of Robinson's from that era] remembered friends in Pasadena taunting him about going to JewCLA." Robinson did have one experience of common prejudice. When he and black track star Kenny Washington and two Jewish athletes were in a competition at the University of Southern California, the two black athletes were lampooned in a carnival exhibit as characters in a minstrel scene, while their Jewish running mates were depicted as merchants in "Cantor and Cohen's Grocery Store." Black and Jewish organizations protested.[41]

Robinson's first real Jewish friends were Sam and Belle Maltin, neighbors in Montreal. Rachel Robinson, herself a new homemaker, learned Jewish cooking, among other skills, from Belle. Sam Maltin, a liberal journalist, chronicled Robinson's experiences in 1946 in articles that were commissioned by the *Pittsburgh Courier* and often referenced in *The Daily Worker*. The move to Brooklyn the following year provided an opportunity for Robinson to live among Jews for the first time. In his autobiographies, Robinson made reference to how comfortable he felt in Jewish Flatbush. Rampersad noted that the family liked living among the Jewish community, with its "synagogues, yeshivas, kosher bakeries and butcher shops, delicatessens, and the like." Almost everyone in their Flatbush neighborhood was Jewish and Robinson recalled that his son, Jackie, Jr., began to believe that he was Jewish, too.[42]

The Robinsons' closest friends in Brooklyn were a Jewish couple, Sarah and Arch Satlow. Sarah and Rachel became lifelong friends, and their children played together. The Satlows stood out in the predominantly Jewish neighborhood on Tilden Avenue because several years earlier they had refused to sign (and deeply resented) a petition to keep a black woman from purchasing the house that the Robinsons would later rent. Sarah Satlow recalled the anger of some of her neighbors when she refused to sign the petition, and Robinson also wrote extensively about this problem. While for some Jews the passion for social justice was the center of their Jewish identity, others were more concerned about losing the Jewish character of their neighborhood and were afraid of blacks moving in.[43]

Robinson recalled learning about Jewish customs during this period. He and Rachel assumed that the Satlows didn't have a Christmas tree in their home because they couldn't afford one, and so the Robinsons bought them a tree. Sarah decided to keep the tree and to decorate it for the holiday, despite the distress to her Russian immigrant parents. Robinson recalled everyone being more amused than upset by the misunderstanding, and it was handled quite graciously on all sides.[44]

Robinson maintained strong connections with Jews throughout his adult life, supported Jewish causes, and believed that there was a special connection between Jews and blacks that united them. In "The Jackie Robinson I Remember,"

Roger Kahn recalled telling Robinson the story of being called "Izzy" (a "not terribly subtle code word for Jew") at prep school, and described Robinson's response:

> We barely knew each other, but to use George Washington's noble phrase, Jackie Robinson gave 'bigotry no sanction.' He hated anti-Semitism just as he hated prejudice against Blacks—without qualification and from the gut.

According to Kahn, Robinson would tolerate no slurs against anyone; he would even express his contempt if someone so much as told a "Polish joke." Robinson exemplified the "unitary theory of bigotry" that brought Jews and blacks together in common cause.[45]

Robinson's relationships with Jews continued throughout his life. Among the Jews with whom Robinson had close personal ties were Bea and Andre Baruch; the Dodger announcer Frank Schiffman and his son Bobbie, who owned the Apollo Theatre; Robinson's lawyers, financial counselors, and business partners like Martin Stone; Caroline and David Wallerstein; and Jennie Grossinger, who welcomed the Robinsons frequently at her Catskill resort. Robinson believed that he had these relationships because Jews were more inclined than other groups to support efforts at integration and to mix with the Robinsons socially.[46]

Robinson saw Jews both as supporters of civil rights and as good role models for blacks to emulate in their struggle for full equality. He defended Jews against charges of racism, even in the 1960s when to do so was extremely unpopular in the black community. He certainly was aware of Jewish racism, experiencing it in the Jewish neighborhood in which he lived in Brooklyn and later when he moved to a wealthy, predominantly white, religiously mixed neighborhood in Connecticut. But he was unwilling to condemn it.

Instead, Robinson praised the Jews who helped them move to previously segregated North Stamford, Connecticut, where Jews themselves had long been excluded. Robinson described his experience at the High Ridge Country Club (in Pound Ridge, N.Y.), where his Jewish friend, Carl Rosen, took him to play. The club had been organized by Protestants, Catholics, and Jews because there were no clubs in Stamford where Jews or Catholics were welcome. It was a rude shock to Robinson and to Rosen when the leadership of the club, which boasted a 75 percent Jewish membership, expressed concern that Rosen was bringing Robinson as a guest too often. When Rosen responded by putting Jackie up for membership, the board rejected the application. Some members resigned, but some continued playing golf there. Robinson reflected:

> [T]hese were friends who loved golf, who had long been barred from other clubs, and we wondered how much right we had to ask them to

resign, to give up what they had now achieved, as a gesture of friendship to us.

Robinson clearly put Jews and their complicated response to the black cause in
a different category from other whites, whose racism he was quick to point
out.[47]

Robinson not only had personal relationships with Jews but worked with
Jewish groups that were fighting anti-Semitism and racism. In 1950 he became
interested in the work of the Anti-Defamation League (ADL). He met frequently
with its head, Arnold Forster, and learned about the methods Jewish leaders
were using to fight anti-Semitism. Robinson became convinced that the ADL's
strategies of confrontation and exposure, as well as working behind the scenes,
were a model that would work in the civil rights movement. His goal was to
duplicate the ADL's successes in the black struggle for civil rights. When Robinson
died, Forster wrote an obituary:

> Most Americans knew Jackie Robinson as the legend of the sports
> pages....But the Anti Defamation League knew the...human being
> behind the legend. For more than 20 years he worked shoulder to
> shoulder with ADL to abolish discrimination, wipe out prejudice, and
> strengthen relationships between the black and Jewish communities.

Robinson maintained the ideal of Jewish-black cooperation throughout the rest
of his life. His personal connections with Jews had translated into a plan of
action for blacks, and Robinson would always be grateful to Jewish people and
supportive of Jewish causes. As his wife Rachel Robinson confirmed in her memoirs, "Jack believed that positive relations between Blacks and Jews were critical
to both."[48]

Times were changing, and Robinson's allegiance to the Jews would be tested
in the 1960s. He was challenged frequently by the emerging black power
movement for his conservative views and his support of Jews. Until almost the
very end of his life, when Robinson began to despair, he believed that America
would ultimately accept blacks as they had accepted Jews. He worked to promote
social integration and black economic empowerment as a means to that end.
This allowed him to maintain a positive image of Jews even when they tried to
keep him out of their neighborhoods and country clubs. From the perspective of
black militants, Robinson was pursuing the wrong agenda and had made the
wrong alliances. But Robinson was part of the African American elite who disdained militant strategies.[49]

In 1962, Frank Schiffman, a friend of Robinson's who owned the Apollo
Theater, decided to support a Jewish businessman, Sol Singer, who wanted to
open a chain restaurant steakhouse on the same block as a similar black-owned

restaurant. Black militants charged that Schiffman was undercutting local black businesses in the area. They referred to Schiffman as the Merchant of Venice and picketed the Apollo with signs that read "Jew go away—black man stay." Robinson believed that for every story of exploitation that was told about Schiffman, he could find another story about his generosity and goodness. Robinson decided to speak out:

> Anti-Semitism is as rotten as anti-Negroism. It is a shame that, so far, none of the leaders of Harlem have yet had the guts to say so in tones which could be heard throughout the city.

He criticized black leaders who formerly sought help from Schiffman, making new use of arguments that had been a staple of the campaign to bring blacks into the major leagues:

> Here we are, a group as persecuted as anyone in the world. Yet, we stand passively or turn our heads in the other direction when a handful of Negroes mouth the kind of thing which Hitler popularized in Nazi Germany.[50]

Robinson reported that black militants began calling him an "oreo" when he went to the aid of an elderly employee of Blumstein's Department Store whom the militants had knocked to the ground. He supported Blumstein's and their employees' right to be in Harlem, in full awareness of the fact that, it was "the very cliché of the usurious, exploitive, Jewish white" business. Ironically, this was the store that Effa Manley had picketed in the 1930s for refusing to hire black employees. In response to Robinson's support of Jewish business, black nationalists picketed the company Robinson worked for, Chock Full o' Nuts, at their store in Harlem, carrying signs that said "Jackie is a classified so called Negro" and "Who Picked Jackie Robinson for our leader" and chanting "Old black Joe, Jackie must go." Robinson received many letters supporting his stand against anti-Semitism, as well as praise from Martin Luther King, Jr. Robinson did not back down, despite the threats. He told the owner of Chock Full o' Nuts that the militants needed to be confronted.[51]

Robinson wrote a second newspaper column to tell readers about the picketing, and also to commend civil rights leaders like Roy Wilkins of the NAACP and A. Philip Randolph, as well as the pastors of several local churches, who had come to Robinson's defense. Robinson did make peace with the militants, appearing on a radio program with black power leader and Harlem bookstore owner Lewis Michaux. He recollected that despite an angry exchange, at the end "Mr. Michaux disavowed anti-Semitism and on that basis I agreed to his right . . . to picket."[52]

Subsequently, Robinson reiterated his sense of connection with Jews. He wrote a column about David Levenson, a Jewish lawyer from Philadelphia, who for fifty-nine years tried cases "in defense of the Constitutional rights of Negro people," for which he never accepted a fee. Robinson commented that Levenson, "in fighting for the Negro... fights his own battle as an American and a member of a minority group." In another column in the *Amsterdam News*, he wrote an open letter criticizing Adam Clayton Powell, Jr., the prominent Harlem politician, for suggesting a boycott of organizations, like the NAACP, that continued to have white (and especially Jewish) leadership on their boards. Robinson defended Jewish supporters, naming Arthur Spingarn and Kivie Kaplan, who were prominent in the legislative efforts that resulted in the Civil Rights Acts of 1964 and 1965. He wrote to Powell:

> You also know that people like the Spingarns and Kivie Kaplan have been doing dedicated jobs and organized more moral and financial support for this cause than any ten Negroes, including yourself.[53]

Robinson again responded when, in 1966, black power leader Clifford Brown spoke out in anger at a meeting of the school board in Mt. Vernon, N.Y. Brown was quoted widely as saying that Hitler hadn't killed enough Jews. Robinson condemned Brown as a "black bigot." Robinson's absolute willingness to attack anti-Semitism reinforced the Jewish community's sense that the historic connections between Jews and blacks, which seemed to be fraying, could be kept alive.[54]

But in the last few years of his life, as the black-Jewish alliance began to rupture badly, Robinson spoke out against Jewish militants who took extreme positions in opposition to the battles blacks were waging for equal rights. In a 1969 television interview, he criticized the New York Board of Rabbis for demanding the removal of a black official, William H. Booth, as Chairman of the City Human Rights Commission. The *Jewish Post and Opinion* commented on the "strong denunciation from a usually patient Jackie Robinson." The newspaper reported that Robinson "contended that the Board of Rabbis had no right to ask for the removal of a Black official, and defended the right of Negroes to be anti-Semitic and to make anti-Semitic statements." By this time, Robinson felt a need to criticize Jewish positions that exaggerated the danger of black anti-Semitism. In 1972, the *Jewish Post and Opinion* reported that "The famous Negro athlete, Jackie Robinson, generally considered a moderate, has uttered a warning and a threat to... Jews opposing the Forest Hills low-income housing project." By this time even moderate blacks had trouble keeping their commitments to Jewish interests, as the relationship turned to bitter enmity in the 1970s.[55]

The last years of Robinson's life—he died in 1972 at the age of fifty-three—were marked by many tragedies: his failing health, his elder son's death in a car accident after recovering from a serious drug problem, his break with Martin Luther King over King's opposition to the Vietnam War, and his disillusionment with baseball's lack of commitment to integration, with the Republican Party for the same reasons, and with America's inability to fulfill the promise of equal rights for blacks. Yet Robinson continued his efforts for intergroup understanding and his connections with the Jews. He joined Hank Greenberg as two of only three former major leaguers to testify on behalf of Curt Flood in his challenge to major league baseball's unfair labor practices in 1970. He was an honorary sponsor of the National Interreligious Consultation on Soviet Jewry, and he participated in a memorial service at ADL headquarters to honor the Israeli athletes murdered at the Munich Olympics. Robinson's commitment to Jewish causes far outweighed any contribution Jews made to the integration of baseball, and they made him a hero to a generation of Jews.[56]

## Denouncing the "Communist Plot"

The postwar era would be a difficult time for the Jewish communist sportswriters. The organizations fighting discrimination were compelled to publicly disavow communism. They did not want their cause to be challenged by the right-wing forces that led the fight against communism and had, in the past, associated Jews and blacks with far-left politics. The claim that discrimination wasn't patriotic had to be accompanied by the claim that blacks and Jews were opposed to anything that wasn't American.

*The Daily Worker* sportswriters carried on their campaign despite the strong surge of anticommunism, arguing that their efforts on behalf of integration were on the side of democracy. Lester Rodney encouraged other owners to hire black players. Now that Benswanger was gone, he singled out Frank McKinney of the Pirates. McKinney claimed that he wanted to scout black talent, but simply couldn't find any players he thought would succeed in the major leagues. Maybe, Rodney suggested sarcastically, the Pirate scouts didn't know where to look. Had they heard about Monte Irvin and Larry Doby? Mardo also wrote angrily about Clark Griffith's open contention that "there aren't any n—s who could help him presently." It began to appear that Rickey was the only executive who would hire black players.[57]

Then, in July of 1947, just a few months after Robinson's debut for the Dodgers, *The Worker* staff happily reported the signing of Larry Doby by Bill Veeck, the new owner of the Cleveland Indians. "And the walls come tumbling down," Mardo wrote, and he suggested that his readers go to Newark that day to celebrate Independence Day by watching Doby play his last Negro League game for Effa Manley's Newark Eagles.

Emboldened by the Doby signing, Mardo and Rodney contrasted the democratic nature of integrating baseball with the undemocratic proceedings that were being held in the U.S. Congress by the House Un-American Activities Committee (HUAC). John Rankin, the committee's chair, was a congressman from Mississippi, a notorious and outspoken antiblack racist and anti-Semite as well as a rabid anticommunist. Rodney and Mardo sent him a mock telegram on the sports page that said, "If you consider signing of Doby a slap in the face— you're so right, 'congressman.'" The Doby signing brought Mardo and Rodney hope that there were positive forces at work in the country, exemplified in the world of baseball.[58]

The following day Rodney corrected a comment by Cleveland manager Lou Boudreau, who described Doby's signing as a "routine matter." Rodney noted that it *should* be routine, but for now it was a "smashing victory for democracy" and a challenge to what they began to call the "Un-American" committee.[59]

*The Worker* staff needed the good news, as the communists would find themselves under siege. They could no longer put political differences aside. Rickey began making public statements that accused communists of opposing democracy. Mardo and Rodney believed that their fight for baseball's integration was the essence of democracy. By 1947 communists and their enemies were both proclaiming that the other side would surely bring an end to democracy and make America into a fascist nation. Mike Gold claimed that if the right wing prevailed,

> the Negro, the Jew, all national minorities, all trade unions, all free science, free art and culture would have no place. The whole traditional democracy would have to be destroyed, as it was in Germany.

Mardo tried to make the best of this difficult dilemma, and proclaimed that despite Rickey's antipathy towards *The Worker*'s politics, they would continue to support Rickey "whether he likes it or not."[60]

In February of 1948 Rickey gave a famous speech at Wilberforce University, a historically black college in Ohio. *The Worker* reported only briefly on the aspect of the speech that made headlines in the daily press—Rickey's claim that owners had voted against his integration plan, fifteen to one, in 1945. Rodney and Mardo were much more concerned that Rickey also said "even now the communists are trying to steal the credit for Negro players being in organized baseball." Deeply hurt, Mardo and Rodney asserted that it wasn't "credit" they desired, but "democracy and equal rights." Ever the optimists, they also quoted Rickey's inadvertent admission that he was aware of *The Worker* efforts, even as he discounted their value:

> In a single day in 1944 I received 30 telegrams, all of which proved after thorough investigation to be from either Communist dominated groups or from individuals associated with them to pressure me to employ a Negro baseball player.[61]

While Mardo and Rodney adamantly protested that they were only interested in democracy and didn't care whether they received credit, they also frequently pointed out the importance of the role that they played. They never failed to remind their readers of their campaign for Satchel Paige, their conversations with Negro League players and major league managers and owners, and their efforts to secure tryouts. They wanted to be sure that it was understood that the communists were a powerful force in this effort, and that they, unlike other white journalists, kept the issue at the forefront of their concerns for many years. They also wanted to emphasize communists' longstanding support of racial equality.[62]

Rickey continually sought to downplay their role. He was opposed to communism and did not want the Party to get credit for something he believed was his own doing. In support of Rickey's contention, Wendell Smith wrote a long and detailed column denouncing *The Worker*'s claims. By this time Smith was working for Rickey and may have joined the ranks of anticommunists himself. But the article vilified *The Worker* in much stronger terms than Rickey did. Smith asserted that its writers were an impediment in the long campaign for integration. He claimed that he wanted to make sure that it was "straight for the record," so that someone writing the history of integration would not mistake the communists' "vicious propaganda" about their role in baseball integration for the truth. Smith denied that Rodney made any contribution. *The Worker* didn't interview managers; it only picked up the stories the *Courier* had printed and then tried to take credit. Smith challenged Rodney's claim that *The Worker* "went to bat for Satchell Paige," despite significant evidence to the contrary both in the pages of *The Worker* and from Paige himself. Smith did admit that *The Worker* sportswriters were involved, but "the most they did was bungle the campaign up at times when it appeared that some headway was being made. Like a bad penny, they always turned up when least wanted." He wrote that the communists were to blame for the owners' reluctance, doing "more to delay the entrance of Negroes in big league baseball than any other single factor." While the communists "hooted and howled," the owners saw the campaign as a "Communistic plot," and evaded the issue for that reason. Their desire to take credit was the only reason *The Worker* sent a reporter to Robinson's first spring training. The Dodgers told Robinson to avoid him so that they would not be able to "steal the glory for their own political purposes."[63]

This was the first time Smith had been so explicitly anticommunist, although he had shunned and denounced *The Worker* before. While he may have shared Rickey's anticommunist perspective at this point, he hadn't in the past. He praised Judge Landis for inviting Paul Robeson to speak to the owners in 1943, identifying him as the "famous stage artist," and never expressed concern about him as a communist sympathizer. Anticommunism was not his only motive for wanting to diminish the role of *The Worker* reporters. As a black man, he did not want to share the credit for baseball's integration with the white sports reporters from *The Worker*. Smith was very much aware of *The Worker*'s deep commitment to this cause and consistently tried to downplay their accomplishments. To Smith, Mardo, Low, and Rodney were not allies but competitors. Rodney later assumed that Smith's shunning was "in keeping with the times and the generally conservative views of his paper—and possibly in deference to the cooperation he was getting from the baseball establishment." In 1947 Smith was Rickey's employee and following Rickey's orders. But Rodney underestimated Smith's rivalry with *The Worker*. He did not consider that a proud black man would not want white Jewish allies getting credit for this important victory. Rodney, Mardo, and Low meant well, but they did not comprehend how important it was to black journalists to fight their own fight. What to well-meaning Jews appeared to be cooperation and support was easily construed as interference by Wendell Smith.[64]

## Abe Saperstein: "Negro" Scout

Abe Saperstein adapted to postwar changes in a variety of ways. By 1947, the Harlem Globetrotters were gaining recognition and making money. Many of the Negro League players Saperstein supported were playing baseball for him in the summer and basketball for the Globetrotters in the winter, and others had become involved in management in Saperstein's agency. Saperstein knew early on that the integration of major league baseball would mean the end of the Negro Leagues, a business he had never wholeheartedly supported and often undermined. Although he maintained a connection to the business until 1951, these next years would find Saperstein working to get talented black players into white organized baseball. But he would also be the main force in keeping basketball segregated.

Like Branch Rickey, Bill Veeck's plan included signing as many black players as possible. Unlike Rickey, who avoided working through the Negro Leagues by scouting black players in high school and college, Veeck saw professional teams as the primary source for players. In May 1948, Veeck announced that his friend Abe Saperstein was "appointed to head the search for Negro talent for the Cleveland Indians." Saperstein's job was to find young talent for the Indians' farm system, not to sign stars who would refuse to spend time in the minor leagues. According to Wendell Smith, Saperstein used his own Globetrotters baseball team as a training ground. Black sportswriters Fay Young and Dan Burley, who were strong Saperstein supporters, wrote enthusiastically about his new role. As Young wrote, "Veeck named the right man. No one else could or would give the time and energy. If the public will have a little patience, results will be seen. If Abe can't do it, we don't know who can."[65]

But not all of the black sportswriters responded so enthusiastically. Sam Lacy was appalled at the "antics of . . . the Jewish promoter." A. S. "Doc" Young, one of Saperstein's most outspoken critics, wrote that racial progress for blacks in America was frequently held back by "parasites who spawn and get fat 'on the cause' under the thin guise of being 'race helpers.'" Although delighted that Veeck and the Indians were taking the lead in signing Negro League players to major league contracts, he cautioned that there would be "a nullification of our gains . . . if Saperstein is the door through which our stars must step." Saperstein's boast that he had done more for black athletes than anyone else in history incensed Young, who wondered where Saperstein was "when Satchel Paige was in his prime," and answered: "Just like Moses when the light went out! In the dark!" Young wondered why Veeck didn't use veteran Negro League players as scouts. They were the ones who really knew the players; Saperstein would turn scouting into "a petty hustle." Young believed that blacks should not have to go through Jewish middlemen on their way to the big leagues. But Veeck trusted Saperstein, and he would play that role.[66]

Saperstein recommended several players who would go on to significant careers in the major leagues. Luke Easter was a highly touted prospect who called Saperstein "the fairest man in baseball." Jose Santiago, Patricio Scantelbury, Art Wilson, and Joe Bankhead were also prospects Saperstein claimed to have found for Cleveland. He also scouted Orestes "Minnie" Miñoso, who went on to have a stellar career in the majors. According to Wendell Smith, it was Saperstein who convinced the Cuban standout to sign a contract to play in the majors despite the language barrier because "base hits speak louder than words.'" In total, Saperstein claimed to have scouted fourteen players for the Indians.[67]

## Saperstein and Satchel Paige

The most valuable of Saperstein's acquisitions for Cleveland was Satchel Paige. Paige did not need to be "scouted." He was by far the best-known player in the Negro Leagues. But Paige was also, many thought, past his prime. Paige and Veeck both named Saperstein as the person who was responsible for persuading Veeck to bring Paige to the majors. Paige believed that Veeck was skeptical about whether he could still pitch and credited Saperstein with encouraging Veeck to sign him. For his efforts, Saperstein received a $20,000 bonus after Cleveland won the World Series, with Paige making an important contribution. Encouraging Veeck to take Paige seriously may have been Saperstein's greatest (and single most lucrative) contribution to blacks in baseball.[68]

Rodney and Mardo were overjoyed, especially with the fact that Paige finally got to pitch in the World Series and "democracy was once again on the public stage." For Rodney's year-end summary, Doby's winning hit in the World Series and the interracial embraces that followed were the "perfect climax of the most exciting day of the sports year."[69]

## The Artie Wilson Case

Signing Negro League players often involved complex business arrangements, as illustrated by the case of Art Wilson. Wilson was playing for the Birmingham Black Barons and leading the Negro American League in hitting in 1948, and Saperstein was making plans to sign him for Cleveland. The following winter in Puerto Rico, Wilson was also scouted by the Yankees, who announced an agreement to sign him to a minor league contract with their farm team, the Newark Bears. The Yankees' press release indicated that Wilson had signed for five hundred dollars a month, lower than the salary he was making with Birmingham. The Yankees said they had negotiated the deal with Barons owner Tom Hayes, although Wilson himself had made no commitment. But the *Pittsburgh Courier* reported that Hayes had accepted Bill Veeck's offer of fifteen thousand dollars for Wilson, not the Yankees' verbal commitment.[70]

Saperstein was at the center of the controversy. He had been in Alaska with the Globetrotters when the Yankees made the announcement. Saperstein had assumed Wilson was going to play for the Indians, since he had scouted him the year before. He immediately phoned Hayes and Veeck, and brokered the better offer from Cleveland. Positioning himself as a trusted ally of black players and confidante of black journalists, rather than a friend of wealthy owners, he reported having a good laugh with Fay Young over orchestrating "two white millionaires fighting over a Negro ball player."[71]

While Saperstein was focused on the financial deal, Lester Rodney was looking at the Wilson story from a different perspective. In an open letter to Veeck, he expressed his wish that the Yankees had signed Wilson to bring integration into one of the nine remaining "lily white organizations." Unfortunately for Wilson, Rodney would get his wish. The Yankees filed a grievance with the Commissioner, and Wilson's contract was awarded to the Yankees. But they were not really interested in keeping him and sent him to the independent Oakland Oaks of the Pacific Coast League, where Wilson would remain for the rest of his career.[72]

## Segregated Basketball

Saperstein committed himself to the task of bringing black players into major league baseball, functioning as the middleman between Bill Veeck and Negro League players and owners. But as a central figure in the business of basketball he was the major impediment to the integration of the game as it became professional. When the NBA finally began to integrate in 1950, Saperstein's livelihood as the owner of the best black team in basketball was threatened. With blacks in professional basketball, Saperstein's Globetrotters would no longer have a monopoly on black talent. In the late 1940s, the popular Globetrotters had kept the NBA afloat by appearing in doubleheaders with the professional teams, and the lines of segregation remained in place. Team owners supported Saperstein by not drafting excellent black college players even though the integration of baseball made it logical for the new professional basketball league to follow suit.[73]

Saperstein tried to purchase the poorly performing Chicago Stags in 1950. Because of his long association with black sports, the black press assumed that Saperstein would integrate the team, but the purchase fell through before he was tested. Alvin E. White of the Associated Negro Press thought Saperstein should have placed Globetrotters in the NBA rather than looking for another team to purchase. White surmised that the Globetrotters "will continue to furnish the gilt to enable Mr. Saperstein to branch out into other fields." Using the Yiddish word for money, "gilt" (i.e., *gelt*), and comparing him to Ed Gottlieb and Lew Leslie, also a Jew and a theater promoter of "Negro extravaganzas" who didn't use blacks in his vaudeville shows, were coded references to White's distrust of Jewish owners in black sports and entertainment who were using their power in a world in which they were no longer welcome. Even Saperstein's major supporters in the black press were dismayed with his silence on the subject of hiring black players for the Stags or bringing the Globetrotters into the NBA.[74]

Yet many in the black press assumed Saperstein's good faith, and his reputation was not appreciably changed by this episode. After Saperstein bought stock in the Philadelphia Warriors basketball team in 1952, some reporters even raised the hope that Saperstein would persuade Ed Gottlieb to integrate the team. When Gottlieb again failed to integrate that season, the black press held both Saperstein and Gottlieb accountable. Their unwillingness to integrate professional basketball when they had the power and resources to do so disappointed those who assumed, given the benefits Saperstein and Gottlieb derived from black baseball, that they would welcome the opportunity to support the ambitions of black basketball players.[75]

## Saperstein and the Negro Leagues

Saperstein continued to scout black ballplayers for the Cleveland Indians. After Bill Veeck left the team in 1950, Saperstein worked for Hank Greenberg, who succeeded Veeck as general manager and part owner. Greenberg, who continued to bring African American talent to the Indians, saw Saperstein as a conduit to Negro League owners and the person who had opened his eyes to the talent in the Negro Leagues. He recalled accompanying Saperstein to an East-West All-Star game at Comiskey Park that drew "55,000 fans, four or five white." Greenberg credits that experience with helping him see that black players were not "just a bunch of clowns" as he had been "brainwashed" to assume.[76]

Saperstein remained a presence in the Negro Leagues, purchasing the Chicago American Giants in 1951 and keeping control over ballparks in the Midwest. The Negro League owners assumed he stayed involved so that he could have access to the black players who were prospects for the majors, keeping the pipeline open for Greenberg's Indians and the team Veeck purchased in 1951, the St. Louis Browns. It was rumored that Saperstein was among the Browns' stockholders. The Chicago American Giants became an unofficial farm team of the Browns. Saperstein brought Satchel Paige, who had been barnstorming after his release from the Indians when Veeck left in 1949, to pitch for the Chicago team, in preparation for his return to the major leagues with the Browns later that season. Both Veeck and Saperstein were at home with comedy baseball and used Ed Hamman to clown for the Giants, while Max Patkin entertained at Browns home games. Although interest in the Negro Leagues was waning, Saperstein managed to get publicity for the Giants in the white press. Publicity was Saperstein's gift.[77]

Saperstein's business associates in the Negro Leagues were disappointed that he didn't turn the Giants into a farm team for a major league team. Doing so might have served as a model for Negro League teams to become part of the minor league system, but Saperstein was never really interested in the institutions of black baseball. His allegiance was only to individual players, and they appreciated his support. Winfield Welch, Tommy Sampson, Double Duty Radcliffe, Ted Strong, Satchel Paige, Parnell Woods, Art Wilson, Luke Easter, Paul Hardy, Piper Davis, and William Cornelius all spoke glowingly in their reminiscences about the support and friendship Saperstein provided. Radcliffe called him "the best friend I ever had, black or white." He claimed that Saperstein helped many black players beyond finding them employment, paying their gambling debts, and financing their funerals. Saperstein's generosity to individuals was unsurpassed, but it did not translate into a commitment to racial equality.[78]

## *The Worker* Continues the Fight

One of the players Saperstein scouted, Luke Easter, was playing for a Cleveland farm team, the San Diego Padres, in 1949, when Nat Low began reporting from the West Coast for *The Daily Worker*. Low was very impressed with Easter's power, and wrote about his potential to become "the next Babe Ruth." Lester Rodney took exception to Low's high expectations for Easter. Easter might not be the next Babe, and Rodney believed he shouldn't have to be. If blacks were truly equal they would not have to be twice as good (or college-educated, as Jackie Robinson was) in order to make the grade. As it turned out, blacks who were not stars would be discriminated against in the major leagues for decades as most teams preferred to limit the number of blacks on their rosters. Rodney understood these subtle dimensions of racism, and sought to combat them even among his colleagues.[79]

Low became Easter's friend and advocate. He was alarmed that Easter, who was out for several weeks with a knee injury, was forced to return before he was healed, and thought the Padres were jeopardizing his future. Low monitored the situation closely and was relieved that Hank Greenberg came to San Diego to take Easter back to Cleveland for additional surgery and took a special interest in his rehabilitation process. When Easter hit a long home run in his Yankee Stadium debut in 1950, Mardo reiterated Rodney's argument about applying a double standard to black players who were not accepted unless they proved themselves to be above average. Easter's injuries would ultimately curtail his career. But his story provided an opportunity for *The Daily Worker* staff to make a contribution both to an individual player and to the values of equality for which they stood.[80]

## The HUAC Hearings

Anticommunist sentiments were growing in intensity. To expose what they considered subversive activity in the entertainment industry, the House Un-American Activities Committee had targeted a predominantly Jewish group of writers and actors who came to be known as "the Hollywood Ten." In 1949, Paul Robeson also became a target.

In April, in a speech in Paris, Robeson had questioned the wisdom of blacks, who experienced second-class citizenship in the United States, fighting against the Soviet Union should the rapidly escalating cold war turn hot. Jackie Robinson, who had succeeded Robeson as the most famous African American at that time, was called to the committee to testify and was expected to refute Robeson's claim that blacks would not fight for their country. Robinson was conflicted, but Branch Rickey urged him to testify. Lester Rodney was distressed, and concerned that the connection he felt between being a Dodger fan and a communist would be tested.

Rodney was present at Robinson's press session prior to the hearings, and reported that Robinson did say he'd "fight an aggressor...including the Russians." Rodney dismissed this because in his naive estimation, the Soviet

Union was a peace-loving country incapable of aggression. *The Worker*'s sports page did not cover Robinson's actual testimony, although it was front-page news in the *New York Times*. Instead, the following day *The Worker*'s front page carried Robeson's statement that he had no quarrel with Robinson, since they both stood for peace. On the sports page was a photo of Robeson accompanied by a comment he had made several years prior about the importance of the campaign to integrate the major leagues, *The Worker*'s subtle message to Robinson about loyalty. Their coverage of the event reflected their disappointment that Robinson was willing to testify.[81]

*The Worker* found an opportunity to enlist Robinson on their side the following month. When local residents, anticommunists, and anti–civil rights groups attacked people on their way to attend a Robeson concert in Peekskill, New York, Mardo sought out Jackie Robinson and showed him a newspaper account of the riot. Mardo described Robinson reading the article slowly and carefully, and then responding "angrily" that:

> It's Robeson's right to do or be or say as he believes. They say here in America you're allowed to be whatever you want. I think those rioters ought to be investigated and let's find out if what they did is supposed to be the democratic way of doing things.

Robinson, although he disagreed with Robeson's politics, agreed that Robeson should have the right to believe what he wanted, since communism wasn't against the law. Robinson had already expressed this idea in his HUAC testimony. Mardo's report ended, "Robinson sighed. 'Anything progressive is called communism.'" For *The Worker*, this interview was crucial. It was unthinkable that Robinson, their hero, would not defend their rights.[82]

As a way of celebrating Robinson's patriotism and the HUAC testimony, Branch Rickey, with the assistance of writer Arthur Mann and his connections in the movie industry, produced a Hollywood film, *The Jackie Robinson Story*, starring Robinson playing himself and noted actress Ruby Dee as his wife. When preliminary news about the film was released, Rodney expressed his displeasure that it would include Robinson's HUAC testimony, and also that the story was framed with Rickey as the "lone ranger" who acted in "some magic vacuum." Of course, he argued, Rickey deserved credit, and of course, at this point in time, after the Hollywood Ten, no screenwriter would put the communists in the picture. But it was more than he could bear that a film would show HUAC, "this fascist-minded group . . . in a favorable light." Rodney was relieved when the film was released that the ending had Robinson simply "going to Washington" and speaking about how democracy is worth defending, a "sentiment on which all fighters for peace and democracy can certainly agree."[83]

## Leaving Black Baseball Behind

In 1950 Rodney congratulated the White Sox for signing their first black player, Sam Hairston of the "Indianapolis team." He credited the campaign of the DuSable, Illinois, edition of *The Worker* for playing a role in protests orchestrated by the black leaders in Chicago that led to the signing. The Hairston sale was rare for the Clowns. In general, Syd Pollock pursued the policy of keeping his older players and not trying to find young prospects to sell to the majors. The Clowns' most famous prospect, Hank Aaron, was an exception. But Pollock fully expected the Clowns to survive.[84]

That same year Ed Gottlieb told Wendell Smith that there was no hope for Negro baseball, although the Stars continued to play in the league for two more seasons. Gottlieb's partner Ed Bolden died after the 1950 season. Given Gottlieb's statements about the future of Negro League baseball, it is surprising that he chose to continue to operate the team. But Gottlieb reassured the other owners at the American League meeting that he was working on arrangements with Bolden's daughter, Dr. Hilda Bolden, a physician in Washington, D.C., to continue for another year. Gottlieb had tried to buy her shares, but Dr. Bolden did not like Gottlieb's offer, so she declined to sell. The Stars did not do well at the gate. Gottlieb and Bolden held on for one more season, but decided to quit league play after 1952. Gottlieb made the announcement in March, saying he could no longer withstand the operating losses. His contacts with black baseball were over, and only revived again when he was chosen to be one of two white members of the first committee to select Negro Leaguers to enter the Baseball Hall of Fame in 1969.[85]

By 1952, *The Daily Worker*'s sports page was reduced to a single column written by Lester Rodney. But Rodney kept track of teams as they signed African American players. Disillusioned with communism, he would leave the newspaper three years before the Boston Red Sox became the last team to integrate in 1959. Although the Negro Leagues were gone, Rodney sought to keep their legacy alive. Long before Negro League researchers made these claims, Rodney passionately criticized an Associated Press poll that named Jim Thorpe and Babe Ruth the best athletes of the twentieth century:

> The past 50 years has notoriously hidden and shackled so many great Negro athletes.... [W]ho could say for sure that Josh Gibson might not have proved a better home run hitter?... [W]here would Satchel Paige have finished in such a poll had this matchless pitcher been allowed to show his wondrous talent in mixed competition?

As a member of the (still all-white) Baseball Writers Association, Rodney wrote in a vote for Satchel Paige on the Hall of Fame ballot in 1951, although he had not yet been out of major league baseball long enough to be eligible. Rodney would also have nominated Josh Gibson had he played in the majors, and agitated to change the rules so that Negro Leaguers could be voted into the Hall. Twenty years later, when Paige was elected, some people still wanted to create a separate wing for him and the other Negro Leaguers who were finally going to be recognized. Rodney was true to his cause and ahead of his time.[86]

In 1954 Abe Saperstein made his last foray into black baseball to once again support Satchel Paige. He organized a Harlem Globetrotters baseball team, with Satchel Paige pitching, serving as the general manager, and making a good share of the profits as well. As Paige pointed out, "I can make 25 to 30K with this team during the coming season. So why should I pitch in organized baseball for less?"[87]

Black baseball could not sustain itself past the mid-1950s. Other segregated institutions, like the black press and historically black colleges, were able to stay in business. Saperstein's Harlem Globetrotters basketball team survived because he shifted from an entertaining and competitive team to one that focused exclusively on entertainment, displaying basketball skill through clowning. The Globetrotters were recreated as emissaries of the American dream, touring the globe as a demonstration that blacks were respected and equal citizens of the United States. Perhaps transferring the Globetrotters to black ownership or differences between baseball as the national pastime and basketball as a new interest was what allowed the team to succeed.

White minor league baseball teams survived by developing players and made their money by selling those players to the major leagues, giving them control of the market of less-skilled players. Negro League owners were not able to follow that model. Although some black owners sought minor league status for their teams, they got no support from organized baseball, where black ownership was not welcomed.

The Jewish businessmen used different exit strategies. Abe Saperstein became a key transitional figure as the middleman who identified Negro League talent for the major leagues. Eddie Gottlieb left the world of black baseball to concentrate on his professional basketball team. Only Syd Pollock remained committed to comedy baseball, continuing to operate a predominantly black team throughout the 1950s. But being a "shrewd" Jewish businessman who traded in stereotypes would no longer be an acceptable way to express Jewish identity.

## The End

When the integration of major league baseball began after World War II, the world of black baseball entered a slow decline, and the opportunities Jews experienced in the segregated world they inhabited but in which they did not belong disappeared. The social changes that permitted baseball's integration after the war also had a profound impact on Jewish American identity. The postwar Jewish community capitalized on these changes in a variety of ways that would put an end to the way Jews in black baseball expressed their identities through radicalism, minstrelsy, and blackness.

Jews and blacks began to work cooperatively during this "golden age of black-Jewish relations." Jewish organizations like the Anti-Defamation League created alliances with black groups like the NAACP to fight for legal rights that would put an end to discrimination in voting, education, housing, and employment. Jackie Robinson's relationship with the Jews was symbolic of this era. Jewish organizations subscribed to the "unitary theory of bigotry" and assumed that supporting rights for blacks would also bring an end to anti-Semitism. In this era, altruism and self-interest went hand in hand. Whether or not it was as a consequence of this stance, anti-Semitism would radically diminish during this era. Judaism came to be viewed primarily as a religious identity, and arguments against discrimination based on "race, creed, or color" were crafted to include Jews on the basis of their beliefs along with blacks on the basis of race.

Jewish and black community organizations also identified with political liberalism and supported cold war antiradicalism. Postwar America defined itself as a society antithetical not only to the racism of Hitler but to the communism of Stalin and Soviet Russia. Blacks and Jews were compelled to adhere to the anti-communism of the age to counteract prevalent assumptions that both groups were controlled by political radicals who sought to undermine American patriotism. They deeply feared the idea, perpetrated originally by right-wing anti-Semites like Henry Ford, that connected Jews with communism. Jewish organizations did not protest when Jews who formed the majority of the Hollywood Ten and Julius and Ethel Rosenberg were singled out and accused of disloyalty, losing their jobs in the former instance and their lives in the latter. Black groups took the same position towards renowned black radicals W. E. B. DuBois and Paul Robeson. The communist sportswriters, despite the success of their campaign, would be forgotten and their efforts unappreciated because of the power of anticommunism.

Jewish ethnic identity also underwent changes. In validation of their solidarity with the movement for black civil rights, Jews had to deal with their own discriminatory practices and work to eradicate the minstrel-based humor that stereotyped and demeaned black people. Just as humor that demeaned blacks was coming to be viewed as shameful, the schmaltzy Yiddish borscht belt entertainment of comedians like Max Patkin that defined the Jewish immigrant generation would also become embarrassing reminders of an immigrant past that postwar Jews left behind in order to truly take their place as part of serious, tolerant, white America.

All these changes made the various manifestations of the Jews of black baseball an embarrassment to the postwar Jewish community. Abe Saperstein, Ed

Gottlieb, and Syd Pollock, the businessmen who made their living from a segregated institution and traded in old-style Jewish vaudevillian humor with traces of minstrelsy, did not fit into a Jewish community that emphasized liberal religious values and the importance of working against discrimination.

The communist Jews were likewise unwelcome. While Lester Rodney, Nat Low, and Bill Mardo campaigned for the same values that undergirded postwar American Jewish life—the end of segregated baseball as an affront to American democracy—their affiliation with the Communist Party put them outside the range of phenomena that the Jewish community wanted to claim as its own.

H. Z. Plummer had given up on his involvement in professional baseball many years before, although his community of Hebrew Israelites continued to play recreationally and provide housing for visiting players and teams through the 1950s. Ironically, one additional consequence of blacks and Jews working together politically was that the Jews working in relation to blacks could only be white; what else could "black-Jewish relations" mean? In that context, black Jews could not be Jewish. Their particular blend of Jewish and African ethnoreligion would remain unrecognized because Jews were fully white, a successful group of immigrants in a pluralistic society.

# Aftermath

Although none of the ways Jews negotiated their identities through black baseball would survive the postwar era, the 1960s would again bring many changes. The alliance between black and Jewish organizations fell apart under the pressure of a reconfigured black politics, which saw that legal rights would not end discrimination and demanded black agency and power to forge their place in society. Baseball, as a reminder of the segregated world of the past, would continue to diminish in importance for blacks. Even in the twenty-first century, there are still no black-owned teams, few black managers, and few teams with more than a handful of black players. Jews, on the other hand, overcame whatever anti-Semitism existed in the upper echelons of the business of baseball. The two most influential men in baseball over the years, Marvin Miller, who revolutionized labor practices as the head of the players' union, and Bud Selig, baseball owner and current commissioner, are publicly identified as Jewish. Sandy Koufax, arguably the greatest left-handed pitcher in baseball history, provided Jews with a hero when he refused to pitch in the World Series on Yom Kippur in 1965, announcing that a sports hero could make Jewish religion an accepted part of the fabric of American culture. Black Jews in baseball also became visible. Jews were eager in the 1960s to claim Hall of Fame infielder Rod Carew, a darkskinned Panamanian who had married a Jew, raised Jewish children, wore a Jewish star, and began to study for conversion, as a member of the Jewish people. Jews also proudly included Elliott Maddox, a black man from New Jersey who was raised among Jews and felt so much of an affinity for Judaism that he underwent a traditional conversion in the 1970s while playing for the New York Yankees, as a Jewish ballplayer. In these ways, the complicated legacy of Jews in black baseball lived on.

Baseball, like history, tells stories of winners and losers. The Jews of black baseball ended in obscurity, their customs and practices no longer acceptable. But as the children of immigrants and descendents of slaves, they accomplished more than was expected of them. Their lives and legacies confirm the complexity of black and Jewish identities and relationships, and underscore the importance of baseball as a location for understanding mid-twentieth-century America.

# NOTES

## Chapter 1

1. Robinson actually reintegrated baseball; some blacks played in predominantly white professional leagues until 1887. Much has been written about Robinson's entry into baseball. The best works are still Tygiel, *The Great Experiment* and Rampersad, *Jackie Robinson*.
2. See Alpert, "Jewish Icon."
3. Greenberg, *Troubling*, 2.
4. Sundquist, *Strangers*, 25.
5. Early, "Unpopular Answer to a Popular Question" interview.
6. Eig, *Opening Day*, 142.
7. Black baseball is often referenced as the "Negro Leagues," and I will use this term in reference to these segregated leagues. But the various Negro Leagues were only a small part of a larger group of teams comprised of black players that played independently as well as in leagues from the late nineteenth century until the 1960s.
8. Tygiel, *Past Time*, 132.
9. Pittsburgh Pirate owner Barney Dreyfuss is also in the Hall of Fame. Depending on how broadly you define "Jew," there are two other Jewish hall of famers: Lou Boudreau, born of a Jewish mother but raised by his French Canadian father, and Rod Carew, married for many years to a Jewish woman and father to Jewish children but never an official convert, so considered by some a "Jew by association." For more information about Greenberg, see Simons, "Standard Bearer," and Aviva Kempner's film *The Life and Times*. The story of Koufax's Jewish connections is best told by Leavy, *Koufax*.
10. Riess, *Sports*, 13; *Touching*, 98.
11. Burgos, *Playing*, 5.

12. The Yiddish word for black, often used derogatorily.

13. Lewis, *In Their Own Interests*, tells the story of this competition in Norfolk, Virginia, especially 1910–1930, 42.

14. Lomax, *Entrepreneurs/Community*.

15. For different approaches to definitions, see Gitelman, "Conclusion," 304 and 309, and Slavet, *Racial Fever*, 96 and 169.

16. Goldscheider, "Judaism, Community" 274 and 285.

17. The literature on Jewish white identity is vast. See Rogin, *Blackface*; Goldstein, *The Price*, 1; Roediger, *Working Toward*, 18; Jacobsen, *Whiteness*; Brodkin, *When the Jews*; Freedman, *Klezmer America*; Slavet, *Racial Fever*, 153. See also Sundquist, *Strangers*, 29. See Neal Gabler's *Empire of Their Own* for the definitive discussion of Jews in Hollywood, and Michael Alexander's *Jazz Age Jews* for a discussion of the Jewish role in sports gambling.

18. This journalist was not alone in characterizing Strong as a "Hebrew." He was called the "Hebrew" who can "exact a heavy [financial] toll" from all the black baseball teams in the East in a related article (BAA February 11, 1921). I am grateful to Michael Lomax for pointing out this citation to me from his forthcoming work, "Black Baseball Entrepreneurs, 1902–1931: The Rise and Decline of the Negro National and Eastern Colored Leagues." Syracuse University Press.

19. See www.ancestry.com for 1910, 1920, 1930 census, draft card; Lowenfish, "When All Heaven"; Jaher, "Antisemitism."

20. Tygiel, *Past Time*, 132. See also Lanctot, *Rise and Ruin*, 95; Goldfarb, "Harlem's Team," 11; Barthel, *Peerless*, 105. Only Burgos identifies Strong as "Irish American" based on a 1947 interview that Negro League owner Alex Pompez gave to Jose Alvarez de la Vega in *Puerto Rico Deportivo* 4:7–8 (July-August 1947): 16, translated by Adrian Burgos, 301 note 2, "Left Out."

21. NYT October 6, 1910.

22. Goldfarb, "Harlem," 19.

23. Lomax, *Entrepreneurs*.

24. Lomax, *Black Baseball*, 386.

25. Greenberg, *Troubling*, chap. 5; Weingarten, *Jewish Organizations*, chap. 3; Muller, *Capitalism*, chap. 3; Gabler, *Empire*, 351–386; Litvak, *The Un-Americans*. Liebman, "Ties that Bind," suggests that Jews made up the majority of the American Communist Party from 1920 to after World War II, when their allegiance was compromised by Soviet anti-Semitism and a focus on Zionism. He also points out that while the majority of leftists were Jewish, the majority of Jews were not of the left.

26. *Life* magazine reference quoted in Carr, *Hollywood*, 354. On the Jewish role in the Black Sox scandal, see Nathan, "Anti-Semitism"; Alexander, *Jazz Age*, 48–54; Carr, *Hollywood*, 72, 87.

27. He was generous to Jewish organizations, leaving bequests to the United States Committee of Sports for Israel, the Jewish Basketball League Alumni (a group he served as president), Congregation B'nai Abraham, Congregation Beth Tovin, the Allied Jewish Appeal, Congregation Temple Israel of Wynnefield, and the National Jewish Hospital in Denver in memory of his father. *Evening Bulletin* obituary, Gottlieb Files, Urban Archives and Year: 1920; Census Place: Philadelphia Ward 4, Philadelphia, Pennsylvania; Roll T625_1616; Page: 3A; Enumeration District: 101; Image: 7. ancestry.com. See also Rich Westcott's biography of Gottlieb, *Mogul*.

28. www.ancestry.com 1910; Census Place: MT Pleasant, Westchester, New York; Roll T624_1089; Page: 2A; Enumeration District: 48; Image: 83; Pollock, *Barnstorming*, 44–45, and Year: 1920; Census Place: North Tarrytown, Westchester, New York; Roll T625_1276; Page: 8B; Enumeration District: 67; Image: 558.

29. Year: 1910; Census Place: Chicago Ward 26, Cook, Illinois; Roll T624_271; Page: 17B; Enumeration District: 1122; Image: 1062; Year: 1920; Census Place: Chicago Ward 26, Cook (Chicago), Illinois; Roll T625_336; Page: 2B; Enumeration District: 1532; Image: 1128. Year: 1930; Census Place: Chicago, Cook, Illinois; Roll 490; Page: 7A; Enumeration District: 1769; Image: 672.0 www.ancestry.com. 1910, 1920, 1930 United States Federal Census [database online]. See also Green, *Spinning*, chap. 1.

30. Green, *Spinning*, 147; NYT, December 15, 1974.

31. Year: 1920; Census Place: Philadelphia Ward 39, Philadelphia, Pennsylvania; Roll T625_1640; Page: 3A; Enumeration District: 1420; Image: 539; Passon Files, EB March 3, 1954, Urban Archives.

32. PC July 21, 1923; August 29, 1942; ADW February 12, 1932; "Cum Posey's Pointed Paragraphs," PC February 13, 1932.

33. See Heaphy, *Negro Leagues* for a comprehensive picture of the many leagues that were formed during the course of black baseball history.

34. Landing, *Black Judaism*; Dorman, "A True Moslem," 133; Isaac, "Orienting Afro-American Judaism," 514.

35. Translation from Jewish Publication Society, 1917. Levine, *Black Culture*, 50; Raboteau, *Slave Religion*, 33; Dvorak, "After Apocalypse," 175.

36. Brooks, *Prince Hall*, 197, 203; Wallace, "Are We Men?" 416.

37. Muraskin, *Middle Class Blacks*, 59.

38. Raboteau, *Slave Religion*, 109; *1906 Census of Religious Bodies*, 202.

39. Church of God, *History*, 39–44.

40. I witnessed these practices at Sabbath services in Belleville and Philadelphia, and gleaned information from conversations with community members, the church history, and their website, www.cogasoc.org. Many of their practices are reminiscent of classical Reform Judaism, including

the interchangeable use of "Hebrew" and "Israelite" as terms of identification, recitation of the Lord's Prayer, and collection taking. NJG April 26, 1951.

41. His WWII registration card lists his birth in Eritrea in 1892, his religious affiliation as Hebrew, and his occupation as Rabbi. Roll WW2_2369422; Local board: Brooklyn, New York. www.ancestry.com. U.S. World War II Draft Registration Cards, 1942; CD June 3, 1922; WP October 4, 1923; BAA November 7, 1942; CD June 5, 1943; NJG, August 21, 1943. On representations of black Jews in the Jewish and black press, see Gold, "The Black Jews of Harlem." That deKollscritta taught them Yiddish, the language of Ashkenazi Jews, indicates a consciousness of how Jews are represented in America as being of Eastern European descent. DeKollscritta claimed to be fluent in 28 languages, so it is not surprising that Yiddish would be included among them.

42. Diner, *In the Almost*, 20; Greenberg, *Troubling*, 134.

43. See Norwood, "Going to Bat."

44. Forman, *Blacks in the Jewish Mind*, 26.

45. Forman, *Blacks in the Jewish Mind*, 26.

## Chapter 2

1. Walker, *History of Black Business*, 185.

2. See Winter and Haupert, "The East-West Game"; Lomax, *Entrepreneurs*; Ruck, *Sandlot Seasons*, 117–122.

3. Haupert, "The Old Fellows," 80.

4. Haupert, "The Old Fellows"; Snyder, *Well Paid Slave*; and Mathewson, "Monopoly."

5. Haupert, "Pay, Performance, and Race," 38–40.

6. EB, June 1, 1929, in Gottlieb Files; Westcott, *Mogul*, 26. Gottlieb kept his offices above Passon's store until 1944. Letter from Ed Gottlieb to Effa Manley, January 24, 1944, NEP.

7. Westcott, *Mogul*, 67; *Philadelphia Record*, September 24, 1939, in Gottlieb Files; CD July 7, 1928 describes the annual pilgrimage of the House of David to Philadelphia to play against Hilldale.

8. Pollock, *Barnstorming*, 47; Middletown (N.Y.) *Daily Herald*, July 15, 1924, Kenyon Files.

9. Pollock, *Barnstorming*, 56; NYAN April 25, 1928; González Echevarría, *Pride of Havana*, 126; Brock, "Not Just Black," 179.

10. PC June 30, 1928; AA June 2, 1928; NYAN June 4, 1930.

11. NYAN July 31, 1929, and August 14, 1929; PC August 24, 1929.

12. NYAN May 25, 1932; AA May 16, 1925; Sam Leaden Bernstein, telephone conversation with author, October 15, 2008; NYA August 1, 1925, Goldfarb, "Lincoln Giants"; PC July 8, 1933; "Ku Klux Klan Faces Hebrews Labor Day," *Washington Post*, September 1, 1926.

13. Church of God, *History*, 48–50; Oral histories conducted by the author with members of the Belleville community, June 2008.

14. Bruce, *Monarchs*, 14–17; Rives, "Baird."

15. PC March 6, 1932; Thomas Burt, former Negro League player, face-to-face interview with author, June 2008.

16. Joel Wagner, face-to-face conversation with author, June 2008; NJG July 23, 1932.

17. NJG May 7, July 23, and September 3, 1932; Leonard, *Buck Leonard*, 18–19.

18. W. Rollo Wilson, "Sport Shots," PC February 6, 1932; February 13, 1932.

19. ADW March 2, 1932.

20. PC June 4, 1932; ADW June 7, 1932; CD June 25, 1932; PC June 25, 1932; ADW and NYAN June 29, 1932. Also in PT June 30 and BAA July 9, 1932.

21. Bill Gibson, "Hear Me Talkin to Ya," AA July 1, and July 29, 1933; PC July 29, 1933; CD July 22, 1933.

22. NYAN June 15, 1932.

23. See Gay, *Satch, Dizzy & Rapid Robert* for a history of interracial play.

24. CD January 29, 1932 and September 16, 1933.

25. McNary, "North Dakota"; Paige, *Pitchin' Man*, 51; Roper, "Another Chink," 75–89.

26. Lester, *National Showcase*.

27. Radcliffe claimed that Comiskey wasn't open to Negro League games before that, but games had been played there occasionally: CD August 18, 1928; McNary, *Radcliffe*, 135; Chester Washington, "Sez Ches," PC September 15, 1934; Dan Burley, "Sports Secret Service Department," CD June 13, 1936.

28. EB June 12, 1931, Harry Passon Files; PC April 9, 1932; "The Bacharach Giants," *Colored Baseball and Sports Monthly* 1935, Carter Files; NYAN April 5, 1933.

29. Randy Dixon, "Sports Bugle," PC, June 8, 1940; Holway, *Voices*, 82; Lanctot, *Rise*, 30.

30. BAA February 25, 1933; Rust, *Get That Nigger*, 55; PC September 30, 1933 and March 25, 1935; NYAN August 3, 1935.

31. John Clark, PC January 5, 1935; PC February 17, 1934; Cum Posey, "Posey's Pointed Paragraphs," PC March 3, 1934; NYAN March 17 and July 7, 1934; AA March 16, 1935.

32. "The Bacharach Giants," Carter Papers; W. Rollo Wilson, "Sport Shots," PC October 13, 1934; PT March 26 and June 25, 1936.

33. NJG July 16, 1938.

34. NJG, June 16, July 2, July 16, August 20, September 3, and September 10, 1938.

35. NJG July 16, 1938; letter from John B. Johnson to Abe Manley, August 3, 1938 NEP; NJG August 27, 1938.

36. CD June 13, 1936; Martin, *New Jersey*, 65–66.

37. CD and AA January 28, 1939; Art Carter, "From the Bench" AA February 18, 1939; BAA February 25, 1939; NYAN March 11, 1939.

38. Letters from John B. Johnson to Mr. and Mrs. Abe Manley, February 3, 1939 and to Abe Manley, February 25, 1939, NEP; Sam Lacy, Richmond AA, May 6, 1939.

39. NJG May 27, 1939; D. E. Ellis, "Cruising Along the Baseball Front with the ECL," NYA May 27, 1939.

40. NJG May 13, 1939 and June 8, 1940; NYAN March 29, 1947 and March 11, 1950.

41. Sam Lacy, BAA June 3, 1939.

42. Ibid.

43. NJG, June 10, 1939; NYA June 24, 1939.

44. Howard, *Sunday*, 25; NJG July 1, 1939; telegram from Brady Johnson to Abe Manley, August 2, 1939 NEP.

45. Kelley, *Negro Leagues Revisited*, 124.

46. BW September 12, 1944; Kelley, *Negro Leagues Revisited*, 126.

47. Negro Baseball Players Biography Sheet, Carter Papers; CD March 9, 1941; CD August 2, 1947.

48. Pollock, *Barnstorming*, 152; George Haskins, Haywood's nephew, telephone conversation with author, October 16, 2008.

49. NJG May 5, 1934; April 29, 1933; CD April 20, 1935; NYA, May 20, 1939.

50. Kelley, *Revisiting*, 109; Pollock, *Barnstorming*, 112–113.

51. Pollock, *Barnstorming*, 243.

52. Carl Haywood, telephone conversation with author, November 3, 2008; Rabbi Curtis Caldwell, face-to-face conversation with author, November 5, 2008.

53. Art Carter to Mr. L. Z. Plummer, The Bellevue [sic] Grays, Portsmouth, Va., March 28, 1940, Carter Papers; Richmond AA, April 13, 1940.

54. NJG May 18, 1940; letter from Art Carter to Joe Lewis, May 30, 1940; letter from Art Carter to H. Z. Plummer, June 8, 1940; Art Carter to Joe Miles, June 10, 1940, Carter Papers.

55. Richmond AA, July 20, 1940; telegram from Joe Lewis to Art Carter, July 10, 1940; letter from Art Carter to Joe Miles, August 23, 1940, Carter Papers.

56. PC June 8, 1940.

57. Oral histories conducted by the author with members of the Belleville community, June 2008.

58. Cum Posey, "Posey's Points," PC January 22, 1938; letter from Effa Manley to Ed Gottlieb, May 23, 1939, NEP; 1938 memo to "All Owners of NNL Clubs" from Tom Wilson, n.d. NEP.

59. Letter from Gottlieb to Mrs. A. Manley, April 4, 1939, NEP; letter from Gottlieb to Effa Manley, April 18, 1939; letter from Effa Manley to Rufus Jackson, April 29, 1939; letters from Gottlieb to Effa Manley, May 27, 1939 and December 4, 1939, NEP; PC August 31, 1940.

60. CD July 16, 1938; PC February 4, 1939; Rust, *Get That Nigger*, 54.

61. NYAN February 24, 1940; PC February 10, 1940.

62. CD February 10, 1940.

63. PT February 15, 1940; Cum Posey, PC February 24, 1940.

64. CD February 24, 1940; "Reports on Sports by Daniel," NYAN March 2, 1940; PT April 11, 1940; Posey, "Posey's Points," PC January 4, 1941.

65. Ed Harris, "Happy Days are Here Again," PT February 15, 1940; Randy Dixon, "The Sports Bugle," February 17, 1940; PT April 11, 1940.

66. Fay Young, "The Stuff Is Here," CD February 24, 1940; BAA February 10, 1940.

67. BAA April 27, 1940.

68. CD February 18, 1939.

69. CD May 9, 1936; AA May 16, 1936.

70. Scott, *Sons of Sheba's Race*, 13, 21; NYAN September 21, 1935.

71. ADW, February 19, 1937; Pollock, *Barnstorming*, 84–86; CD May 1 and May 22, 1937; ADW April 8, 1937.

72. PC May 29, 1937.

73. NYAN August 13, 1938; ADW October 29, 1938; CD March 18, 1939; Young, "The Stuff Is Here," CD April 8, 1939.

74. Posey, "Posey's Points," PC March 9, 1940.

75. Jones, ADW March 17, 1940; BAA March 2, 1940.

76. CD May 25, 1940.

77. PC August 31, 1940.

78. CD September 14 and August 3, 1940.

79. NYAN May 24, 1941.

80. Young, "The Stuff Is Here," CD March 29, 1941.

81. Letter from Syd Pollock to Effa Manley, March 28, 1941, NEP.

82. PC June 28, 1941.

83. PC September 28, 1940 and August 16, 1941.

84. NJG August 23, 1941; Posey, "Posey's Points," PC November 1 and October 11, 1941.

85. Posey, "Posey's Points," PC April 5, 1941; PT April 10, 1941; ADW April 23, 1941; CD June 21 and 28, 1941; PT September 13, 1941; CD August 23, 1941.

86. ADW December 31, 1941; BAA January 3, 1942; CD January 3, 1942.

## *Chapter 3*

1. Lanctot, *Rise and Ruin*, 127–128; NYT June 5, 1942; DW June 27, 1942.

2. PC January 11, 1941; letters from Ed Gottlieb to Effa Manley, May 16 and July 21, 1941; letters from Effa Manley to See Posey, July 28 and August 1, 1941, NEP.

3. Leuschner was not Jewish, according to cemetery records. (Letter to author, R. Stutzmann and Sons, April 17, 2009.) He was never presumed to be Jewish in contemporary sources, despite his association with Nat Strong.

4. NYAN August 30 and August 16, 1941; PC November 21, 1942.

5. PT March 14, 1940; letter from Cum Posey to Effa Manley, November 17, 1941.

6. Telegram from Abe Saperstein to Effa Manley, February 20, 1942; letter from Effa Manley to Abe Saperstein, February 22, 1942, NEP.

7. Letter from Abe Saperstein to Effa Manley, February 24, 1942; letter from Syd Pollock to Effa Manley, February 26, 1942, NEP.

8. Letter from Abe Saperstein to Effa Manley, March 7, 1942; letter from Effa Manley to Abe Saperstein, March 11, 1942; letter from Abe Saperstein to Effa Manley, March 14, 1942, NEP.

9. PV February 21, 1942; Dan Burley, "Confidentially Yours," PV September 17, 1942.

10. ADW February 1, 1942; NYAN March 28, 1942; CD December 19, 1942. Campbell died the following December. CD March 28, 1942.

11. Joe Sephus, "Cullings," *Cumberland* (Md.) *Evening Times*, April 27, 1942. J Michael Kenyon files; CD March 23, 1940; Wendell Smith, PC February 28, 1942.

12. Cum Posey, "Posey's Points," PC April 4, 1942; PC February 28, 1942.

13. Wendell Smith, "Smitty's Sports Spurts," PC April 25, 1942; CCP March 28, 1942; PC May 16, 1942.

14. NYA and BAA, March 7, 1942. Saperstein did have real power in St. Louis. By 1945, he was involved with running the Stars himself. Kelley, *Revisited*, 127; NYAN March 3, 1945; PV March 28, 1942.

15. NJG May 9, 1942.

16. ADW July 30, 1942; BW July 31, 1942; CD August 8, 1942.

17. Burley, "Confidentially Yours," NYAN October 17, 1942; PV October 24, 1942; Posey, "Posey's Points," PC October 31, 1942.

18. BW March 7, 1941; letter from Effa Manley to Abe Saperstein, March 4, 1944; Bob Williams, "Sports Rambler," CCP July 29, 1944.

19. Holway, *Voices*, 182; CD, February 26, 1944; BW March 21, 1944; NAL Minutes, March 5, June 13, December 15, 1944 in T. Y. Baird Files 4.12.

20. PC January 30, 1943; ADW April 14 and 17, 1943.

21. BAA May 8, 1943; BAA July 24, 1943; NYAN June 19, 1943.

22. PV February 27, 1943.

23. Emory Jackson, "Hits and Bits," ADW August 24, 1943; Smith, "Smitty's Sports Spurts," PC December 18, 1943; balance sheet from East-West Game, August 1, 1943, Baird Collection 4.12. Saperstein continued to receive payments for his publicity work. He was paid $1,250 in both 1945 and 1946, $767.49 in 1951, and $816.91 in 1952. See Lester, *National Showcase*, 466, 468, 477.

24. Letter from Effa Manley to Ed Gottlieb, November 7, 1942, and Ed Gottlieb to Effa Manley, November 10, 1942, NEP.

25. PV January 30, 1943, February 6, and May 8, 1943; NYAN May 15, 1943; IR October 2, 1943.

26. Westcott, *Mogul*, 94, 106–109; Holway, *Voices*, 84–85, Rust, *Get That Nigger*, 54.

27. CD March 11, 1944.

28. Letter from Abe Saperstein to Effa Manley, May 24, 1944, and night letter from Abe Saperstein to Abe Manley, June 3, 1944, NEP; PT March 25, 1944.

29. Posey, "Charge Clown's White Agent Jips Players," PT, BAA July 1, 1944; PC July 8, 1944.

30. Burley, NYAN July 29, 1944; Smith, "Smitty's Sports Spurts," PC July 29, 1944.

31. PV August 12, 1944.

32. ADW September 8, 1944; Posey, "Posey's Points," PC November 21, 1944; PC December 16, 1944.

33. Quoted in Green, *Spinning*, 173.

34. NAL minutes, December 15, 1944, Baird Collection 4.12.

35. CD December 23, 1944; letter from Syd Pollock to Art Carter, Carter Papers.

36. Smith, "Smitty's Sports Spurts," PC March 17 and March 31, 1945.

## Chapter 4

1. Wolinsky, "Arlie Latham," online.

2. Brunson, *Early*, 149. White baseball imitated some of those black traditions in its early phases. James Brunson argues convincingly that white come-

dians developed routines in imitation of black aesthetic style that, translated into the white idiom, inevitably changed and misrepresented it.

3. Brunson, "Mirthful," 26.

4. Brunson, *Early*, 130, 149.

5. In *Love and Theft*, Eric Lott supported the idea that minstrelsy parodied and misinterpreted authentic traditions, while Robert Toll (*Blacking Up*) saw minstrel traditions as completely based in the white imagination.

6. Watkins, *Real Side*, 65; Levine, *Black Culture*, 305–380.

7. Watkins, *Real Side*, part one.

8. Stewart, *Migrating to the Movies*, 202.

9. Watkins, *Real*, 126–131.

10. Watkins, *Real*, 36.

11. Toll, *Blacking Up*, 196; Stewart, *Migrating to the Movies*, 6.

12. Nasaw, *Going Out*, 54 and 75.

13. See Distler, "Exit the Racial Comics"; Erdman, *Staging the Jew*, 144; Rogin, *Blackface, White Noise*.

14. Snyder, *The Voice of the City*, 156; Melnick, *A Right to Sing*, 41, 63.

15. Carr, *Hollywood*, 188; Erdman, *Staging*, 145.

16. See Ely, *Adventures*.

17. Watkins, *Stepin Fetchit*, 262.

18. Schacht, *Screwball*, 34, 60, 88.

19. Schacht, *Screwball*, 96.

20. Schacht, *Screwball*, 115, 138, 175, 210; Schacht, Oral History, June 1, 1980.

21. Schacht, *Screwball*, 222; Oral History, 39.

22. PM July 7, 1942.

23. Patkin, *Clown Prince*, 2–3.

24. Peterson, *Only the Ball*, 70; NYAN May 15, 1929; CD August 31, 1929.

25. Peterson, *Only the Ball*, 149.

26. Eugene OR *Register-Guard*, July 17, 1931 in Kenyon files.

27. Peterson, *Only the Ball*, 151; PC August 29, 1925; notices about the Detroit Clowns appear in the black press through the 1934 season. Holway, *Voices*, 256–257; Barthel, *Peerless*, 97; Holway, *Voices*, 96.

28. Taylor, House of David trustee, telephone conversation with author, May 21, 2009; Barthel, *Peerless*, 96. Pepper games were banned from some parks because they were considered dangerous.

29. Chadwick, *When the Game*, 113. Mark Ribowsky, *Complete History*, called them "the traveling salesmen of faith" who used baseball for missionary purposes, noting that they wore the Jewish side curls known as "pais," 64. John Klima refers to them as the "famous Jewish team" as late as 2009 in *Willie's Boys*, 18. Taylor, telephone conversation. See also "House of David Echoes Base Ball Club" online.

30. I discuss the film at length below.

31. Badham, "Director's commentary." According to Badham, Cohen orchestrated this scene predicated on the idea that the House of David was "totally Jewish baseball players." Erdman, *Staging the Jew*, 107.

32. James Sturm, telephone conversation with the author, September 14, 2009.

33. Sturm, *Golem*, 13, 32.

34. PC, June 2, 1928.

35. PC, March 9, 1929.

36. PC, February 16, 1929.

37. See Green, *Spinning*, for a discussion of the beginnings of the Globetrotters. Saperstein claimed to invent the genre of basketball comedy, but its origins remain in doubt.

38. CD August 23, 1930; Heward, *Clowns*, 74; AA January 1, 1931.

39. NYAN March 3, 1926; AA April 11, 1931, March 31, 1934; Marion Jackson, "Hits and Bits," ADW May 16, 1936; Pollock, *Barnstorming*, 84. Double Duty Radcliffe remembered asking Saperstein to help him out by booking the "Cuban Zulus" for a game to help attract a crowd. McNary, *Double Duty*, 130.

40. CD May 9, 1936; Pollock, *Barnstorming*, 84; CD April 3, 1937.

41. ADW February 19, 1937; CD May 22, 1937; NYAN September 17, 1938.

42. ADW April 29, 1939.

43. ADW May 12, 1939.

44. IR July 22, 1939; CD July 29, 1939.

45. CD September 16, 1933; CD June 17, 1939; PC April 14, 1962; ADW June 8, 1939, April 12, 1940, June 26, 1940.

46. NYAN December 26, 1936; CD July 9, 1938; NYAN July 16, 1938; DW April 2, 1951; Baker, *Jesse Owens*, 155–156, 169; Owens, *Blackthink*, 50; Owens, *I Have Changed*, 56. In 1944, Saperstein sent the first Harlem Globetrotters baseball team to play on the west coast, including games against the House of David, in 1944, and also got involved in creating a league in the Northwest (Wilson, *Sunday*, 120). Jesse Owens was vice president of operations, but also put on running exhibitions as part of the promotion package (Kelley, *Voices*, 127; ADW, September 4, 1945). As Double Duty Radcliffe recalled, "We barnstormed with the House of David and had Jesse Owens running against a horse—we made money!" (McNary, *Double Duty*, 187).

47. Paige, *Pitchin' Man*, 64; NYT May 8, 1941.

48. Holway, *Voices*, 103.

49. Silber, *Press Box*, 63; NYAN August 6, 1949. Recent research on Paige has focused on the craft of his self-invention for economic gain. See Tye, *Satchel*.

50. NYAN July 1, 1939.

51. ADW February 20, 1940; *Chester* (Pa.) *Times*, June 17, 1940, Kenyon files. Joe Jacobs was the Jewish promoter who managed German boxing champion Max Schmeling in the 1930s.

52. Jones, "Slants on Sports," ADW April 27, 1940; NJG August 17, 1940.

53. NJG April 25, 1942.

54. CD March 22, 1941.

55. ADW March 13, 1941; IR May 17, 1941, May 23, 1941, June 7, 1941; CD May 31, 1941.

56. CD June 14, 1941.

57. Young, "The Stuff Is Here," CD June 14, 1941; Posey, "Posey's Points," PC November 1, 1941.

58. Posey, "Posey's Points," PC, July 5, 1941.

59. PC June 28, 1941, July 5, 1941; ADW July 7, 1941.

60. ADW July 2, July 7, and July 8, 1941.

61. DP August 3, 1941, BW, August 26, 1941.

62. Carberry, "The Second Guess," DP August 14, 1941.

63. PC February 28, 1942; Graves, "From the Press Box," NJG March 28, 1942.

64. Smith, "Smitty's Sports Spurts," PC, April 25, 1942, May 16, 1942; Graves, "From the Press Box," NJG May 23, 1942.

65. Smith, "Smitty's Sports Spurts," PC June 30, 1942.

66. CD May 23, 1942, June 20, 1942, August 22, 1942; ADW August 11, 1942, September 8, 1942.

67. PC and CD, January 9, 1943; Smith, "Smitty's Sport Spurts," PC January 23, 1943, Posey, "Posey's Points," PC May 8, 1943.

68. Pollock, *Barnstorming*, 134–135.

69. Wilson, "The Eyes," PC July 11, 1953; Bostic, "The Scoreboard," NYAN July 17, 1954; Motley, *Ruling*, 120.

70. CD July 18, 1942; PT September 5, 1942; McNary, *Double Duty*, 140; BW May 2, 1941; ADW August 26, 1943; Patkin, *Clown*, 90.

71. "Negro Leagues Baseball 1946," *Treasures*.

72. Holway, *Voices*, 340–341.

73. NJG, August 21, 1943.

74. CD April 8, 1944; ADW April 18, 1944; CD July 26, 1947.

75. Roberts, "Reports from Courier Sports Experts," PC July 12, 1947.

76. Ibid.; NYAN, July 12, 1947.

77. CD July 17, 1948; letter from Syd Pollock to Art Carter, July 25, 1948, Carter Papers.

78. CD September 18, 1948; PT March 5, 1949.

79. CD April 30, 1949; ADW January 16, 1952 and reprinted in PT January 19 and CD January 26; PC September 12, 1953.

80. ADW April 23, 1955.

81. Smith, "Smitty's Sports Spurts," PC May 13 and July 1, 1944.

82. Don Deleighbur [Burley's pseudonym], "Behind the Play," IR and NJG June 24, 1944.

83. CD, November 3, 1945.

84. NYAN April 13, 1946; NJG September 20, 1946.

85. Letter from Effa Manley to Syd Pollock, February 6, 1946 NEP; CD September 7, 1946 and August 9, 1947.

86. Press release, Negro Baseball Players Biography Sheet 1948, Carter Papers; Sampson interview in Kelley, *Revisted*, 125–128.

87. Pollock, *Barnstorming*, 116, and letter from Syd Pollock to Art Carter, July 25, 1948, Carter Papers; Jacox, "From the Press Box," NJG April 9, 1949.

88. NAL Minutes 1949, Baird Collection 4.12; ADW April 9, 1949; IR July 9, 1949.

89. "Wendell Smith's Sports Beat," PC December 16, 1950; Pollock, *Barnstorming*, 383; ADW July 22, 1950; PT June 7, 1958.

90. CD April 23, 1949; Debnam, "Sports-I-View," PT July 16, 1949; Marion Jackson, "Sports of the World," ADW July 29, 1949, NYAN August 6, 1949; PT September 6, 1949.

91. ADW October 10, 1950; PT November 25, 1950; McNary, *Black Baseball*, 221.

92. ADW July 1, 1951; PT July 10, 1951; AA July 14, 1951; PT August 4, 1951; CD September 22, 1951; ADW June 21, 1952.

93. NYAN July 12 and August 2, 1952; PT August 19, 1953.

94. ADW February 22, 1953 and May 31, 1953; NYAN July 4, 1953; PT July 21, 1953; CD August 8, 1953.

95. Pollock, *Barnstorming*, 97.

96. Motley, *Ruling*, 149–150.

97. Pollock, *Barnstorming*, 112; NYAN July 18, 1953.

98. Pollock, *Barnstorming*, 252.

99. PT March 9, 1954; CD August 28, 1954; Poindexter, "Sports I View," PT September 11, 1954.

100. Jackson, "Sports of the World," ADW April 14, 1954; Overbea, "Beating the Gun," PT May 8, 1954.

101. Pollock, *Barnstorming*, 277; Saunders, "The Sports Broadcast," PT January 25, 1955; letter from T. Y. Baird to J. B. Martin, March 6–7, 1955, Baird Collection 1.3; PT, February 15, 1955.

102. ADW, April 2, 1955; PT June 21, 1955; ADW July 9, 1955; PC March 5, 1955; Jackson, "Sports of the World," ADW August 23, 1957; PT September 18, 1956.

103. For a history of the Clowns later years, see Heward, *Clowns*, and Kimball, "Integrated Baseball."

104. Brashler, *Bingo Long*, xiv.

105. Silber, *Press Box Red*, 57; NPC August 7, 1976.

106. Lanctot, *Rise and Ruin*, 161 and 370–371.

107. Pollock, *Barnstorming*, 283.

108. Mohl, "Clowning Around," 62.

## Chapter 5

1. See Burgos, *Playing*, chap. 1. The famous case of Charlie Grant, who was presented as an Indian until the fact that he played in the Negro Leagues was uncovered, well illustrates this phenomenon.

2. PT September 11, 1926; AA May 14, 1927. For a thorough account of Landis's role, see Pietrusza, *Judge and Jury*.

3. PC February 18, 1933.

4. AA March 11, 1933; CD, September 16, 1933.

5. CD September 16, 1933; Levine, *Ellis Island*, 108–116.

6. PC September 30, 1933.

7. CD September 2, 1933, and reprinted in PC and NYAN September 13, 1933.

8. In Owens' case, one of his Olympic medals came at the expense of two Jewish members of the track team, Marty Glickman and Sam Stoller, who were replaced by Owens and another black runner, Ralph Metcalfe, on the four-man relay team at the last minute. Although the reason for the substitution has never been proven conclusively, Glickman has surmised that the U.S. Olympic Committee, represented by the track coaches, was only willing to go so far in embarrassing Hitler. It was bad enough that American blacks dominated track at the Berlin Olympics. Louis, managed by Jewish promoter Mike Jacobs, lost to German heavyweight boxer Max Schmeling (managed by Jewish promoter Joe Jacobs) in 1936, but beat him in the rematch two years later.

9. CD May 30, 1936.

10. Jules Tygiel, Arnold Rampersad, and Joe Dorinson all wrote works that were published to coincide with the fiftieth anniversary of Jackie Robinson's entrance into baseball that restored awareness of the contribution of *The Worker*. On the other hand, Rusinack, "Radical Agenda," and Fetter, "Stooge to Czar," argue that *The Worker*'s impact was negligible.

11. Greenberg, *Troubling the Waters*, 150; Maxwell, *New Negro*, 7.

12. Silber, *Press Box*, 20–28; Lester Rodney, e-mail communication with author, August 5, 2004.

13. Silber, *Press Box*, 5, 13.

14. SW August 16 and 23, 1936.

15. Silber, *Press Box*, 9; SW August 30, 1936.

16. DW January 18 and 21, 1937.

17. DW May 3 and June 23, 1937.

18. DW September 13, 1937.

19. DW September 16, 1937.

20. DW March 19 and June 15, 1938. Like many other publications of the era, *The Worker* often spelled Satchel with two l's.

21. Rodney, "From the Press Box," DW May 24 and September 22, 1938; December 16, 1939.

22. DW July 8, 1938.

23. PC December 10, 1938.

24. PC February 25, 1939; DW March 26 and 27, 1939.

25. DW March 26 and 27, 1939. Although there were Jewish players in the early baseball era, Johnny Kling, who played for the Chicago Cubs in the early 1900s, was not one of them, although he was married to a Jewish woman and was often mistakenly identified as a Jew.

26. PC, weekly articles, July 22–September 2, 1938.

27. DW July 19 and 30, 1939; PC July 29, 1939.

28. DW August 6, 1939 and March 10, 1940.

29. DW August 19, 1939 and April 3, 1950; AA August 29, 1936.

30. CD August 29, 1936; DW August 23, 1936; PC February 12, 1938.

31. PC February 11, 1939.

32. DW August 7, 1939; AA August 19, 1939; ADW August 21, 1939.

33. DW July 25 and 31, 1939, October 11, 1939; PT December 21, 1939.

34. DW February 26, March 6, April 2 and 5, May 14, 1940.

35. CD May 18, 1940.

36. DW August 24, 1940.

37. DW February 24, 1941.

38. DW April 18 and October 1, 1941.

39. DW January 23, 28, March 2, April 20, 1942.

40. DW June 5, 1942.

41. "Bill Mardo's Farewell to Low," DW February 12, 1946; Lester Rodney, "On the Scoreboard," DW October 22, 1951. Bill Mardo and Ruth Ost contributed other details about Low's life and friendship. Ost and Mardo telephone conversation with author, November 16, 2009.

42. DW June 29, July 16, 1942; Campanella, *Good to Be Alive*, 98–100.

43. DW June 6, 7, 18, 19, July 15, 30, 1942.

44. DW August 13, 1942.

45. DW June 24, July 18–19, 1942.

46. NYAN July 18, 1942; DW and ADW July 20, 1942; NYAN, CD and PC July 25, 1942.

47. DW July 27, 1942, October 22 and 25, 1951; Campanella, *Good to Be Alive*, 96.
48. BW July 31, 1942; NYAN August 1, 1942.
49. PC, August 1, 1942.
50. ADW August 2, 1942; CD August 8, 1942.
51. DW August 4, 1942.
52. Posey, "Posey's Points," PC August 15, 1942.
53. ADW August 16, 1942; DW August 21 and 24, 1942.
54. Smith, "Smitty's Sports-Spurts," PC August 29, 1942.
55. PV September 5, 1942; NYAN September 12 and 19, 1942; CD September 26 and October 10, 1942.
56. DW September 1 and December 10, 1942; Smith, "Smitty's Sports-Spurts," PC January 2, 1943, April 28, May 19, 1945.
57. Campanella, *Good to Be Alive*, 97.
58. October 14 and December 5, 1942.
59. DW December 8, 1942.
60. DW January 20, 23, February 2, April 3, 13, 1943.
61. DW February 25, 1943.
62. Veeck, *Veeck*, 141; SN August 13, 1942. Jordan, et al., "Baseball Myth," argued that Veeck made up the story, while Tygiel, "Revisiting Bill Veeck," did not think they made a strong enough case to reject Veeck's claims. But the story remains impossible to corroborate. In the minutes of the National League meetings of November 4, 1942, Nugent mentions Veeck, representing a group in Milwaukee, as a possible buyer, but assumes Veeck doesn't have access to the $400,000 asking price. NL Minutes, HOF.
63. Povich, *All Those Mornings*, 151–152; CD, August 14, 1954; SN August 13, 1942.
64. Red Smith, NYT January 13, 1980; DW February 21, 1949; National League Minutes, January 17, 1942, HOF.
65. Kuklick, *Everything*, 146; Westcott, *Mogul*, 125.

## Chapter 6

1. DW June 12, August 11 and 13, September 15, 1943.
2. ADW December 12, 1943; NYAN January 15, 1944. Reporters Wendell Smith and Dan Burley, who took credit for authoring the recommendations, accompanied them.
3. Lacy, *Fighting*, 45–46; Tygiel, *Great Experiment*, 410; Mardo, "Robinson—Robeson," 102; PC December 11, 1943; Duberman, *Robeson*, 282.
4. DW January 3, 1944.

5. DW November 27, 1944; Pietrusza, *Judge and Jury*, 417.

6. DW January 13, 1945; Silber, *Press Box Red*, xi; Dodson, "Integration," 73.

7. Mann, *Branch Rickey*, 247. Trautman became the president of the minor league organization, and was himself instrumental in ending segregation in the Southern Cotton League in 1953.

8. DW February 6 and March 7, 1945.

9. DW April 7, 1945; October 22, 1951.

10. DW April 9, 10, 13, 1945; Durocher, *The Dodgers and Me*, 207–208.

11. Smith, "Smitty's Sports Spurts," PC April 14, 1945. In addition to Low, Bostic recalled being accompanied by an African American photographer, Harold Stovall, not Jimmy Smith. NYAN November 11, 1950; Polner, *Branch Rickey*, 147.

12. CD March 24, 1945; IR April 7, 1945; PC March 24, 1945.

13. PC April 14 and 21, 1945; DW April 17 and 18, 1945.

14. DW April 29, 1948.

15. Rowan, *Wait*, 97; Tygiel, *Great Experiment*, 43; Rampersad, *Jackie Robinson*, 119.

16. Norwood, "Going to Bat," 124–125; Bryant, *Shut Out*, 36.

17. Bryant, *Shut Out*, 36–38.

18. *Congressional Record*, March 2, 2005.

19. Mann, *Rickey*, 218; Thorn and Tygiel, "Jackie Robinson's Signing: The Real, Untold Story," accessed at MrBaseball.com.

20. DW May 9, 1945.

21. DW July 7, 1945.

22. DW July 11, August 14 and 20, September 25, 1945.

23. DW October 25, 1945.

24. DW October 26, 1945.

25. DW February 5 and 12, 1946; Mardo, "Robinson—Robeson," 99.

26. DW February 21 and April 1, 1946.

27. DW January 23, 1947.

28. DW July 11, 1946; Kelly, "Integrating America," 1028.

29. PC December 22, 1945.

30. PC October 12 and December 21, 1946.

31. BAA January 4, 1947.

32. Smith, "Sports Beat," PC January 11 and 25, 1947.

33. BAA January 11, 1947; Burley, "Confidentially Yours," NYAN February 1, 1947; Joe Bostic, "Sports Extra," NYAN February 15, 1947.

34. PT October 24, 1953.

35. DW April 11 and 12; May 10, 12, 14; June 11, 1947.

36. NYT May 18, 1947.

37. PC May 25, 1947.

38. Greenberg, *Hank Greenberg*, 191.

39. Ibid.

40. Robinson, *My Own Story*, 146–147; Tygiel, *The Great Experiment*, 192.

41. Rampersad, *Robinson*, 67; PT December 21, 1939.

42. Rampersad, *Robinson*, 152, 197; Robinson, *My Own Story*, 208.

43. Robinson, *I Never*, 1995; Rowan, *Wait Til Next Year*, 305.

44. Robinson, *I Never*, 74. Robinson's daughter Sharon tells this story of inter-faith tolerance and connection, from the perspective of Steven, the Satlow's son, in a children's book, *Jackie's Gift*.

45. Kahn, "The Jackie Robinson I Remember," 89; Kahn face-to-face interview with author, January 15, 2005.

46. Rampersad, *Robinson*, 221.

47. Robinson, *I Never*, 107; Rowan, *Wait Til Next Year*, 321.

48. Rampersad, *Robinson*, 220; ADL obituary typescript, 1972, Robinson Papers; Rachel Robinson, *Jackie Robinson*, 162.

49. McDowell, "In the Same Boat," 231.

50. Rampersad, *Robinson*, 364; Robinson, "Home Plate," NYAN July 14, 1962.

51. Kahn, *Boys of Summer*, 402; letter from Dan Blumenthal to Isidore Lapan, July 17, 1962, and Jackie Robinson to Mr. William Black, July 16, 1962, Robinson Papers; Martin Luther King, Jr. Address at Hall of Fame Dinner, July 16, 1962, typescript in Robinson files, HOF.

52. NYAN July 28, 1962 and Robinson, *First Class Citizenship*, 148–150.

53. Robinson, NYAN April 6 and 13, 1963.

54. Rampersad, *Robinson*, 404. Robinson, "We Also Have Black Bigots," NYAN February 19, 1966.

55. "Protests Widen on Anti-Semitism," 1969; "Jackie Robinson Calls Jews Racist," 1972, clippings, Robinson Papers.

56. Rampersad, *Robinson*, 455–457. Jim Brosnan was the other player. Bill Veeck also testified. See Snyder, *Well-Paid Slave*, for a full discussion of the Flood case. Although Flood's challenge to the reserve system failed in the courts, modifications followed via a 1975 arbitration decision that upheld players' rights to free agency. The matter has been further negotiated via collective bargaining. Rudin, "In Memory of Jackie Robinson," November 26, 1972, Robinson Papers; Alpert, "Jewish Icon."

57. DW June 24, September 16, 1947.

58. DW July 4, 1947.

59. DW July 5, 1947.

60. DW February 8 and November 12, 1947.

61. Rickey's claim against the owners turned out to be exaggerated. He was referring to a brief comment in a long document that owners agreed to but probably never read. Only MacPhail and Connie Mack ever spoke out

against Rickey's plan. Lowenfish, *Branch Rickey*, 451; NYT February 18 and 19, 1948.

62. DW February 18, 1948.

63. Smith, "The Sports Beat," PC August 23, 1947.

64. PC December 11, 1943; Silber, *Press Box Red*, 68.

65. DW May 5, 1948; Wendell Smith File, HOF, n.d.; ADW May 7, 1948; CD May 15, 1948.

66. Lacy, "From A to Z," AA June 25, 1949; A. S. "Doc" Young, "Sportivanting," CCP May 15, 1948.

67. NYAN June 26 and August 3, 1946; "Wendell Smith's Sports Beat," PC April 16, 1949.

68. PC July 17, 1948; Veeck, *Veeck as in Wreck*, 183–184; Paige, *Pitchin Man*, 12; "Wendell Smith's Sports Beat," PC January 14, 1961.

69. DW October 12 and 18, December 31, 1948.

70. NYAN June 26, 1948; PC February 19, 1949; CD September 24, 1949.

71. Young, "Fay Says," CD February 19, 1949; "Wendell Smith's Sports Beat," PC February 19, 1949. It is likely that Fay Young was on Saperstein's payroll at this time.

72. DW February 11, 1949; DW March 3, 1949; CD May 14, 1949; letter from Saperstein to Hayes, February 15, 1949; Hayes to Saperstein June 29, 1949, Saperstein to Hayes, July 28, 1949; Parker Carroll to T. H. Hayes, August 27, 1949; Hayes to Saperstein, September 12, 1949, Hayes Collection, Box I, folder 4.

73. Green, *Spinning*, 229–233.

74. NYAN June 24, 1950; ADW June 28, 1950; Burley, "Confidentially Yours," PT September 16, 1950.

75. PC May 24 and December 27, 1952.

76. Greenberg, *Hank Greenberg*, 249.

77. Letter from T. Y. Baird to J. B. Martin, undated. Baird Collection, 1.3; PC June 30, September 8, 1951.

78. Holway, *Voices*, 181–186, 248; Rosengarten, "Reading the Hops," 71; McNary, *Double Duty*, 130, 136.

79. DW April 11, 12, 22, 1949; "From the Press Box," DW April 27, 1949. Black stars offset the financial losses in ticket sales to white fans who no longer attended games by bringing in others who would come to see a winning team. Bench players did not provide a financial incentive, and owners were less likely (given their lack of enthusiasm for integration) to hire them. Hanssen, "The Cost of Discrimination," 606. See also Lanning, "Productivity, Discrimination, and Lost Profits."

80. DW June 2, 23, 27, September 1, 1949; May 5, 1950.

81. DW July 11 and 20, 1949.

82. DW August 29, 1949.

83. DW February 14 and May 15, 1950.

84. DW August 3, 1950.

85. "Wendell Smith's Sports Beat," PC May 6, 1950; PT January 9, 1951; letter from Ed Gottlieb to Hilda Bolden, May 3, 1951, Bolden Papers; ADW August 4, 1951; PT March 14, 1953; Poindexter, "Sports I View," PT July 21, 1953.

86. DW January 12, 1950; January 22 and 30, 1951; January 13 and 25, February 14 and 22, 1954.

87. NYAN May 8, 1954.

# BIBLIOGRAPHY

## Newspapers

AA/BAA *[Baltimore] Afro-American*

ADW *Atlanta Daily World*

BW *Birmingham World*

CCP *Cleveland Call and Post*

CD *Chicago Defender*

DW *Daily Worker*

EB *Evening Bulletin*

IR *Indianapolis Recorder*

NYA *New York Age*

NYAN *New York Amsterdam News*

NJG Norfolk *Journal and Guide*

NYT *New York Times*

PM *PM*

PV *People's Voice*

PT *Philadelphia Tribune*

PC *Pittsburgh Courier*

SN *Sporting News*

SW *Sunday Worker*

WP *Washington Post*

## Archival Resources

NEP—Newark Eagle Papers, Newark Public Library

Clipping Files, Baseball Hall of Fame

Negro League Collection, Baseball Hall of Fame

Wendell Smith Papers, Baseball Hall of Fame

Art Carter Collection, Moorland-Spingarn Research Center, Howard University

Ed Bolden Collection, Moorland-Spingarn Research Center, Howard University

T. Y. Baird Papers, Spencer Library, University of Kansas

Jackie Robinson Papers, Manuscript Division, Library of Congress, Washington, D.C.

Oral Histories, American Jewish Committee, American Jews in Sports Collection, New York Public Library

Ed Gottlieb Files, Urban Archives, Temple University, Philadelphia, Pa.

Harry Passon Files, Urban Archives, Temple University, Philadelphia, Pa.

J Michael Kenyon Files, private collection

T. H. Hayes Collection, Memphis Public Library

## Interviews

Leaden Bernstein
Thomas Burt
Curtis Caldwell
Roger Kahn
Bill Mardo
Ruth Ost
Hannah Penner
Jerry Pollock
Lester Rodney
James Sturm
R. J. Taylor

Adelson, Bruce. *Brushing Back Jim Crow: The Integration of Minor-League Baseball in the American South*. Charlottesville: University Press of Virginia, 1999.

Alexander, Michael. *Jazz Age Jews*. Princeton: Princeton University Press, 2001.

Alpert, Rebecca. "Jackie Robinson, Jewish Icon." *Shofar: An Interdisciplinary Journal of Jewish Studies* 26.2 (2008): 42–58.

Ardell, Jean Hastings. *Breaking into Baseball: Women and the National Pastime*. Carbondale: Southern Illinois University Press, 2005.

Badham, John. *The Bingo Long Traveling All-Stars & Motor Kings*. Universal City, Ca. Universal Studios, 1976.

Baer, Hans A., and Merrill Singer, eds. *African American Religion: Varieties of Protest and Accommodation*. 2nd ed. Knoxville: University of Tennessee Press, 2002.

Bak, Richard. *Turkey Stearnes and the Detroit Stars: The Negro Leagues in Detroit, 1919–1933*. Detroit: Wayne State University Press, 1994.

Baker, William J. *Jesse Owens: An American Life*. New York: Free Press, 1986.

Barthel, Thomas. *Baseball's Peerless Semipros: The Brooklyn Bushwicks of Dexter Park*. Haworth, N.J.: St. Johann Press, 2009.

Boles, John B. *Masters & Slaves in the House of the Lord: Race and Religion in the American South, 1740–1870*. Lexington: University Press of Kentucky, 1988.

Brashler, William, and introduction Peter C. Bjarkman. *The Bingo Long Traveling All-Stars and Motor Kings*. Urbana: University of Illinois Press, 1993.

Brock, Lisa, and Bijan Bayne. "Not Just Black: African-Americans, Cubans, and Baseball." In *Between Race and Empire: African-Americans and Cubans before the Cuban Revolution*, edited by Lisa Brock and Digna Castañeda Fuertes, 168–204. Philadelphia: Temple University Press, 1998.

Brooks, Joanna. "Prince Hall, Freemasonry, and Genealogy." *African American Review* 34.2 (2000): 197–216.

Brown, Phil. *The Harlem Globetrotters.* Columbia Picture Corporation, Burbank, Ca. 1951.

Bruce, Janet. *The Kansas City Monarchs: Champions of Black Baseball.* Lawrence: University Press of Kansas, 1985.

Brunson, James E. *The Early Image of Black Baseball: Race and Representation in the Popular Press, 1871–1890.* Jefferson, N.C.: McFarland, 2009.

———. "'A Mirthful Spectacle': Race, Blackface Minstrelsy, and Base Ball, 1874–1888." *NINE: A Journal of Baseball History and Culture* 17.2 (2009): 13–30.

Bryant, Howard. *Shut Out: A Story of Race and Baseball in Boston.* New York: Routledge, 2002.

Burgos, Adrian, Jr. "Left Out: Afro-Latinos, Black Baseball, and the Revision of Baseball's Racial History." *Social Text* 27.1 (Spring 2009): 37–58.

———. Playing America's Game: Baseball, Latinos, and the Color Line. Berkeley: University of California Press, 2007.

Burns, Ken. *Baseball. Fifth Inning, 1930–1940, Shadow Ball.* PBS Home Video, Alexandria, Va. 1994.

Campanella, Roy. *It's Good to Be Alive.* New York: Little, Brown, 1959.

Carnes, Mark C. *Secret Ritual and Manhood in Victorian America.* New Haven: Yale University Press, 1989.

Carr, Steven Alan. *Hollywood and Anti-Semitism: A Cultural History Up to World War II.* New York: Cambridge University Press, 2001.

Carroll, Brian. "Early Twentieth-Century Heroes: Coverage of Negro League Baseball in the *Pittsburgh Courier* and the *Chicago Defender.*" *Journalism History* 32.1 (2006): 34–42.

———. *When to Stop the Cheering: The Black Press, the Black Community, and the Integration of Professional Baseball.* New York: Routledge, 2007.

Chadwick, Bruce. *When the Game was Black and White: The Illustrated History of the Negro Leagues.* New York: Abbeville Press, 1992.

Chireau, Yvonne Patricia, and Nathaniel Deutsch, eds. *Black Zion: African American Religious Encounters with Judaism.* New York: Oxford University Press, 2000.

Church of God and Saints of Christ, and Historical Committee. *History of the Church of God and Saints of Christ.* Suffolk, Va.: The Church, 1992.

Church of God and Saints of Christ, Temple Beth El website, http://www.cogasoc. com/.

Clark, Dick, Larry Lester, and Society for American Baseball Research Negro Leagues Committee, eds. *The Negro Leagues Book.* Cleveland: Society for American Baseball Research, 1994.

"Connie Morgan." *Sport Magazine,* July 1954: 88.

Cripps, Thomas. *Slow Fade to Black: The Negro in American Film, 1900–1942.* New York: Oxford University Press, 1977.

Curtis, Edward E., and Danielle Brune Sigler, eds. *The New Black Gods: Arthur Huff Fauset and the Study of African American Religions*. Bloomington: Indiana University Press, 2009.

Debono, Paul. *The Indianapolis ABCs: History of a Premier Team in the Negro Leagues*. Jefferson, N.C.: McFarland, 1997.

Dickson, Paul, et al. *The Dickson Baseball Dictionary*. 3rd ed. New York: W.W. Norton, 2009.

Diner, Hasia R. *In the Almost Promised Land: American Jews and Blacks, 1915–1935*. Westport, Conn.: Greenwood Press, 1977.

Dinnerstein, Leonard. *Antisemitism in America*. New York: Oxford University Press, 1994.

Distler, Paul Antonie. "Exit the Racial Comics." *Educational Theatre Journal* 18.3 (1966): 247–254.

Dixon, Phil, and Patrick J. Hannigan. *The Negro Baseball Leagues, 1867–1955: A Photographic History*. Mattituck, N.Y.: Amereon House, 1992.

Dodson, Dan W. "The Integration of Negroes in Baseball." *Journal of Educational Sociology* 28.2 (1954): 73–82.

Dorinson, Joseph, and Joram Warmund, eds. *Jackie Robinson: Race, Sports, and the American Dream*. Armonk, N.Y.: M. E. Sharpe, 1998.

Duberman, Martin B. *Paul Robeson*. New York: Knopf, 1988.

Dumenil, Lynn. *Freemasonry and American Culture, 1880–1930*. Princeton: Princeton University Press, 1984.

Durocher, Leo. *The Dodgers and Me: The Inside Story*. Chicago: Ziff-Davis, 1948.

Dvorak, Katherine. "After Apocalypse, Moses." In Boles, *Masters & Slaves*, 1988, 173–191.

Early, Gerald. "Unpopular Answer to a Popular Question." *108 Magazine*, Spring 2007 [formerly at http://news-info.wustl.edu/news/page/normal/9233.html; no longer online].

Echevarría, Roberto González. *The Pride of Havana: A History of Cuban Baseball*. New York: Oxford University Press, 1999.

Eig, Jonathan. *Opening Day: The Story of Jackie Robinson's First Season*. New York: Simon & Schuster, 2007.

Ellison, Ralph. *Invisible Man*. New York: Random House, 1952.

Ely, Melvin Patrick. *The Adventures of Amos 'n' Andy: A Social History of an American Phenomenon*. Charlottesville: University Press of Virginia, 2001.

Erdman, Harley. *Staging the Jew: The Performance of an American Ethnicity, 1860–1920*. New Brunswick: Rutgers University Press, 1997.

Everbach, Tracy. "Breaking Baseball Barriers: The 1953–1954 Negro League and Expansion of Women's Public Roles." *American Journalism* 22.1 (2005): 13–33.

Falkner, David. *Great Time Coming: The Life of Jackie Robinson, from Baseball to Birmingham*. New York: Simon & Schuster, 1995.

Fetter, Henry. "From 'Stooge' to 'Czar': Judge Landis, the *Daily Worker*, and the Integration of Baseball." *American Communist History* 6.1 (2007): 29–63.

Forman, Seth. *Blacks in the Jewish Mind: A Crisis of Liberalism*. New York: New York University Press, 1998.

Frank, Stanley Bernard. *The Jew in Sports*. New York: Miles, 1936.

Franklin, V. P., ed. *African Americans and Jews in the Twentieth Century: Studies in Convergence and Conflict*. Columbia: University of Missouri Press. 1998.

Freedman, Jonathan. *Klezmer America: Jewishness, Ethnicity, Modernity*. New York: Columbia University Press, 2008.

Freedman, William. *More Than a Pastime: An Oral History of Baseball Fans*. Jefferson, N.C.: McFarland, 1998.

Fuchs, Robert S., and Wayne Soini. *Judge Fuchs and the Boston Braves, 1923–1935*. Jefferson, N.C.: McFarland, 1998.

Gabler, Neal. *An Empire of Their Own: How the Jews Invented Hollywood*. New York: Doubleday, 1989.

Gay, Timothy. *Satch, Dizzy & Rapid Robert: The Wild Saga of Interracial Baseball before Jackie Robinson*. New York: Simon & Schuster, 2010.

Gitelman, Zvi Y. "Conclusion: The Nature and Viability of Jewish Religious and Secular Identities." In *Religion or Ethnicity: Jewish Identities in Evolution*, edited by Zvi Y. Gitelman, 303–322. New Brunswick: Rutgers University Press, 2009.

Gold, Roberta S. "The Black Jews of Harlem: Representation, Identity, and Race, 1920–1939." *American Quarterly* 55.2 (2003) 179–225.

Goldfarb, Jim. "Harlem's Team: The New York Lincoln Giants." *Afro-Americans in New York Life and History* 26.2 (2002): 7–65.

Goldscheider, Calvin. "Judaism, Community, and Jewish Culture in American Life: Continuities and Transformations." In *Religion or Ethnicity: Jewish Identities in Evolution*, edited by Zvi Y. Gitelman, 267–285. New Brunswick: Rutgers University Press, 2009.

Goldstein, Eric L. *The Price of Whiteness: Jews, Race, and American Identity*. Princeton: Princeton University Press, 2006.

Green, Alfred. *The Jackie Robinson Story*. Twentieth Century Fox, Beverly Hills, Ca. 1950.

Green, Ben. *Spinning the Globe: The Rise, Fall, and Return to Greatness of the Harlem Globetrotters*. New York: Amistad, 2005.

Greenberg, Cheryl Lynn. *Troubling the Waters: Black-Jewish Relations in the American Century*. Princeton: Princeton University Press, 2006.

Greenberg, Hank, and Ira Berkow, eds. *Hank Greenberg: The Story of My Life*. New York: Times Books, 1989.

Gubar, Susan. *Racechanges: White Skin, Black Face in American Culture*. New York: Oxford University Press, 1997.

Hanssen, Andrew. "The Cost of Discrimination: A Study of Major League Baseball." *Southern Economic Journal* 64.3 (1998): 603–627.

Haupert, Michael J., and Kenneth Winter. "The Old Fellows and the Colonels: Innovation and Survival in Segregated Baseball." *Black Ball* 1.1 (Spring 2008): 79–92.

Haupert, Michael J. "Pay, Performance, and Race During the Integration Era." *Black Ball* 2.1 (Spring 2009): 37–51.

Heaphy, Leslie A. *Black Baseball and Chicago: Essays on the Players, Teams, and Games of the Negro Leagues' Most Important City.* Jefferson, N.C.: McFarland, 2006.

———. *The Negro Leagues, 1869–1960.* Jefferson, N.C.: McFarland, 2003.

———. *Satchel Paige and Company: Essays on the Kansas City Monarchs, Their Greatest Star and the Negro Leagues.* Jefferson, N.C.: McFarland, 2007.

Heward, Bill, and Dimitri V. Gat. *Some Are Called Clowns: A Season with the Last of the Great Barnstorming Baseball Teams.* New York: Crowell, 1974.

Hietala, Thomas R. *The Fight of the Century: Jack Johnson, Joe Louis, and the Struggle for Racial Equality.* Armonk, N.Y.: M. E. Sharpe, 2002.

Holway, John B. *Black Diamonds: Life in the Negro Leagues from the Men Who Lived It.* Westport, Conn.: Meckler, 1989.

———. *Voices from the Great Black Baseball Leagues.* Rev. ed. New York: Da Capo Press, 1992.

Howard, Darrell J. *"Sunday Coming": Black Baseball in Virginia.* Jefferson, N.C.: McFarland, 2002.

Howe, James Wong. *Go Man Go.* United Artists, Beverly Hills, Ca. 1954.

Inter-university Consortium for Political and Social Research., ed. *Censuses of Religious Bodies, 1906–1936 United States Department of Commerce Bureau of the Census.* Ann Arbor: Inter-university Consortium for Political and Social Research [distributor], 1984.

Isaac, Walter. "Orienting Afro-American Judaism: A Critique of White Normativity in Literature on Black Jews in America." In *A Companion to African-American Studies,* edited by Lewis R.Gordon and Jane Anna Gordon, 512–542. Malden, Mass.: Blackwell Pub, 2006.

Jacobson, Matthew Frye. *Whiteness of a Different Color: European Immigrants and the Alchemy of Race.* Cambridge: Harvard University Press, 1998.

Jaher, Frederic Cople. "Antisemitism in American Athletics." *Shofar: An Interdisciplinary Journal of Jewish Studies* 20.1 (2001): 61–73.

"Jesus' Boys: Israelite House Of David Baseball," available at www.maryscityof-david.org/html/baseball.html.

Jordan, David M., Larry R. Gerlach, and John P. Rossi. "Bill Veeck and the 1943 Sale of the Phillies: A Baseball Myth Exploded." *The National Pastime* 18 (1998): 3–12.

Kahn, Roger. "The Jackie Robinson I Remember." *The Journal of Blacks in Higher Education* 14 (1996): 88–93.

———. *The Boys of Summer.* New York: Harper & Row, 1972.

Kelley, Brent P., ed. *The Negro Leagues Revisited: Conversations with 66 More Baseball Heroes*. Jefferson, N.C.: McFarland, 2000.

———. *Voices from the Negro Leagues: Conversations with 52 Baseball Standouts of the Period 1924–1960*. Jefferson, N.C.: McFarland, 1998.

Kelly, John. "Integrating America: Jackie Robinson, Critical Events and Baseball Black and White." *The International Journal of the History of Sport* 22.6 (2005): 1011–1035.

Kempner, Aviva. *The Life and Times of Hank Greenberg*. Twentieth Century Fox Home Entertainment, Beverly Hills, Ca. 2001.

Kimball, Richard Ian. "Beyond the 'Great Experiment': Integrated Baseball Comes to Indianapolis." *Journal of Sport History* 26.1 (1999): 142–162.

Klima, John. *Willie's Boys: The 1948 Birmingham Black Barons, the Last Negro League World Series, and the Making of a Baseball Legend*. Hoboken: John Wiley & Sons, 2009.

Krzemienski, Ed. "On the Initial Sack: Goose Tatum—Two-Sport Star." *NINE: A Journal of Baseball History and Culture* 14.2 (2006): 59–67.

Kuklick, Bruce. *To Every Thing a Season: Shibe Park and Urban Philadelphia, 1909–1976*. Princeton: Princeton University Press, 1991.

"Ku Klux Klan Faces Hebrews Labor Day," *Washington Post*, September 1, 1926, available at http://jeffreygoldberg.theatlantic.com/archives/2009/05/what_a_game.php.

Kuska, Bob. *Hot Potato: How Washington and New York Gave Birth to Black Basketball and Changed America's Game Forever*. Charlottesville: University of Virginia Press, 2004.

Lacy, Sam, and Moses J. Newson. *Fighting for Fairness: The Life Story of Hall of Fame Sportswriter Sam Lacy*. Centreville, Md.: Tidewater Publishers, 1998.

Lamb, Chris. *Blackout: The Untold Story of Jackie Robinson's First Spring Training*. Lincoln: University of Nebraska Press, 2004.

Lanctot, Neil. *Fair Dealing and Clean Playing: The Hilldale Club and the Development of Black Professional Baseball, 1910–1932*. Jefferson, N.C.: McFarland, 1994.

———. *Negro League Baseball: The Rise and Ruin of a Black Institution*. Philadelphia: University of Pennsylvania Press, 2004.

Landing, James E. *Black Judaism: Story of an American Movement*. Durham: Carolina Academic Press, 2002.

Lanning, Jonathan A. "Productivity, Discrimination, and Lost Profits During Baseball's Integration." *The Journal of Economic History* 70.4 (2010): 940–63.

Leavy, Jane. *Sandy Koufax: A Lefty's Legacy*. New York: Harper Collins, 2002.

Lederhendler, Eli. *Jewish Immigrants and American Capitalism, 1880–1920: From Caste to Class*. New York: Cambridge University Press, 2009.

Leonard, Buck, and James A. Riley. *Buck Leonard: The Black Lou Gehrig: The Hall of Famer's Story in His Own Words*. New York: Carroll & Graf, 1995.

Lester, Larry, Sammy J. Miller, and Dick Clark, eds. *Black Baseball in Detroit*. Chicago: Arcadia, 2000.

Lester, Larry, and foreword by Joe Black. *Black Baseball's National Showcase: The East-West All-Star Game, 1933–1953*. Lincoln: University of Nebraska Press, 2001.

Levine, Lawrence W. *Black Culture and Black Consciousness: Afro-American Folk Thought from Slavery to Freedom*. New York: Oxford University Press, 1977.

Levine, Peter. *Ellis Island to Ebbets Field: Sport and the American Jewish Experience*. New York: Oxford University Press, 1992.

Lewis, David Levering. "Parallels and Divergences: Assimilationist Strategies of Afro-American and Jewish Elites from 1910 to the Early 1930s." *The Journal of American History* 71.3 (1984): 543–564.

Lewis, Earl. *In Their Own Interests: Race, Class, and Power in Twentieth-Century Norfolk, Virginia*. Berkeley: University of California Press, 1991.

Liebman, Arthur. "Ties That Bind: The Jewish Support for the Left in the United States," *American Jewish Historical Quarterly* 66.2 (December 1976): 285–321.

Liscio, Stephanie. *Integrating Cleveland Baseball: Media Activism, the Integration of the Indians, and the Demise of the Negro League Buckeyes*. Jefferson, N.C.: McFarland, 2010.

Litvak, Joseph. *The Un-Americans: Jews, the Blacklist, and Stoolpigeon Culture*. Durham: Duke University Press, 2010.

Lomax, Michael E. *Black Baseball Entrepreneurs, 1860–1901: Operating by Any Means Necessary*. Syracuse: Syracuse University Press, 2003.

———. *Black Baseball Entrepreneurs, 1902–1931: The Rise and Decline of the Negro National and Eastern Colored Leagues*. Syracuse University Press, forthcoming.

———. "Black Baseball, Black Entrepreneurs, Black Community." PhD diss., Ohio State University, 1996.

———. "Black Entrepreneurship in the National Pastime: The Rise of Semi-professional Baseball in Black Chicago, 1890–1915." *Journal of Sport History* 25.1 (1998): 43–65.

Lott, Eric. *Love and Theft: Blackface Minstrelsy and the American Working Class*. New York: Oxford University Press, 1993.

Lowenfish, Lee. *Branch Rickey: Baseball's Ferocious Gentleman*. Lincoln: University of Nebraska Press, 2007.

———. "When All Heaven Rejoiced: Branch Rickey and the Origins of the Breaking of the Color Line." In *Out of the Shadows: African American Baseball from the Cuban Giants to Jackie Robinson*, edited by Bill Kirwin, 15–30. Lincoln: University of Nebraska Press, 2005.

Luke, Bob. *The Baltimore Elite Giants: Sport and Society in the Age of Negro League Baseball*. Baltimore: The Johns Hopkins University Press, 2009.

Mann, Arthur William. *Branch Rickey: American in Action*. Boston: Houghton Mifflin, 1957.

Mardo, Bill. "Robinson—Robeson." In Dorinson, *Jackie Robinson*, 1998. 98–106.

Marshall, William. *Baseball's Pivotal Era, 1945–1951*. Lexington: University Press of Kentucky, 1999.

Martin, Alfred M., and Alfred T. Martin. *The Negro Leagues in New Jersey: A History*. Jefferson, N.C.: McFarland, 2008.

Mathewson, Alfred Dennis. "Major League Baseball's Monopoly Power and the Negro Leagues." *American Business Law Journal* 35.2 (1998): 291–318.

Maxwell, William J. *New Negro, Old Left: African-American Writing and Communism between the Wars*. New York: Columbia University Press, 1999.

McDowell, Winston C. "Keeping Them 'In the Same Boat Together'?: Sufi Abdul Hamid, African Americans, Jews, and the Harlem Jobs Boycotts." In Franklin, *African Americans and Jews*, 1998. 208–236.

McNary, Kyle P. *Black Baseball: A History of African-Americans & the National Game*. New York: Sterling, 2003.

———. *Ted "Double Duty" Radcliffe: 36 Years of Pitching & Catching in Baseball's Negro Leagues*. Minneapolis: McNary, 1994.

———. "North Dakota Baseball History," available at http://www.pitchblackbaseball.com/northdakota.html.

McNeil, William F. *The California Winter League: America's First Integrated Professional Baseball League*. Jefferson, N.C.: McFarland, 2002.

Melnick, Jeffrey Paul. "Some Notes on the Erotics of 'Black-Jewish Relations.'" *Shofar: An Interdisciplinary Journal of Jewish Studies* 23.4 (2005): 9–25.

———. *Black-Jewish Relations on Trial: Leo Frank and Jim Conley in the New South*. Jackson: University Press of Mississippi, 2000.

———. *A Right to Sing the Blues: African Americans, Jews, and American Popular Song*. Cambridge: Harvard University Press, 1999.

Mendelsohn, Ezra, ed. *Jews and the Sporting Life*. New York: Oxford University Press, 2008.

Merwin, Ted. *In Their Own Image: New York Jews in Jazz Age Popular Culture*. New Brunswick: Rutgers University Press, 2006.

Miñoso, Minnie, and Herb Fagen, eds. *Just Call Me Minnie: My Six Decades in Baseball*. Champaign, Ill.: Sagamore, 1994.

Mohl, Raymond A. "Clowning Around: The Miami Ethiopian Clowns and Cultural Conflict in Black Baseball." *Tequesta: The Journal of the Historical Association of Southern Florida* 62 (2002): 40–67.

Moore, Deborah Dash. *At Home in America: Second Generation New York Jews*. New York: Columbia University Press, 1981.

Motley, Bob, and Byron Motley. *Ruling over Monarchs, Giants & Stars: Umpiring in the Negro Leagues & Beyond*. Champaign, Ill.: Sports, 2007.

Muller, Jerry Z. *Capitalism and the Jews*. Princeton, N.J.: Princeton University Press, 2010.

Muraskin, William A. *Middle-Class Blacks in a White Society: Prince Hall Freemasonry in America*. Berkeley: University of California Press, 1975.

Nance, Susan. "Mystery of the Moorish Science Temple: Southern Blacks and American Alternative Spirituality in 1920s Chicago." *Religion and American Culture* 12.2 (2002): 123–166.

Nasaw, David. *Going Out: The Rise and Fall of Public Amusements*. New York: BasicBooks, 1993.

Nathan, Daniel A. "Anti-Semitism and the Black Sox Scandal." *Nine: A Journal of Baseball History and Social Policy Perspectives* 4.1 (1995): 94–101.

Norwood, Stephen H., and Harold Brackman. "Going to Bat for Jackie Robinson: The Jewish Role in Breaking Baseball's Color Line." *Journal of Sport History* 26.1 (1999): 115–141.

Overmyer, James. *Effa Manley and the Newark Eagles*. Metuchen, N.J.: Scarecrow Press, 1993.

Owens, Jesse, and Paul G. Neimark, eds. *Blackthink My Life as Black Man and White Man*. New York: William Morrow, 1970.

———. *I Have Changed*. New York: William Morrow, 1972.

Paige, Satchel, and David Lipman, eds. *Maybe I'll Pitch Forever: A Great Baseball Player Tells the Hilarious Story Behind the Legend*. Garden City: Doubleday, 1962.

Patkin, Max, and Stan Hochman. *The Clown Prince of Baseball*. Waco, Tex.: WRS, 1994.

Peterson, Robert. *Only the Ball Was White*. Englewood Cliffs, N.J.: Prentice-Hall, 1970.

Pietrusza, David. *Judge and Jury: The Life and Times of Judge Kenesaw Mountain Landis*. South Bend: Diamond Communications, 1998.

Pollock, Alan J., and James A. Riley. *Barnstorming to Heaven: Syd Pollock and His Great Black Teams*. Tuscaloosa: University of Alabama Press, 2006.

Polner, Murray, and foreword Branch B. Rickey. *Branch Rickey: A Biography*. Rev. ed. Jefferson, N.C.: McFarland, 2007.

Povich, Shirley, ed. *All those Mornings...at the Post: The Twentieth Century in Sports from Famed Washington Post Columnist Shirley Povich*. New York: Public Affairs, 2005.

Powell, Larry. *Black Barons of Birmingham: The South's Greatest Negro League Team and Its Players*. Jefferson, N.C.: McFarland, 2009.

Quirk, James P., and Rodney D. Fort, eds. *Hard Ball: The Abuse of Power in Pro Team Sports*. Princeton: Princeton University Press, 1999.

Raboteau, Albert J. *Slave Religion: The "Invisible Institution" in the Antebellum South*. New York: Oxford University Press, 1980.

Rampersad, Arnold. *Jackie Robinson: A Biography*. New York: Knopf, 1997.

Reisler, Jim, and foreword Don Newcombe. *Black Writers/Black Baseball: An Anthology of Articles from Black Sportswriters Who Covered the Negro Leagues*. Rev. ed. Jefferson, N.C.: McFarland, 2007.

Ribowsky, Mark. *A Complete History of the Negro Leagues, 1884 to 1955*. Secaucus: Carol Publishing Group, 1995.

———. *Don't Look Back: Satchel Paige in the Shadows of Baseball*. New York: Simon & Schuster, 1994.

———. *The Power and the Darkness: The Life of Josh Gibson in the Shadows of the Game*. New York: Simon & Schuster, 1996.

Riess, Steven A. *Sports and the American Jew*. Syracuse: Syracuse University Press, 1998.

———. *Touching Base: Professional Baseball and American Culture in the Progressive Era*. Westport, Conn.: Greenwood Press, 1980.

Riley, James A. *The Biographical Encyclopedia of the Negro Baseball Leagues*. New York: Carroll & Graf Publishers, 1994.

Robinson, Frazier, and Paul Bauer, eds. *Catching Dreams: My Life in the Negro Baseball Leagues*. Syracuse: Syracuse University Press, 1999.

Robinson, Jackie, and Alfred Duckett. *Breakthrough to the Big League: The Story of Jackie Robinson*. New York: Harper & Row, 1965.

———. *I Never Had It Made: An Autobiography*. Hopewell, N.J.: Ecco Press, 1995.

Robinson, Jackie, and Wendell Smith. *Jackie Robinson, My Own Story, as Told to Wendell Smith*. New York: Greenberg, 1948.

Robinson, Jackie, and Michael G. Long, eds. *First Class Citizenship: The Civil Rights Letters of Jackie Robinson*. New York: Times Books, 2007.

Robinson, Rachel. *Jackie Robinson: An Intimate Portrait*. New York: Harry Abrams, 1996.

Robinson, Sharon. *Jackie's Gift*. New York: Viking, 2010.

Roediger, David R. *Working toward Whiteness: How America's Immigrants Became White: The Strange Journey from Ellis Island to the Suburbs*. New York: Basic Books, 2006.

Rogin, Michael Paul. *Blackface, White Noise: Jewish Immigrants in the Hollywood Melting Pot*. Berkeley: University of California Press, 1996.

Rogosin, Donn. *Invisible Men: Life in Baseball's Negro Leagues*. New York: Atheneum, 1983.

Roper, Scott. "Another Chink in Jim Crow: Race and Baseball on the Northern Plains, 1900–1935." *Nine: A Journal of Baseball History* 2.1 (1993): 75–89.

Rosengarten, Theodore. "Reading the Hops, Recollections of Lorenzo Piper Davis and the Negro Baseball League." *Southern Exposure* 5.2–3 (1973): 62–79.

Ross, Andrew, and David Dyte. "Dexter Park." 2010. Available at http://www.covehurst.net/ddyte/brooklyn/dexter.html.

Rothstein, Edward. "A Tip of the Hat to Pokes in the Eye." *New York Times*, August 28, 2009, Movies: 21.

Rowan, Carl Thomas. *Wait Till Next Year: The Life Story of Jackie Robinson*. New York: Random House, 1960.

Ruck, Rob. *Sandlot Seasons: Sport in Black Pittsburgh*. Urbana: University of Illinois Press, 1993.

Rusinack, Kelly Elaine. "Baseball on the Radical Agenda: The Daily and Sunday Worker on the Desegregation of Major League Baseball, 1933 to 1947." MA thesis, Clemson University, 1995.

Rust, Art, Jr. *"Get That Nigger Off the Field!": A Sparkling, Informal History of the Black Man in Baseball*. New York: Delacorte Press, 1976.

Salzman, Jack, and Cornel West, eds. *Struggles in the Promised Land: Toward a History of Black-Jewish Relations in the United States*. New York: Oxford University Press, 1997.

Schacht, Al, and Edward Keyes. *My Own Particular Screwball: An Informal Autobiography*. Garden City, N.Y.: Doubleday, 1955.

Scott, William R. *The Sons of Sheba's Race: African-Americans and the Italo-Ethiopian War, 1935–1941*. Bloomington: Indiana University Press, 1993.

Silber, Irwin, and Lester Rodney. *Press Box Red: The Story of Lester Rodney, the Communist Who Helped Break the Color Line in American Sports*. Philadelphia: Temple University Press, 2003.

Simons, William M. "The Athlete as Jewish Standard Bearer: Media Images of Hank Greenberg." *Jewish Social Studies* 44.2 (1982): 95–112.

Slavet, Eliza. *Racial Fever: Freud and the Jewish Question*. New York: Fordham University Press, 2009.

Snyder, Brad. *Beyond the Shadow of the Senators: The Untold Story of the Homestead Grays and the Integration of Baseball*. Chicago: Contemporary Books, 2003.

———. *A Well-Paid Slave: Curt Flood's Fight for Free Agency in Professional Sports*. New York: Viking, 2006.

Snyder, Robert W. *The Voice of the City: Vaudeville and Popular Culture in New York*. Chicago: I. R. Dee, 2000.

Staub, Michael E. *Torn at the Roots: The Crisis of Jewish Liberalism in Postwar America*. New York: Columbia University Press, 2002.

Stewart, Jacqueline Najuma. *Migrating to the Movies: Cinema and Black Urban Modernity*. Berkeley: University of California Press, 2005.

Stout, Glenn, and Dick Johnson. *Jackie Robinson: Between the Baselines*. San Francisco: Woodford Press, 1997.

Sturm, James. *The Golem's Mighty Swing*. Montreal: Drawn and Quarterly, 2001.

Sundquist, Eric J. *Strangers in the Land: Blacks, Jews, Post-Holocaust America*. Cambridge: Belknap Press of Harvard University Press, 2005.

Swanton, Barry. *The ManDak League: Haven for Former Negro League Ballplayers, 1950–1957*. Jefferson N.C.: McFarland, 2006.

Thorn, John, and Jules Tygiel. "Jackie Robinson's Signing: The Real, Untold Story." 2010. Available at http://www.mrbaseball.com/index.php?Itemid=57&id=23&option=com_content&task=view

Toll, Robert C. *Blacking Up: The Minstrel Show in Nineteenth Century America*. New York: Oxford University Press, 1974.

Tollin, Michael. *Hank Aaron Chasing the Dream*. Turner Home Entertainment, Atlanta, Ga. 1995.

*Treasures from American Film Archives Encore Edition Program 2*. Scott Simmon, Curator. United States. Image Entertainment, 2000.

Tye, Larry. *Satchel: The Life and Times of an American Legend*. New York: Random House, 2009.

Tygiel, Jules. "Revisiting Bill Veeck and the 1943 Phillies." *The Baseball Research Journal* 35 (2007): 109–114.

———. *Baseball's Great Experiment: Jackie Robinson and His Legacy*. New York: Oxford University Press, 1983.

———. *Past Time: Baseball as History*. New York: Oxford University Press, 2000.

U. S. Congress. *Congressional Record*. Vol. 151, March 2, 2005. E333–35.

Veeck, Bill, and Edward Linn, eds. *Veeck as in Wreck: The Autobiography of Bill Veeck*. Chicago: University of Chicago Press, 2001.

Walker, Corey D. B. *A Noble Fight: African American Freemasonry and the Struggle for Democracy in America*. Urbana and Chicago: University of Illinois Press, 2010.

Walker, Juliet E. K. *The History of Black Business in America: Capitalism, Race, Entrepreneurship*. New York: Macmillan Library Reference, 1998.

Wallace, Maurice. "'Are we Men?': Prince Hall, Martin Delany, and the Masculine Ideal in Black Freemasonry, 1775–1865." *American Literary History* 9.3 (1997): 396–424.

Watkins, Mel. *On the Real Side: Laughing, Lying, and Signifying: The Underground Tradition of African-American Humor that Transformed American Culture, from Slavery to Richard Pryor*. New York: Simon & Schuster, 1994.

———. *Stepin Fetchit: The Life and Times of Lincoln Perry*. New York: Pantheon Books, 2005.

Weingarten, Aviva. *Jewish Organizations' Response to Communism and to Senator McCarthy*. London: Vallentine Mitchell/European Jewish Publication Society, 2008.

Westcott, Rich. *The Mogul: Eddie Gottlieb, Philadelphia Sports Legend and Pro Basketball Pioneer*. Philadelphia: Temple University Press, 2008.

White, Sol. *Sol White's History of Colored Base Ball, with Other Documents on the Early Black Game, 1886–1936*. Lincoln: University of Nebraska Press, 1995.

Wilson, Lyle Kenai. *Sunday Afternoons at Garfield Park: Seattle's Black Baseball Teams, 1911–1951*. Everett, Wash.: Lowell, 1997.

Wilson, Nick. *Voices from the Pastime: Oral Histories of Surviving Major Leaguers, Negro Leaguers, Cuban Leaguers, and Writers, 1920–1934*. Jefferson, N.C.: McFarland, 2000.

Winter, Kenneth, and Michael Haupert. "The East-West Game: More than Meets the Eye?" Paper presented at 21st Cooperstown Symposium on Baseball and American Culture. Cooperstown, New York, June 3–5, 2009.

Wolinsky, Russell. "Arlie Latham: 19th Century Clown Prince of Baseball." <http://209.23.71.87/library/columns/rw_040618.htm>. Not available.

Wynia, Elly M. *The Church of God and Saints of Christ: The Rise of Black Jews*. New York: Garland, 1994.

Zanuck, Darryl. *Gentleman's Agreement*. Twentieth Century Fox Film Corporation, Beverly Hills, Ca. 1993.

# INDEX

CPSIA information can be obtained at www.ICGtesting.com
Printed in the USA
BVOW05s2337060516

447078BV00002B/2/P